The Mindfulness Revolution

A SHAMBHALA SUN BOOK

THE
MINDFULNESS
REVOLUTION

Leading Psychologists, Scientists, Artists,
and Meditation Teachers on the Power
of Mindfulness in Daily Life

Edited by Barry Boyce
and the editors of the *Shambhala Sun*

SHAMBHALA
Boston & London · 2011

Shambhala Publications, Inc.
Horticultural Hall
300 Massachusetts Avenue
Boston, Massachusetts 02115
www.shambhala.com

9 8 7 6 5 4 3 2 1

First Edition
Printed in the United States of America

⊗This edition is printed on acid-free paper that meets
the American National Standards Institute z39.48 Standard.
♻This book was printed on 30% postconsumer recycled paper.
For more information please visit www.shambhala.com.

Distributed in the United States by Random House, Inc.,
and in Canada by Random House of Canada Ltd

Library of Congress Cataloging-in-Publication Data

The mindfulness revolution: leading psychologists, scientists, artists,
and meditation teachers on the power of mindfulness in daily life /
edited by Barry Boyce and the editors of the Shambhala Sun.—1st ed.
p.   cm.
ISBN 978-1-59030-889-9 (pbk.: alk. paper)
1. Cognition. 2. Awareness. 3. Perception. 4. Experience.
I. Boyce, Barry Campbell, 1956– II. Title: Leading psychologists, scientists,
artists, and meditation teachers on the power of mindfulness in daily life.
BF311.M55355 2011
294.3'4435—dc22
2010036652

Contents

PART TWO: Mindfulness in Daily Life

PART THREE: Mindfulness, Health, and Healing

Acknowledgments

To prepare an anthology on mindfulness naturally requires at least a little bit of mindfulness, so I want to express my deep gratitude to the many teachers who helped me discover it, including in particular Chögyam Trungpa Rinpoche. I also want to thank the many authors included in this book for being so reasonable and helpful in bringing it to fruition.

I want to thank my colleagues at the Shambhala Sun Foundation for all their help in making this book possible. Editor-in-chief Melvin McLeod has provided immeasurable guidance every step of the way. My lifelong friend and colleague, publisher James Gimian, is an ever-present strategic thought partner. Andy Karr kicked around many ideas with me that helped to shape the content. Editors Andrea Miller and Liam Lindsay brought a can-do attitude to this endeavor that made it a joy to show up for work.

Thanks to my many friends and guides at Shambhala Publications, foremost among them Eden Steinberg, whose intelligence and care helped bring this book the focus and flow it needed. I continue to rely on the friendship and support of Peter Turner, president of Shambhala, and vice president Jonathan Green.

Thanks finally to my wife, Judi, who provided countless hours of help in pulling details together and who waited for me many nights when this book made me very late for dinner.

Introduction

Anyone Can Do It, and It Changes Everything

Mindfulness. It's a pretty straightforward word. It means the mind is fully attending to what is at hand, what you're working on, the person you're talking to, the surroundings you're moving through. It is a basic human capacity. It's not a talent. We all have it. We all need it. And yet, it is so often elusive. Our mindfulness can slip away from us in an instant, and we are lost in distraction or engrossed in obsessive thoughts or worries about the future. Even in the midst of the intense pain that can come from an injury, illness, or loss—as much as such moments seemingly captivate our attention—mindfulness can fade so that we become more caught up in our inner story than what we are actually experiencing.

Given that it's so easy for us to stray from our awareness of the present moment, mindfulness long ago became a discipline. By taking time away from the pressures and needs of daily life to work only on mindfulness, with no other project at hand, we refresh our ability to be mindful when we return to our everyday activities: taking care of a household, raising children, working, exercising, playing sports, volunteering, and so on. This practice has often been called *meditation*, but since that term also covers a number of other types of practices, we use the term *mindfulness* as shorthand for "mindfulness meditation practice."

This book is about how to engage in that practice, which anyone can do since the only requirement is to pay attention to your breath and your body. This book is also about how just taking part in this simple practice can enhance all areas of your life and—dare I say—change how you approach life. It's not necessarily a monumental change; it's more a small shift that can make a difference day in, day out. As one new practitioner put it, "My mindfulness practice provides me with a way to observe the stressful situations around me and not become caught up in them. It has taught me how to pause, and then in that moment, I can make the *choice* whether to respond or react to what's going on."

Historically, the most prominent practitioner was the Buddha, and mindfulness became the basis for the spiritual tradition that bears his name. The practice existed in various forms in southern Asia prior to his time, and it seems likely that similar forms of practice focusing on an awareness of body and mind in the present moment have existed in many cultures. In the last thirty years, the practice of mindfulness has been taught as a secular discipline detached from any involvement in Buddhism or any other faith tradition. It can be practiced equally by people of any religious faith and those who have no religious faith, based as it is on fundamental mental and physical capabilities that all human beings have, irrespective of any ideological views they may hold.

The pioneer in establishing mindfulness as a secular discipline is Jon Kabat-Zinn. In 1979, Kabat-Zinn, trained as a molecular biologist at the Massachusetts Institute of Technology, had been a yoga and meditation practitioner for many years. He took some time off from his job in the gross anatomy lab at the University of Massachusetts (UMass) Medical Center in Worcester to do a meditation retreat. It occurred to him while he was practicing that hospital patients could use some mindfulness. It was one of those so-obvious but so-brand-new realizations that happen to scientists in labs every day: take the mindfulness to the hospital because that's where the pain is.

In the early years, the Mindfulness-Based Stress Reduction (MBSR) program he founded was modest. His sessions were held in a basement. He taught mindfulness and related techniques in a program of eight weekly two-hour classes and one daylong session that included paying attention to breathing, eating, stress in the body, communication, and caring. This eight-week program continues to this day with small variations. In 1990, Kabat-Zinn put out his first book, *Full Catastrophe Living*, which contained detailed descriptions of and instructions for all facets of the program he had developed in his stress-reduction clinic at UMass. It spurred a lot of interest. In 1993, Bill Moyers's documentary *Healing and the Mind* featured ordinary folks practicing at the clinic, and inquiries soared. So it was no surprise that Kabat-Zinn's second book, the shorter and more poetic *Wherever You Go There You Are,* became an immediate best seller when it was released in 1994. This was the beginning of what we now can call the "mindfulness revolution."

An umbrella organization called the Center for Mindfulness in Medicine, Health Care, and Society exists to chart the course of MBSR. The center does not exert any strong control on how mindfulness, a practice that can't be trademarked, spreads around the world. It does, however, ask that people respect the integrity of the MBSR program itself, and if they create a variation of it, that they give it another name. Many variations have sprung up, including Mindfulness-Based Childbirth and Parenting, Mindfulness-Based Cognitive Therapy, Mindfulness-Based Eating Awareness Training, and Mindfulness-Based Art Training for Cancer Patients, to name just a few. All of them combine a mindfulness component with preexisting ways of helping people who have particular problems and ailments.

MBSR and its offshoots are by far the largest source of secular mindfulness training today. MBSR programs taught by certified MBSR teachers exist in more than five hundred hospitals and clinics worldwide, and more than nine thousand MBSR teachers have graduated from Oasis, the Center for Mindfulness's professional training program. More than eighteen thousand people have graduated from the stress reduction clinic at UMass alone, and an inestimable number have taken MBSR courses in their hometowns and logged in millions of hours of mindfulness practice. Somebody somewhere is learning it for the first time right now.

In addition to MBSR programs, many groups and programs teach mindfulness in diverse settings. For example, the Mindful Awareness Research Center (MARC) at the University of California–Los Angeles (UCLA) offers six-week mindfulness classes to students, faculty, staff, and the general public. Integrative Health Partners in Chicago offers four-week programs in mindfulness and stress reduction. In Philadelphia, you can take part in a wide variety of mindfulness-based classes offered by the Penn Program for Mindfulness. Online courses and audio and video programs are widely available as well. Please see the Resources section for more details.

One of the core reasons for the growing acceptance of mindfulness as a beneficial practice that doesn't require any religious training is that from the earliest days of MBSR, Kabat-Zinn and others sought to prove the practical effectiveness of the technique through scientific studies. In a paper presented by Margaret Cullen, a longtime MBSR teacher who develops mindfulness curricula, at "The State of Contemplative Practice in America," a dialogue held at the Fetzer Insitute in Kalamazoo, Michigan, in June 2010, she wrote, "There are hundreds of research papers on the effects of mindfulness-based interventions on physical and mental conditions including, but not limited to depression and relapse prevention, anxiety, substance abuse, eating disorders, insomnia, chronic pain, psoriasis, type 2 diabetes, fibromyalgia, rheumatoid arthritis, attention-deficit/hyperactivity disorder, HIV, cancer, and heart disease." A comprehensive literature review of four of the largest health science databases (EBSCO, CINAHL, PSYCLINE, and MEDLINE) found that "MBSR is an effective treatment for reducing the stress and anxiety that accompanies daily life and chronic illness." Ten different agencies within the National Institutes of Health are funding almost forty different studies of the effectiveness of mindfulness in ameliorating conditions such as alcoholism, heart disease, and menopause, to name just a few. Compared to the level of support for other methodologies, resources directed to mindfulness are still small. Nevertheless, thirty-five years ago, no one was studying mindfulness.

Discoveries in neuroscience that show beneficial effects on the brain from meditation have also contributed to the increasing popularity of mindfulness. In 1979, at the same time Jon Kabat-Zinn was launching MBSR, the cognitive scientists Francisco Varela and Eleanor Rosch held a conference at the Naropa Institute in Boulder, Colorado, where Western and Eastern approaches to the mind were discussed. The understanding of mind based on meditation became an object of inquiry for scientists, leading to the first meeting sponsored by the newly formed Mind and Life Institute. Called "Dialogues between Buddhism and Cognitive Science," it was held in October 1987 in Dharamsala, India, at the seat of His Holiness the Dalai Lama, who had encouraged these conversations to take place and has been an active participant in almost all of the more than twenty meetings that have occurred since. One of the things His Holiness had hoped would come out of these investigations was proof from a scientific perspective that meditation was beneficial for brain health. As Matthieu Ricard and Daniel Siegel indicate in the pieces excerpted in part 3 of this book, science has indeed confirmed that the brain is "plastic" or changeable throughout life and that mindfulness and other forms of meditation help the brain change—even grow—in positive ways. In May 2010, Richie Davidson, the foremost researcher into the neurological effects of mindfulness and other kinds of contemplative practices, opened the Center for the Investigation of Healthy Minds at the University of Wisconsin–Madison. The new center is dedicated to the study of how contemplative practices might play a useful role in changing the mind in a positive manner. Researchers there will be aided by the sophisticated equipment for studying brain activity housed in the Waisman Laboratory for Brain Imaging and Behavior, where Davidson has carried out his research for many years.

In this book, you will hear from many people, including many of the most authoritative voices in the world of mindfulness. They will take you on a mindfulness journey, beginning with personal instruction, then discussing various ways that practice may be useful in your life, and ending with a short survey of ways that mindfulness practices are starting to make inroads into key sectors of society.

In part 1, "How to Practice Mindfulness," we learn what mindfulness is, how to practice it, and why we may want to practice it. In the first selection, Jan Chozen Bays, MD, an experienced meditation teacher, pediatrician, and author of *Mindful Eating,* describes how mindfulness is "fully paying attention" to everything inside and outside without judgment or criticism. Rather than draining our energy; mindfulness refreshes us. Mindfulness does involve some effort, though, as Susan Smalley and Diana Winston, of MARC at UCLA, point out. While it may be simple, it is not necessarily easy. We have to want to be present and make the effort to do so. Jon Kabat-Zinn gives us plenty of reasons to want to when he talks about how the benefits of mindfulness are more profound than just learning to pay more attention. Because we are more aware of our thoughts, we actually become more aware of our motivations and what we really desire in life.

In part 2, "Mindfulness in Daily Life," we are introduced to a range of ways in which mindfulness can enhance our enjoyment and effectiveness in day-to-day pursuits as diverse as gardening, office work, computing, photography, and playing a musical instrument. Gardener Bob Howard takes us on a mindful walk in the woods that demonstrates how attention to the details of nature can offer surprises and insights that enrich life. Zen cook Edward Espe Brown shows how cooking goes better with mindfulness. Mindfulness helps in the workplace as much as it does at home. Consultant and business coach Michael Carroll, author of *Awake at Work,* tells how the quality of "not-knowing" (the opposite of being a know-it-all), which emerges from mindfulness, can be a great help in our work lives. One of the greatest stressors in life is having to perform. Many of us are less frightened of catastrophic injury than we are of getting up in front of a group of people. Piano teacher Madeline Bruser's advice for musical performers can help us all work with the fear that can overtake us when we face an audience.

In part 3, "Mindfulness, Health, and Healing," we learn how mindfulness is beneficial to many dimensions of physical and emotional health. It helps us think better, regulate our stress, eat better, heal ourselves, avoid overindulgence, and accept the inevitability of aging. Vidyamala Burch, author of *Living Well with Pain and Illness: The Mindful Way to Free Yourself from Suffering,* introduces us to the distinction between the sensation of pain and the mental anxiety associated with it. Mindfulness practice can help lessen the mental kind of pain. Toni Bernhard, a University of California law professor who contracted a debilitating illness that necessitated her retirement, shares a technique she has used to work with the ups and downs of being sick: mindfulness helps her to approach the uncertainty in her life the same way she approaches the uncertainty of the weather and to be more accepting. If it's raining, it's raining; if it's sunny, it's sunny. Saki Santorelli, executive director of the Center for Mindfulness in Medicine, Health Care, and Society, suggests that mindfulness can help the process of healing. If we can learn to stop and be present when we are ill or facing a crisis in our health, we can choose how to respond rather than be driven by fear or habitual neurosis.

In part 4, "Interpersonal Mindfulness," we explore how mindfulness can help us in our relationships—with those we love and those we find difficult—and in raising and teaching children, helping our society, and benefiting humanity. Pema Chödrön, author of many best-selling books on how to cultivate kindness through meditation, explains how natural warmth can emerge from our hearts even when (in fact, especially when) we are experiencing emotional hurt ourselves. Psychologist Ronald Siegel talks about how mindfulness practice makes it more possible for us to actually *be with* the people we are closest to in our lives by helping us see that we are more interdependent than independent. While expecting children to practice mindfulness in the same way as adults is foolish, Susan Kaiser Greenland, author of *The Mindful Child*, presents several hands-on activities that help children cultivate their innate mindfulness. The Dalai Lama, who promotes a universal ethical code that is free of religious doctrine, celebrates our ability to develop "a deep concern for all, irrespective of creed, color, sex, or nationality." If we include in our own pursuit of happiness an understanding of the need for others' happiness, we will practice "wise self-interest" and ultimately act according to the mutual interest of all humanity.

In the final essay in part 4, "Creating a Mindful Society," I introduce you to people I have been reporting on in my Mindful Society department in the *Shambhala Sun* magazine. Mindfulness practitioners are often called "contemplatives," which can conjure up the notion of people who spend their time in solitude, or perhaps just introversion, and have little to do with the outside world. In this essay, I introduce you to people who are fierce contemplatives. They practice mindfulness deeply, but they also are working to transform institutions in society to bring them more in line with values of attention to detail, savoring, listening, cooperation, and caring. Chade-Meng Tan, who started the Search Inside Yourself program at Google, believes world peace begins with peace in the workplace and the home. Linda Lantieri and Patricia Jennings are longtime teachers who believe our schools could become places where children learn not only the information they need to live but also become emotionally resilient and confident of their valuable place in the world. Elizabeth Stanley, a retired Army captain who represents the ninth generation of her family to serve in the United States military, believes troops need more awareness to serve their country in a way that draws on their full human potential. Congressman Tim Ryan, Democrat from the Youngstown-Akron area of Ohio, is a meditator and yoga practitioner who wants to see mindfulness helping ordinary citizens to lead better lives and leaders to become better listeners and more effective advocates for the public good. In a message to a recent gathering of contemplative practitioners, he said, "Washington is starting to understand the power of mindfulness, compassion, and the contemplative.

We need you to knock on our doors and tell us how it benefits the world and what we can do to help."

The mindfulness revolution begins with the simple act of paying attention to our breath, body, and thoughts, but clearly it can go very far. It helps us in our home life, with our family, our friends, and our colleagues. It helps us in our businesses, our volunteer groups, our churches, our communities, and in our society at large. It's a small thing. We all can do it. And it can change the world.

Barry Boyce
Senior Editor, *The Shambhala Sun*
Editor, www.mindful.org

PART ONE

How to Practice Mindfulness

What Is Mindfulness?

Jan Chozen Bays

Mindfulness is a capability we all possess and can cultivate. Yet, so often, we are on autopilot, going through the motions but not really present in our lives. Longtime meditation teacher and physician Jan Chozen Bays tells us how not being present leads to dissatisfaction and unhappiness, while being in the present moment is restful and enjoyable, bringing a sense of discovery to even the most mundane of everyday activities.

MINDFULNESS MEANS deliberately paying attention, being fully aware of what is happening both inside yourself—in your body, heart, and mind—and outside yourself in your environment. Mindfulness is awareness without judgment or criticism. The last element is key. When we are mindful, we are not comparing or judging. We are simply witnessing the many sensations, thoughts, and emotions that come up as we engage in the ordinary activities of daily life. This is done in a straightforward, no-nonsense way, but it is warmed with kindness and spiced with curiosity.

Sometimes we are mindful, and sometimes we are not. A good example is paying attention to your hands on the steering wheel of a car. Remember when you were first learning to drive, and how the car wobbled and wove its way along the road as your hands clumsily jerked the wheel back and forth, correcting and overcorrecting? You were wide awake, completely focused on the mechanics of driving. After a while, your hands learned to steer well, making subtle and automatic adjustments. You could keep the car moving smoothly ahead without paying any conscious attention to your hands. You could drive, talk, eat, and listen to the radio, all at the same time.

Thus arises the experience we have all had of driving on automatic pilot. We open the car door, search for our keys, back carefully out of the driveway, and . . . pull into the parking garage at work. Wait a minute! What happened to the twenty miles and forty minutes between house and job? Were the lights red or green? Our mind took a vacation in some pleasant or distressing realm as our body deftly maneuvered the car through flowing traffic and stoplights, suddenly awakening as we arrived at our destination.

Is that bad? It's not bad in the sense of sin or guilt. If we are able to drive to work on autopilot for years without having an accident, that's pretty skillful! We could say that it's sad, though, because when we spend a lot of time with our body doing one thing while our mind is on vacation somewhere else, it means that we aren't present for much of our life. When we aren't present, it makes us feel vaguely but persistently dissatisfied. This sense of dissatisfaction, of a gap between us and everything and everyone else, leads to unhappiness.

Let's look at it from the other side. When have we really been present? Everyone can recall at least one time when they were completely present, when everything became clear and vivid. We call these peak moments. It can happen when our car skids. Time slows as we watch the accident unfold or not. It often happens at a birth or as someone dies. It doesn't have to be dramatic. It can happen on an ordinary walk as we turn a corner and everything is, for a moment, luminous.

Peak moments are times when we are completely aware. Our life and our awareness are undivided, at one. At these times, the gap between us and everything else closes. We feel satisfied—actually, we are beyond satisfaction and dissatisfaction. We are present.

These moments inevitably fade, and there we are again, divided and grumpy about it. We can't force peak moments or enlightenment to happen. Mindfulness, however, helps close the gap that causes our unhappiness.

Zen master Thich Nhat Hanh has called mindfulness a miracle. It seems like it. When we learn how to use this simple tool and find for ourselves what it can do, it seems miraculous. It can transform boredom into curiosity, distressed restlessness into ease, and negativity into gratitude. Using mindfulness, we will find that anything—*anything*—we bring our full attention to will begin to open up and reveal worlds we never suspected existed. In all my experience as a physician and a Zen teacher, I have never found anything to equal it.

A large and growing body of scientific studies supports the claims about the surprisingly reliable healing abilities of mindfulness. Jon Kabat-Zinn at the University of Massachusetts Medical School has developed a training called Mindfulness-Based Stress Reduction (MBSR). He first taught MBSR techniques to people suffering from chronic pain and disease, people whose doctors had referred them as a last resort after other medical therapies had failed. The results were so good that he began helping people to apply these techniques to other illnesses. Other doctors and therapists learned MBSR techniques and tried them out successfully with a variety of disorders. There are now many articles in medical and psychology journals documenting the benefits of MBSR for illnesses ranging from asthma to psoriasis, heart disease to depression.

Why is mindfulness helpful to us? Left to our own devices, we easily become lost in thoughts about the past and the future. The capacity of the human mind to plan for the future is a unique gift. Unfortunately the mind, in its anxiety for us, tries to make plans for a huge number of possible futures, most of which will never arrive. This constant leapfrogging into the future is a waste of our mental and emotional energy.

The mind also enjoys excursions into realms of fantasy, where it creates an internal video of a "new me," famous, handsome, powerful, talented, successful, wealthy, and loved. The capacity of the human mind to fantasize is wonderful, the basis of all our creativity. It allows us to imagine new inventions, create new art and music, arrive at new scientific hypotheses, and make plans for everything from new buildings to new chapters in our lives. Unfortunately, it can become an escape, an escape from the anxiety of not knowing what is actually moving toward us, the fear that the next moment (or hour or day or year) could bring us difficulties or even death.

When we allow the mind to rest in the present, full of what is actually happening right now, redirecting it away from repeated fruitless excursions into the past or future or fantasy realms, we are doing something very important: conserving the energy of the mind. It remains fresh and open, ready to respond to whatever appears before it.

This may sound trivial, but it is not. Ordinarily the mind does not rest. Even at night it is active, generating dreams from a mix of anxieties and the events of our life. We know that the body cannot function well without rest, so we give it at least a few hours to lie down and relax each night. We forget, though, that the mind needs rest too. Where it finds rest is in the present moment, where it can lie down and relax into the flow of events.

Although mindfulness is becoming an increasingly popular concept, people may easily misunderstand it. First, they may mistakenly believe that to practice mindfulness means to think hard (or harder) about something. In mindfulness, we use the thinking power of the mind to initiate the practice and to remind us to return to the practice when the mind inevitably wanders during the day. But once we follow the mind's instructions and begin the task (following the breath and, when the mind wanders, returning to the breath), we can let go of thoughts. The thinking mind naturally quiets down. We are anchored in the body, in awareness.

The second misunderstanding is to think of mindfulness as a program, a series of forty-five-minute exercises that begin and end during periods of seated meditation. Mindfulness is helpful to the extent that it spreads out into the activities of our life, bringing the light of heightened awareness, curiosity, and a sense of discovery to the mundane activities of life: getting up in the morning, brushing our teeth, walking through a door, answering a phone, listening to someone talk.

Anything that we attend to carefully and patiently will open itself up to us. Once we are able to apply the power of a concentrated, focused mind, anything, potentially all things, will reveal their true hearts to us. It is that heart-to-heart connection with ourselves, with our loved ones, and with the world itself that all of us so dearly long for.

A Receptive, Respectful Awareness

JACK KORNFIELD

When we first start practicing mindfulness meditation, says psychologist and meditation teacher Jack Kornfield, we usually expect to become instantly calm and peaceful. Instead, we most likely are shocked to find out just how much is going on in our minds or how bored we can be just sitting there. The very act of seeing this confusion and irritation begins the process that leads to insight and, ultimately, to relief and relaxation.

THE FILM *GORILLAS IN THE MIST* tells the story of Dian Fossey, a courageous field biologist who managed to befriend a tribe of gorillas. Fossey had gone to Africa to follow in the footsteps of her mentor, George Shaller, a renowned primate biologist who had returned from the wilds with more intimate and compelling information about gorilla life than any scientist before. When his colleagues asked how he was able to learn such remarkable detail about the tribal structure, family life, and habits of gorillas, he attributed it to one simple thing. He didn't carry a gun.

Previous generations of biologists had entered the territory of these large animals with the assumption that they were dangerous. So the scientists came with an aggressive spirit, large rifles in hand. The gorillas could sense the danger around these rifle-bearing men and kept a safe distance. By contrast, Shaller—and later, his student Dian Fossey—entered the territory without weapons. They had to move slowly, gently, and, above all, respectfully toward these creatures. And in time, sensing the benevolence of these humans, the gorillas allowed them to come right among them and learn their ways. Sitting still, hour after hour, with careful, patient attention, Fossey finally understood what she saw. As the African-American sage George Washington Carver explained, "Anything will give up its secrets if you love it enough."

Mindfulness is attention. It is a nonjudgmental, receptive awareness, a respectful awareness. Unfortunately, much of the time, we don't attend in this way. Instead, we react, judging whether we like, dislike, or can ignore what is happening. Or we measure our experience against our expectations. We evaluate ourselves and others with a stream of commentary and criticism.

When people initially come to a meditation class to train in mindfulness, they hope to become calm and peaceful. Usually they are in for a big shock. The first hour of mindfulness meditation reveals its opposite, bringing an unseen stream of evaluation and judgment into stark relief. In the first hour, many of us feel bored and dislike the boredom. We can hear a door slam and wish for quiet. Our knees hurt, and we try to avoid the pain. We wish we had a better cushion. We can't feel our breath, and we get frustrated. We notice our minds won't stop planning, and we feel like failures. Then we remember someone we're angry at and get upset, and if we notice how many judgments there are, we feel proud of ourselves for noticing.

But like George Shaller, we can put aside these weapons of judgment. We can become mindful. When we are mindful, it is as if we can bow to our experience without judgment or expectation. "Mindfulness," declared the Buddha, "is all-helpful."

Peter, a middle-age computer designer, came to a meditation retreat looking for relief. He was coping with a recently failed business, a shaky marriage, and a sick mother. But meditation quickly became an agony. The anger and disappointment that pervaded his current situation rose up in the quiet room to fill his mind. His attempts to quiet himself by sensing his breath felt hopeless; his attention bounced away from his body like water on a hot skillet. Then it got worse. A restless woman seated nearby began to cough loudly and frequently. She began to fidget and move and cough more as the first day wore on.

Peter, who was struggling just to be with his own sorrow, became frustrated and angry, and as the woman continued coughing, he became enraged. He sought out my coteacher and good friend, Debra Chamberlin-Taylor, and insisted that meditation was the wrong approach and told her that he wanted to leave. Debra asked Peter to close his eyes and mindfully notice the state of his body. It was filled with tension and pain. With Debra's help, Peter found he could hold the tension and hurt with a more accepting and kind attention. He breathed, relaxed a little, and recognized that the medicine he needed was nothing other than to understand his own pain.

The next instruction he was given was simple: "As you sit, keep a gentle mindfulness on your body and notice whatever happens." After only a few minutes, his fidgety neighbor began a long coughing spell. With each cough, Peter felt his own muscles clench and his breath stop. Now he became more curious, interested in how his body was reacting. He began to notice that hearing each cough produced an internal clenching and a wave of anger, which subsided as he practiced relaxing between the spells.

Finally, at the end of the sitting period, he got up to walk down to the lunchroom. As he arrived, he noticed this same difficult woman in line just ahead of him. Immediately he noticed how his stomach clenched and his breath stopped—just from seeing her! Again, he relaxed. After lunch, when he returned to the meditation hall, he checked to see what time his name was listed for a private interview with his teacher. Further down the same list, he read the restless woman's name. Still paying attention, he was surprised. Just seeing her name made his stomach clench and his breath tighten! He relaxed again. He realized that his body had become a mirror and that his mindfulness was showing him when he was caught and where he could let go.

As the retreat went on, his attention grew more precise. He noticed that his own anxious and angry thoughts about his family and business problems could trigger the same clenching and tightening as the woman's cough did. He had always tried to have things under control. Now that his life had proved out of control, the habits of anger, blame, and judgment toward himself were tying him in knots. With each reaction, he could feel the knots arise. After each one, he would pause mindfully and bring in a touch of ease. He began to trust mindfulness. By the close of the retreat, he was grateful to the restless woman near him. He wanted to thank her for her teaching.

With mindfulness, Peter found relief. He also discovered the benefit of curiosity and openness, what Zen master Suzuki Roshi famously called "beginner's mind." In Suzuki Roshi's words, "We pay attention with respect and interest, not in order to manipulate, but to understand what is true. And seeing what is true, the heart becomes free."

Is Mindfulness for You?

Susan Smalley and Diana Winston

When we live life mindlessly, we feel dull and disconnected from others, and we can act rashly. Susan Smalley and Diana Winston, of the Mindful Awareness Research Center at UCLA, counsel us to practice present-time awareness, even in the midst of difficult situations. Instead of reacting thoughtlessly to the stimuli in our lives, we can become curious about what's going on in our minds and be kinder and more accepting of ourselves and others.

THE IDEA THAT MINDFULNESS can have meaning for someone with a demanding job, endless responsibilities, and any one of a variety of religious orientations—including Christian, Jewish, Hindu, Buddhist, or no religion at all—might seem absurd. After all, even if there were some benefit to the practice, who has the time? Right away we can dispel the notion that mindfulness is time-consuming. In fact, it is time-*enhancing* and can be practiced anywhere in the blink of an eye. *Mindfulness is the art of observing your physical, emotional, and mental experiences with deliberate, open, and curious attention.* And although it is an "art" that can be cultivated through a daily, formal meditation practice, you can easily practice it instantaneously by remembering to be aware of your present-moment experience anytime in the course of a day.

To incorporate mindfulness into your life does not require that you change your life in any drastic way; you still attend to your normal array of family, work, social, and leisure-time activities. But you can learn to perform all of these activities with a different state of awareness, one that is open, curious, and nonreactive. Mindfulness may at some point lead you to change some behaviors, particularly those that may be harmful to yourself or others, but it is not a self-help methodology per se. In practicing mindfulness, *you are not trying to change who you are but to become more fully present with your experiences*—with your body, thoughts, and feelings, and with their impact on your life. In the process, you are likely to get to know yourself better, learn to relax and detach from stress, and find a way to navigate the intense pressures you may face. Through such increased awareness, you may also become more discerning of your thoughts, feelings, and actions, and that awareness will give you a greater opportunity to make a positive change if you wish to do so. Says Charlie, a thirty-eight-year-old dockworker,

> I'm convinced mindfulness makes me a better father. It's not only that I'm able to listen better to my children, but also it's the fact that I somehow appreciate every moment I have with them more than I ever have in the past. I don't take the time with them for granted anymore. I mean, they're six and eight now, but before I know it, they'll be in college and . . . Well, I get to enjoy them now.

No More Automatic Pilot

Many of us complain that we sometimes miss out on parts of our lives. So often we are not present in what we are doing. We have no idea of what we may or may not have just done, whether it was driving across town, making dinner, or engaging in some other routine behavior. We tend to remember crises or extraspecial events, but much of ordinary life—the daily activities of showering, grocery shopping, getting dressed, and so on— seems to slip by us.

Mindfulness is an antidote to the dullness and disconnection of life lived on automatic pilot. By applying mindfulness, you can counteract that spaced-out feeling you may sometimes have in the midst of your day. You can learn to take an ordinary experience, give it your present-moment attention, and experience it as extraordinary. With many moments of your life taking on extraordinary qualities, you are likely to feel more "alive." Sometimes sights and sounds seem stronger, more varied and textured.

Spicing up life with mindfulness can change the way you approach ordinary activities and bring you new enthusiasm and joy.

One of our meditation students told us about how bored she was with walking her dog. When she began to really pay attention, however, it suddenly became an entirely different experience. She felt more connected to her body, her senses came alive, and she saw her neighborhood as if for the first time. She saw details of trees and flowers she had never noticed. The scents seemed stronger and more varied. She relaxed as she felt the sun on her skin. As she connected to her present-moment experience, she felt a greater sense of appreciation and enjoyment in activities that she had been performing with reluctance. She felt that even her dog could sense the change in her.

MOVING INTO THE PRESENT

If you ask people on the street where their minds are most of the time, they will probably think you are really odd, but then they will answer, "My mind is right here." Is it? Most of us spend a great deal of time lost in thoughts about the past or the future. Many of our thoughts are about things we regret from the past or things we are worried about in the future. We obsess, worry, grieve, imagine the worst happening in the future, and replay situations from the past that caused us pain. Theoretically, it might be wise to replay only pleasant thoughts, but we mostly replay negative thoughts, as if we have broken records in our heads. Most of our thoughts hardly seem to vary. We have been thinking the same (often painful) thoughts day after day! So our minds are often not aware in the present but are living in a different time period, either the past or the future.

Mindfulness can take you out of your habitual thinking by bringing you to what is actually happening at the present time. Stop right now, take a breath, and pay close attention to the present. Exactly in this moment, are things, for the most part, okay? The future has not happened, the past is over, and right now—well, it just is. This foundational technique of learning mindfulness—learning to return your mind to the present no matter what is happening—is tremendously helpful for working with challenging thoughts, emotions, and experiences.

Emma, a twenty-three-year-old aspiring actress, struggled constantly with negative thoughts about herself. After a few weeks of the Mindful

Awareness Practices (MAPs) class we teach at the Mindful Awareness Research Center at UCLA, she came into class elated: "I had an audition today, and for the first time ever, I didn't judge myself. Well, I did notice judgment in my mind, but I just stopped and took a breath and decided to be mindful instead of judgmental. I felt my body, noticed my thoughts, and all the judgment just stopped."

Coming back into the present moment by letting go of thoughts does not require that you eliminate creative ruminations, reflections on the past, or abstract thinking. Mindfulness is more about giving yourself a choice with your thoughts. You can exert some control over them rather than being at their mercy. As you learn to regulate your attention, you also learn when it is useful to focus on the present moment (particularly when working with difficult or negative thinking) and when it is useful to use creativity and other functions of mind.

Sunila, who is a forty-four-year-old internist, tells us,

> As a physician, it's important for me to be able to be really present with patients. But I also have so much I'm juggling, thinking through their case, not to mention the other cases I'm working with that day. Oftentimes I'm trying to come up with an out-of-the-box solution. So I've learned to train my mind. When I'm with patients, I listen with full attention. I focus on them fully. Once I leave the room, I allow my attention to wander, to ponder, to think creatively. It's only since learning mindfulness that I've had some facility doing this, and my patients have noticed a difference.

LESS REACTIVITY

For our purposes here, *reactivity* means responding to stimuli in the world in ways that induce unnecessary stress. For instance, when you are verbally attacked, you may respond automatically, both physically and mentally. When you come into your office and find extra work on your desk, you may get irritated and say or do something you later regret. When your partner has promised to wash the dishes but you come home and find the kitchen a mess, you may react by getting angry, isolating yourself, or trying to make your partner feel guilty. It may feel as though you have no control over your actions. You are behaving automatically—reactively.

Mindfulness offers another way. By practicing present-time awareness, even in the midst of a difficult situation, you can become aware of your impulses (your reactive patterns), stop, perhaps take a breath, and respond skillfully in a way that does not lead to more harm. With such insight into yourself, wise actions are likely to follow, as one meditation student discovered.

Gino, a twenty-eight-year-old graduate student, was running late as he drove down an L.A. freeway; when someone cut him off, he missed his exit. Immediately, a flash of rage swept through his body. In the past, he might have made an angry hand gesture or shouted fruitlessly at the long-departed car. He would have stewed in his anger, with his blood pressure rising, and obsessed about getting back at the other driver. But because he was learning mindfulness, he decided to use this experience as an opportunity to become aware of his reactivity and make a different choice. He took a breath, noticed his body—heart racing, heat in his face, a clenching in his gut—and thought, *Wow, I'm really angry.* After thinking about what a small thing it had been that triggered such massive anger, he was actually able to laugh about it. As he noticed this, his body began to calm down. In that moment, he knew he could respond differently in the situation. He realized that he was still angry but somehow not so overwhelmed. He even thought, *I might let that guy in the pickup into my lane.* Awareness allowed him to make that choice.

DEVELOPING A MINDFUL ATTITUDE

A classic definition of mindfulness often includes the words *nonjudgmental, open, accepting,* and *curious* to describe the attitude you can cultivate when in this state. Mindfulness is an accepting and kind attitude toward yourself and your present-moment experience. So if you are trying to be mindful but have a reaction to your experience—that is, you are aware, but you're disliking, fearing, or judging your experience—then your mindfulness is colored by these reactions. For example, if you are mindful of your breath but thinking, *Wow, this is utterly boring,* or *I'm doing this wrong,* then you are aware, but the quality of accepting things as they are is not present for you. To make it slightly more complicated, if you then notice that you are either bored or doubting your effort but feel curious and open about this experience, even somewhat kind toward yourself for feeling bored or doubting, then your attitude would be accepting!

When you are aware of the present moment in a kind and curious way, accepting it exactly as it is, then you have the direct experience of mindfulness. This is not to say that judgment, aversion, fear, and so forth will not sometimes color your mindfulness, but this is the ideal you can aspire to through practice: to be as kind as possible to yourself and your experience. This is also not to say that if you are truly mindful you will never have judgmental thoughts. Judgments arise unbidden in our minds, so we don't need to judge our judgments! Instead, recognize them for what they are— thoughts passing through your mind. How might this work? Here is what Joan, a fifty-three-year-old musician, has to say:

> When I began my meditation practice, I was convinced I was doing it wrong. I couldn't breathe one breath without a voice telling me that I was breathing wrong! How can you breathe wrong? Anyway, I really worked on practicing kindness with myself, letting myself be okay with each breath, even letting myself be okay with not knowing if I was doing it right. It was like I could bring mindfulness to being unsure. Over time I began to relax, and now I don't judge my meditation so strongly.

Having a kind and open attitude does not mean that you accept all behaviors as equally appropriate. If you say to yourself, "I yelled at my partner when he didn't deserve it, but I was very mindful and kind to myself in the process," you are misunderstanding this attitude. When you have a truly mindful attitude, you see yourself kindly but *clearly,* with no blind spots arising from your own reactive patterns. As you become more mindful, you begin to see more clearly the effect of your behaviors on other people. Through a lens of mindfulness, you recognize behaviors that harm, such as abuse, lying, and malicious gossip, as hurtful to yourself and others, and you may choose to diminish or abandon these behaviors.

Over the long term, you may notice a striking effect: kindness begins to permeate the rest of your life. Unfortunately, many people these days suffer from self-criticism and self-hatred. Learning to develop an accepting attitude through moments of mindfulness helps you develop a kind and compassionate attitude toward yourself and others over the long term. This idea is based on the principle that what you practice, you cultivate. So if you spend many moments of your day learning to be open to experiences with kindness, openness, and curiosity, you are likely, over time, to find these attitudes and behaviors becoming a natural and more incorporated part of who you are.

MINDFULNESS IS SIMPLE BUT NOT EASY

One of our students, Jade, age thirty, sums up how difficult it is to be in the present:

> I was on vacation in Mexico, and the whole time I was there, despite beautiful, sunny weather and an amazing beach, all I could think about was whether or not I should be in Hawaii or maybe another Central American country. Finally, I said to myself, "If I'm not going to be *here,* why bother to go anywhere at all?"

As obvious and simple as mindfulness can be, and despite its beneficial effects, doing it is another story. It is very *simple* to be mindful. Take a moment right now, stop reading, and feel your nose and body take one breath. You are present with that one breath. You are mindful in this single moment in time. It is simple to be mindful, but *remembering* to be mindful can be very difficult.

Modern society tends to condition us to be anything but mindful. The dominant American culture validates virtually mindless productivity, busyness, speed, and efficiency. The last thing we want to do is just be present. We want to do, to succeed, to produce. Those of us who are good at the doing seem to fare well in many of our institutions and corporations. Those who are not—well, they tend to fall behind. But this is life in America in the twenty-first century and, to an increasing degree, around the world. We are so focused on doing that we have forgotten all about being, and the toll this takes on our physical, mental, and emotional health is significant. As the saying goes, we have become "human doings instead of human beings." Mindfulness is a means to rebalance doing and being.

It has become so normal to be incessantly busy that many of us cannot even tolerate the feeling of stopping and slowing down. We know a man who needs to talk on his cell phone or read a book when walking down the street; he cannot face what he perceives as the sheer boredom of no stimulation. Josh, a beginning meditation student, reports that in all his waking hours, he never chooses to be in silence. Even when he is relaxing, he turns on the TV or searches the Internet while ambient music pumps away in the background. His first attempts at mindfulness were quite discouraging for him, because the feeling of being alone with himself was so foreign and uncomfortable.

He could not see the point of spending five minutes in silence with himself when he had so much to do to run a successful business. He assumed that a period of silence and self-inquiry was a waste of time when he had all those "important" things to do.

Learning mindfulness starts wherever you are. Whether you are busy, distracted, anxious, depressed, jealous, peaceful, or tired, all you need to do is take a moment to pay attention to yourself. If you can stop, breathe, and notice what is happening in just this moment, then you have tapped into the power of mindfulness. This simple act, unassuming as it is, can lead to significant changes in your well-being and become a real "seat belt" for your mental health.

PRACTICE

Eating Meditation

This introductory exercise provides an excellent experiential understanding of mindfulness. We recommend that you try this practice with grapes, raisins, or any small bits of fruit.

Assume an upright yet relaxed posture, sitting on a cushion on the floor or in a flat, upright chair with your feet touching the floor. Have two pieces of your fruit nearby—we usually choose grapes. Pick up one of the grapes. Close your eyes, and take a breath or two to relax. The grape you have in front of you didn't magically appear at the supermarket. It actually has a long history. As we describe this, let your mind imagine the history of the grape. Feel free to make other associations on your own.

Some time ago, someone planted a grape seed. That grape seed began to sprout, and it grew into a vine. There was soil, sun, rain, and water, and perhaps fertilizer; there were humans who tended to the vine. The vine grew and grew, and ultimately it began to sprout fruit. The fruit ripened until it was ready to be harvested. Then someone came along and cut the vine, whose grapes may have been packaged at that point, wrapped in plastic, loaded on trucks, and driven to supermarkets, where you purchased them. There are also many secondary connections to reflect on . . . all of the humans involved in this process. There were people who tended, people who harvested, people who drove the trucks. And we don't know the circumstances under which the farmworkers lived and worked; perhaps their lives were quite difficult.

We do know that each person had a set of parents. Their parents had parents, and *their* parents had parents, and so on. And each person was clothed and fed and ate countless amounts of food. Where did that food come from? Let your mind roam and imagine the answer to this question. The truck, for instance—where did *that* come from? Oil and metal and plastic and glass. How about the roads the truck drove on to cart the grapes to market? Who tarred, cemented, and paved those roads? Let your mind consider this. Make one more connection that hasn't been described here.

Now notice what is going on inside yourself. How do you feel? There is no right or wrong answer to this question, which is a really important point with mindfulness. All we do is find out what is true in this moment for us. You might be feeling some sense of appreciation. Or you might be feeling some sadness or sleepiness or anything at all. Just check in with yourself and notice what is happening in this present moment.

Now open your eyes and pick up the grape. Look at it as though you have never seen a grape before—as if you were a little child who has been handed his or her first grape. You can roll it around in your fingers; you can notice the shape and the color and the way the light on it changes; you can find out whether it has a smell or a sound. See if you can look at the grape with the curiosity and wonder a child brings to a first experience—that is mindfulness.

Now bring the grape up close to your mouth and notice as you do so whether something inside you says, *I want to eat it!* Simply be aware of that impulse. Then close your eyes, open your mouth, and put the grape in. Begin to chew, but slow down the process. Use your awareness to feel and sense and taste; there's so much to explore—flavors, textures, sounds. And there's saliva; your teeth and your tongue know exactly what to do.

You also might notice what is going on in your mind. Maybe you are comparing this grape to one you had last week and thinking, *It's not as good,* or *Oh, this one's better than the other one.* Maybe you want another grape immediately. Maybe you are thinking, *Hmmm, this is kind of silly,* or *This is so interesting.* Truly *anything* could be happening. With mindfulness, we simply notice. We become aware.

When you finish the first grape, eat the second grape with the same quality of attention. When you finish the second grape, notice your whole body present here, and when you are ready, open your eyes.

Here, Now, Aware

Joseph Goldstein

"Have you ever stopped to consider what a thought is?" asks author and meditation teacher Joseph Goldstein. The very fact that we are not very aware of our thoughts and how they come into being allows them to dominate our lives. Like little dictators, they tell us to go here, there, and everywhere. Mindfulness breaks the grip our thoughts have on us, allowing us to more often choose whether to act on them or not.

MINDFULNESS IS THE KEY to the present moment. Without it, we cannot see the world clearly, and we simply stay lost in the wanderings of our minds. Tulku Urgyen, a great Tibetan master of the last century, said, "There is one thing we always need, and that is the watchman named mindfulness—the guard who is always on the lookout for when we get carried away by mindlessness."

Mindfulness is the quality and power of mind that is deeply aware of what's happening—without commentary and without interference. It is like a mirror that simply reflects whatever comes before it. It serves us in the humblest ways, keeping us connected to brushing our teeth or having a cup of tea.

Mindfulness also keeps us connected to the people around us, so we don't just rush by them in the busyness of our lives. The Dalai Lama is an example of someone who beautifully embodies this quality of caring attention. After one conference in Arizona, His Holiness requested that all the employees of the hotel gather in the lobby so that he could greet each of them.

Mindfulness is also the basis for wise action. When we see clearly what is happening in the moment, wisdom can direct our choices and actions rather than old habits simply playing out our patterns of conditioning. And on the highest level, the Buddha spoke of mindfulness as the direct path to enlightenment: "This is the direct path for the purification of beings, for the overcoming of sorrow and lamentation, for the disappearing of pain and grief, for the attainment of the Way, for the realization of nirvana."

I began to practice meditation when I was in the Peace Corps in Thailand. At the time, I was very enthusiastic about philosophical discussion. When I first went to visit Buddhist monks, I arrived with a copy of Spinoza's *Ethics* in my hand, thinking to engage them in debate. Then I started going to discussion groups for Westerners, which were held at one of the temples in Bangkok. I was so persistent in my questions that other people actually stopped coming to the groups. Finally, perhaps out of desperation, one of the monks said, "Why don't you start meditating?"

I didn't know anything about meditation at the time, and I became excited by the prospect of what I saw as an exotic Eastern practice. I gathered all the paraphernalia together, sat myself down on a cushion, and then set my alarm clock for five minutes. Surprisingly, something important happened even in those few minutes. For the first time, I realized there was a way to look inward; there was a path for exploring the nature of my mind.

Something connected, and I said to myself, "Yes, I can do this." All of this was so new and interesting to me that, for a while, I'd invite my friends over to watch me meditate. Of course, they didn't often come back.

The Practice of Mindfulness

We can start the practice of mindfulness meditation with the simple observation and feeling of each breath. Breathing in, we notice we're breathing in; breathing out, we notice we're breathing out. It's very simple but not easy. After just a few breaths, we hop on trains of association, getting lost in plans, memories, judgments, and fantasies. Sometimes it seems like we're in a movie theater where the film changes every few minutes. Our minds are like that. We wouldn't stay in a theater where the movies changed so rapidly, but what can we do about our own internal screening room?

This habit of wandering mind is very strong, even when our reveries aren't pleasant and, perhaps, aren't even true. As Mark Twain put it, "Some of the worst things in my life never happened." We need to train our minds, coming back again and again to the breath and simply beginning again.

As our minds slowly steady, we begin to experience some inner calm and peace. From this place of greater stillness, we feel our bodies more directly and begin to open to both the pleasant and unpleasant sensations that might arise. At first, we may resist unpleasant feelings, but generally they don't last that long. They are there for a while, we feel them, they're unpleasant—then they're gone and something else comes along. And even if they come up repeatedly, over a period of time we begin to see their impermanent, insubstantial nature and to be less afraid of feeling them.

A further part of the training is becoming aware of our thoughts and emotions, those pervasive mental activities that so condition our minds, our bodies, and our lives. Have you ever stopped to consider what a thought is—not the content but the very nature of thought itself? Few people really explore the question, "What is a thought?" What is this phenomenon that occurs so many times a day and to which we pay so little attention?

Not being aware of the thoughts that arise in our minds or of the very nature of thought itself allows thoughts to dominate our lives. Telling us to do this, say that, go here, go there—thoughts often drive us like we're their servants.

Once, when I was teaching in Boulder, Colorado, I was sitting quite comfortably in my apartment. Thoughts were coming and going, when one arose in my mind that said, "Oh, a pizza would be nice." I wasn't even particularly hungry, but this thought lifted me out of the chair and took me out the door, down the stairs, into the car, over to the pizza place, back into the car, up the stairs, and into my apartment, where I finally sat back down to eat the pizza. What drove that whole sequence of activity? Just a thought in my mind.

Obviously, there is nothing wrong with going out for pizza. What does merit our attention, though, is how much of our lives is driven by thoughts. Unnoticed, they have great power. But when we pay attention, when we observe thoughts as they arise and pass away, we begin to see their essentially empty nature. They arise as little energy bubbles in the mind rather than as reified expressions of a self.

Just as there was no all-powerful wizard behind the curtain in *The Wizard of Oz,* the only power our thoughts have is the power we give them. All thoughts come and go. We can learn to be mindful of them and not be carried away by the wanderings of the mind. With mindfulness, we can exercise wise discernment: "Yes, I will act on this one. No, I'll let that one go."

WORKING WITH EMOTIONS

In the same way, we can train ourselves to be mindful of emotions, those powerful energies that sweep over our bodies and minds like great breaking waves. We experience such a wide range of emotions, sometimes within quite a short period of time: anger, excitement, sadness, grief, love, joy, compassion, jealousy, delight, interest, boredom. There are beautiful emotions and difficult ones—and for the most part, we are caught up in their intensity and the stories that give rise to them.

We easily become lost in our own melodramas. It's illuminating to drop down a level and look at the energy of the emotion itself. What is sadness? What is anger? Seeing more deeply requires looking not at the emotion's "story," but at how the emotion manifests in our minds and bodies. It means taking an active interest in discovering the very nature of emotion.

The American Buddhist monk Ajahn Sumedho expressed this kind of interest and investigation very well. He suggested that in a moment of anger or happiness, we simply notice, "Anger is like this," or "Happiness is like that." Approaching our emotional lives in this way is quite different than drowning in the intensity of feelings or being caught on the roller coaster of our ever-changing moods. To do this takes mindfulness, attention, and concentration. We need to take care, though, not to misunderstand this practice and end up suppressing emotions or pushing them aside. The meditative process is one of complete openness to feelings. From the meditative perspective, the question is, "How am I relating to this emotion? Am I completely identified with it, or is the mind spacious enough to feel the grief, the rage, the joy, the love without being overwhelmed?"

THE PRACTICE OF LETTING GO

As you meditate, keep bringing your attention back to what is happening in the moment: the breath, a feeling in the body, a thought, an emotion, or even awareness itself. As we become more mindful and accepting of what's going on, we find—both in meditation and in our lives—that we are less controlled by the forces of denial or addiction, two forces that drive much of life. In the meditative process, we are more willing to see whatever is there, to be with it but not be caught by it. We learn to let go.

In some Asian countries, there is a very effective trap for catching monkeys. Trappers make a slot in the bottom of a coconut, just big enough for the monkey to slide its hand in but not big enough for the hand to be withdrawn when it's clenched. Then they put something sweet in the coconut, attach it to a tree, and wait for the monkey to come along. When the monkey slides its hand in and grabs the food, it gets caught. What keeps the monkey trapped? It is only the force of desire and attachment. All the monkey has to do is let go of the sweet, open its hand, slip out, and go free—but only a rare monkey will do that. Similarly, the twentieth-century Japanese Zen teacher Kosho Uchiyama speaks of "opening the hand of thought."

Another quality that develops in meditation is a sense of humor about our minds, our lives, and the human predicament. If you do not have a sense of humor now, meditate for a while and it will come, because it's difficult to watch the mind steadily and systematically without learning to smile.

Some years ago I was on retreat with the Burmese meditation master Sayadaw U Pandita. He is a strict teacher, and everyone on the retreat was being very quiet, moving slowly, and trying to be impeccably mindful. It was an intense time of training. At mealtimes, we would all enter the dining room silently and begin taking food, mindful of each movement.

One day, the person on line in front of me at the serving table lifted up the cover on a pot of food. As he put it down on the table, it suddenly dropped to the floor, making a huge clanging noise. The very first thought that went through my mind was, "It wasn't me!" Now where did that thought come from? With awareness, we can only smile at these uninvited guests in the mind.

Through the practice of meditation, we begin to see the full range of the mind's activities, old unskillful patterns as well as wholesome thoughts and feelings. We learn to be with the whole passing show. As we become more accepting, a certain lightness develops about it all. And the lighter and more accepting we become with ourselves, the lighter and more accepting we are with others. We're not so prone to judge the minds of others once we have carefully seen our own. The poet W. H. Auden says it well: "Love your crooked neighbor with all your crooked heart." Spacious acceptance doesn't mean that we act on everything equally. Awareness gives us the option of choosing wisely: we can choose which patterns should be developed and cultivated and which should be abandoned.

Just as the focused lens of a microscope enables us to see hidden levels of reality, so too a concentrated mind opens us to deeper levels of experience and more subtle movements of thought and emotion. Without this power of concentration, we stay on the surface of things. If we are committed to deepening our understanding, we need to practice mindfulness and gradually strengthen concentration. One of the gifts of the teachings is the reminder that we can do this—each and every one of us.

PRACTICING IN DAILY LIFE

In our busy lives in this complex and often confusing world, what practical steps can we take to train our minds?

The first step is to establish a regular, daily meditation practice. This takes discipline. It's not always easy to set aside time each day for meditation; so many other things call to us. But as with any training, if we practice regularly, we begin to enjoy the fruits. Of course, not every sitting will be concentrated. Sometimes we'll be feeling bored or restless. These are the inevitable ups and downs of practice. It's the commitment and regularity of practice that is important, not how any one sitting feels. Pablo Casals, the world-renowned cellist, still practiced three hours a day when he was ninety-three. When asked why he still practiced at that age, he said, "I'm beginning to see some improvement."

The training in meditation will only happen through our own effort. No one can do it for us. There are many techniques and traditions, and we can each find the one most suitable for us. But regularity of practice is what effects a transformation. If we do it, it begins to happen; if we don't do it, we continue acting out the various patterns of our conditioning.

The next step is to train ourselves in staying mindful and aware of our bodies throughout the day. As we go through our daily activities, we frequently get lost in thoughts of the past and future, not staying grounded in the awareness of our bodies.

A simple reminder that we're lost in thought is the very common feeling of rushing. Rushing is a feeling of toppling forward. Our minds run ahead of us, focusing on where we want to go instead of settling into our bodies where we are.

Rushing does not particularly have to do with how fast you are going. You can feel rushed while moving slowly, and you can be moving quickly and still be settled in your body. Learn to pay attention to this feeling of rushing. If you can, notice what thought or emotion has captured your attention. Then, just for a moment, stop and settle back into your body: feel your foot on the ground, feel the next step.

The Buddha made a very powerful statement about this practice: "Mindfulness of the body leads to nirvana." This is not a superficial practice. Mindfulness of the body keeps us present—and therefore, we know what's going on. The practice is difficult to remember but not difficult to do. It's all in the training: sitting regularly and being mindful of the body during the day.

To develop deeper concentration and mindfulness, to be more present in our bodies, and to have a skillful relationship with thoughts and emotions, we need not only daily training, but also time for retreat. It's very helpful, at times, to disengage from the busyness of our lives for intensive mindfulness practice. Retreat time is not a luxury. If we are genuinely and deeply committed to awakening, to freedom—to whatever words express the highest value we hold—a retreat is an essential part of the path.

We need to create a rhythm in our lives, establishing a balance between times when we are engaged, active, and relating in the world, and times when we turn inward. As the great Sufi poet Rumi noted, "A little while alone in your room will prove more valuable than anything else that could ever be given you."

At first this "going inside" could be for a day, a weekend, or a week. At the Insight Meditation Society in Barre, Massachusetts, we offer a three-month retreat every year, and at the adjacent Forest Refuge, people have come for as long as a year. We can do whatever feels appropriate and possible to find balanced rhythm between our lives in the world and the inner silence of a retreat. In this way we develop concentration and mindfulness on deeper and deeper levels, which then makes it possible to be in the world in a more loving and compassionate way.

Mindfulness Meditation Instructions

Bob Stahl and Elisha Goldstein

Health professionals Bob Stahl and Elisha Goldstein lucidly present a range of mindfulness practices beginning with the body, proceeding through breath and sensations, ending with choiceless awareness of the present moment. These practices are the heart of the Mindfulness-Based Stress Reduction program.

Simply put, mindfulness is the practice of cultivating nonjudgmental awareness in day-to-day life. It involves simple profound practices that can decrease suffering and bring you greater balance and peace. These tools help you maximize your life and experience, even in the midst of stress, pain, and illness. They can also help with the stresses associated with living with illness and medical conditions such as AIDS, arthritis, asthma, cancer, chronic pain, fibromyalgia, gastrointestinal disorders, heart disease, high blood pressure, and migraines.

Mindfulness of Body

It's quite obvious you need a body to live and that you won't get another one in this lifetime. You may perhaps have some parts surgically removed or replaced, but there's no such thing as a total body transplant. The body is the vehicle you live within through the journey of life, and you must care for it to promote its health, wellness, and longevity. Bringing mindfulness to the body can help you learn what your body does and doesn't need in order to thrive. It can also reveal a great deal about your world and your life. Through mindfulness of the body, you can begin to understand how stress and anxiety affect you and also learn how to live better, even with physical pain and illness. You can open the door to greater mindfulness of the body using a time-honored practice: the body scan.

The body scan meditation is a deep investigation into the moment-to-moment experiences of the body. While you may have heard about meditations that create "out-of-body" experiences, the object of the body scan is to have an "in-the-body" experience. If you're like most people, you probably spend a lot of time living outside your body while thinking of the future or the past, imagining all sorts of scenarios, contemplating abstractions, or being otherwise preoccupied with your thoughts.

In the body scan, you methodically bring attention to the body, beginning with the left foot and ending at the top of the head. We suggest lying down while doing the body scan, but if you find yourself sleepy or would rather just sit or stand, you are welcome to do that too. A full body scan can take up to forty-five minutes. It's helpful if you can get some guidance from an instructor or a CD that guides your attention progressively through the parts of your body. (For a list of helpful audio programs on meditation, see page 265.)

As you perform a body scan, you may notice a wide range of physical feelings: itches, aches, tingles, pain, lightness, heaviness, warmth, cold, and more, as well as neutrality. Some of these sensations may be accompanied by thoughts or emotions. As you practice the body scan, this multitude of sensations and internal experiences can be boiled down to three basic feelings: pleasant, unpleasant, and neutral. Since the body is a dynamic organism that's always changing, no two body scans will ever be completely alike. The body has its own wisdom, and if you listen, it can communicate where physical tension, thoughts, and emotions lie within it.

When you practice the body scan, first simply become aware of physical sensations by exploring their felt sense. This is distinct from thinking about your body. There is no need to analyze or manipulate your body in any way; just feel and acknowledge whatever sensations are present. Through this deep investigation, the body may begin to reveal a whole range of feelings. In this way, the body scan can bring you in touch with many aspects of your life.

PRACTICING THE BODY SCAN

Take a few moments to be still. Congratulate yourself for taking this time for meditation practice.

Do a mindful check-in, feeling into your body and mind and simply allowing any waves of thoughts, emotions, and physical sensations to just be.

Perhaps it's been a busy day and this is the first time you're stopping. As you begin to enter the world of being rather than doing, you may notice the trajectory of the feelings you've been carrying within you.

There is no need to judge, analyze, or figure things out. Just allow yourself to be in the moment with all that's there.

When you feel ready, gently shift the focus to the breath.

Now become aware of breathing.

Breathe normally and naturally and focus on the tip of the nose or the abdomen. Breathing in and knowing you're breathing in, and breathing out and knowing you're breathing out.

At times the mind may wander away from awareness of breathing. When you recognize this, acknowledge wherever you went and then come back to the breath, breathing in and out with awareness.

And now gently withdraw awareness from mindful breathing as you shift to the body scan. As you go through the body, you may come across areas that are tight or tense. If you can allow them to soften, let that happen; if you can't, just let the sensations be, letting them ripple in whatever direction they need to go. This applies not only to physical sensations but also to any emotions. As you go through the body be mindful of any physical sensations and any thoughts or emotions that may arise from sensations.

Bring awareness to the bottom of the left foot where you feel the contact of your foot on the floor. It could be the back of the heel or the bottom of the left foot. Sensing into what is being felt. Feeling the heel, ball, and sole of the left foot.

Feel into your toes and the top of the left foot and back into the Achilles tendon and up into the left ankle.

Now move your awareness up to the lower left leg, feeling into the calf and shin and their connection to the left knee. Being present.

Let awareness now rise up to the thigh, sensing into the upper leg and its connection above into the left hip.

And now withdraw awareness from the left hip down to the left foot, shifting it into the right foot and bringing awareness to where you feel the contact of your right foot on the floor. It could be the back of the heel or the bottom of the right foot. Sensing into what is being felt. Feeling the heel, ball, and sole of the right foot.

Feel into the toes and the top of the right foot and back into the Achilles tendon and up into the right ankle.

Now move your awareness up to the lower right leg, feeling into the calf and shin and their connection to the right knee. Being present.

Let awareness now rise up into the thigh, sensing into the upper leg and its connection above into the right hip.

Gently withdraw your attention from the right hip and move into the pelvic region. Sense into the systems of elimination, sexuality, and reproduction. Feeling into the genitals and the anal region. Being mindful to any sensations, thought or emotions.

And now lift the awareness to the abdomen and into the belly, the home of digestion and assimilation, feeling into your guts with awareness and letting be.

Now withdraw your awareness from the belly and move to the tailbone and begin to sense into the lower, middle, and upper parts of the back. Feeling sensations. Allow any tightness to soften and let be what's not softening.

Let the awareness now shift into the chest, into the heart and lungs. Being present. Feeling into the rib cage and sternum and then into the breasts.

Now gently withdraw attention from the chest and shift the awareness into the fingertips of the left hand. Feeling into the fingers and palm, and then the back of the hand and up into the left wrist.

Proceed up into the forearm, elbow, and upper left arm, feeling sensations.

Now shift awareness to the fingertips of the right hand. Feeling into the fingers and palm, and the back of the hand and up into the right wrist.

Proceed up into the forearm, elbow, and upper right arm, feeling sensations.

Let the awareness move into both shoulders and armpits and then up into the neck and throat. Being present to any sensations, thought or emotions.

Now bring your awareness into the jaw and then gently into the teeth, tongue, mouth, and lips. Allowing any resonating sensations to go wherever they need to go and letting be.

Feel into the cheeks, the sinus passages that go deep into the head, the eyes, and the muscles around the eyes. Feel into the forehead and the temples, being present.

Let the awareness move into the top and back of the head. Feeling into the ears and then inside of the head and into the brain. Being present.

Now expand the field of awareness to the entire body from head to toe to fingertips. Connect from the head through the neck to the shoulders, arms, hands, chest, back, belly, hips, pelvic region, legs, and feet.

Feel the body as a whole organism, with its various physical sensations, thoughts, and emotions. Being present.

Breathing in, feel the whole body rising and expanding on an inhalation and falling and contracting on an exhalation. Feel the body as a whole organism. Being present.

As you come to the end of the body scan, congratulate yourself for taking this time to be present.

SITTING MEDITATION

Outwardly, the formal practice of sitting mindfulness meditation is much like the popular conception of meditation: sitting in silent contemplation. You'll soon discover that the practice is quite rich and profound, as you turn your awareness to the ever-changing nature of your experience. By focusing on how the breath, sensations, sounds, thoughts, and emotions are continually forming and then falling away, it allows a glimpse of the transitory nature of all things—and the potential freedom that comes with this awareness. As you simply sit with and acknowledge whatever is with beginner's mind, without evaluation or judgment and without striving for a particular outcome, you'll develop greater equanimity, a deeper capacity for letting things be, and, with time and practice, greater wisdom and compassion.

This practice begins with a focus on posture and the breath and expands outward to sensations, sounds, thoughts and emotions, and finally choiceless awareness.

Time, Place, and Posture

It can be very easy to get caught up in daily routines and not follow through on your intention to practice. Schedule your formal practice in whatever calendar you use for your daily life and try to observe this special time with the same discipline as you would a doctor's appointment. Try to practice at least five days a week. Try to choose an amount of time you are going to practice for and stick to that. Forty-five minutes is a good amount of time for a session, but if you have less time or would like to start out slowly, you may try a half hour or fifteen minutes. You may use an alarm or stick of incense to measure the time. The amount of time you practice in each session may increase as you become more familiar with the practice. Instructions from a mindfulness teacher or CD will help guide you in starting your practice.

Find a relaxing environment without distractions, such as a phone, television, or the noise of other people. It's advisable to sit up with the spine as straight as possible. You may sit on the floor, on a meditation cushion, or on a chair. You can also sit on a folded towel or blanket or cushions from your couch.

Most people meditate with their eyes closed, but if you prefer or are more comfortable doing so, you can keep them partially open. If you choose to keep them open, please remember the focus is on whatever meditation you are practicing.

You can fold your hands on your lap or place them on your thighs.

Position yourself so you can remain alert yet comfortable. Just as the strings on an instrument can be wound too tight or too loose, a meditator can sit too rigidly, causing a lot of discomfort. This may result in not sitting for very long. Conversely, a meditator whose posture is too relaxed may end up falling asleep.

Mindfulness of Breathing

Sitting meditation often begins with mindfulness of breathing. By being aware of the shifting quality of the breath as you inhale and exhale, you can learn a great deal about the nature of impermanence and life. Much like the ebb and flow of the ocean's waves, the breath is constantly in a state of change, coming in and going out. This is a powerful teacher that underscores how everything changes in life and that it's possible to go with the flow rather than fighting it. It also brings a recognition that the stronger the resistance, the greater the suffering. It's natural to go after what you want and try to hold on to it and, conversely, to push away what you don't want. However, this self-limiting definition often fuels a push-and-pull relationship between what you want and don't want and can make you feel restless and ill at ease; in short, it leads to suffering. For example, if you try to resist the process of breathing, you'll find that discomfort arises almost instantly and can rapidly develop into suffering! Simply being with your breath as you practice mindfulness meditation allows you to experience firsthand the ever-changing quality of your experience and helps you open up to going with the flow of life with less grasping and aversion and with a greater sense of space and freedom.

Mindfulness of Sensations

After spending some time with the breath, you'll expand your awareness to the field of physical sensations. You simply open awareness to whatever sensations are predominant or distinct in each moment. Noticing the coming and going of sensations throughout the body in this way makes this practice much more fluid and reflective of the direct experience of the present moment. The human body is a dynamic organism with sensory receptors that are essentially in a perpetual state of fluctuation, experiencing a wide array of sensations (itching, tingling, warmth, coolness, dryness, moisture, heaviness, lightness, pain, and so on) that may be either pleasant, unpleasant, or neutral. If you aren't feeling any distinct sensations, you can bring awareness to any point of contact, such as your body touching the chair, your feet on the floor, or your hands making contact with your lap— wherever you feel contact. In mindfulness meditation, there's nothing to analyze or figure out about these sensations. Simply maintain attention on the field of sensory experience, noticing as each sensation arises and then recedes. Directly focusing on the transitory quality of physical sensations will deepen your understanding of the nature of change.

Mindfulness of Hearing

Next, you'll extend your mindful awareness to hearing. By listening to various sounds rise and fall, you come into direct contact with impermanence in yet another way. Mindfulness of sounds can be very useful. As with mindfulness of the breath, most of us can engage in this practice almost anytime and anywhere, since so many of us live in noisy, busy environments where sounds are almost always coming and going. If a particular sound is persistent and possibly even annoying, such as a car alarm, loud music, kids screaming, traffic, or airplanes, simply bring attention to the sound itself without evaluation. On a more elemental level, the mind simply hears sound waves. Auditory phenomena are always present; you cannot escape them. Even if you isolated yourself in a deep cave or a soundproof room, you'd still hear the internal sounds of your pulse, your heartbeat, or ringing in your ears. Whatever your auditory environment, try not to judge the sounds as good or bad. Simply notice how they arise and recede as impermanent events.

As you turn your focus to hearing, you can begin to transform any irritation with sounds. There is no need to like or dislike them; they're just sounds. You may hear sounds outside or indoors, or as your concentration deepens, you may be aware of sounds within the body. All of these are just sounds, appearing and disappearing. There's no need to analyze them or figure them out; simply maintain bare attention on the ever-changing field of auditory experience.

Mindfulness of Thoughts and Emotions

After meditating on sounds, you'll shift to mental events (thoughts and emotions) as the object of meditation, directing attention to the mind and the thought process itself. As well as seeing and experiencing the content of your thoughts and emotions, sometimes known as the "ten thousand joys and sorrows," you'll begin to see that thoughts and emotions are always changing, just like the breath, sensations, and sounds. Rather than getting involved in the contents of the mind, you can become more interested in just experiencing the process. As you become aware of the stories you spin and the traps you create, you can begin to disengage from them.

Mindfulness cultivates the ability to observe and experience thoughts and emotions as they arise, develop, and recede. There's no need to analyze them or figure them out; simply view them as mental formations that come and go. It's like lying in a meadow watching the clouds float through the sky or like sitting in a movie theater watching the images and sounds changing on the screen. In other words, the practice is simply to experience and be mindful of the changing nature of mental formations that rise and fall away moment to moment.

Here's a helpful metaphor: Many different types of storms arise in the ever-changing atmosphere of our planet—occasionally very powerful storms, such as Category 5 hurricanes. Yet even with the strongest hurricane, the sky doesn't feel the effect of the storms. The virtue of the sky is that it has plenty of space to let the storm run its course. Within this vast space, the storm eventually dissipates. In a sense, mindfulness helps you develop an internal awareness as big as the sky. By practicing mindfulness, you can begin to watch the storms of fear, anxiety, and other emotions and give them the space they need to transform and diminish in intensity. By observing and experiencing thoughts and emotions and allowing them to go wherever they need to go, you can come to see them as transient mental phenomena and understand that you are not your thoughts. Your thoughts are not facts, nor are they a complete definition of who you are. Freeing yourself from your own self-limiting constructions will bring deeper levels of freedom and peace.

Choiceless Awareness

The last and most expansive aspect of this practice of sitting mindfulness meditation is choiceless awareness, or present-moment awareness. In this practice, the present moment becomes the primary object of attention. Choiceless awareness invites you to become mindful of whatever is arising in the unfolding of each moment in the endless succession of present moments—whatever arises in the body and mind, whether sensations, sounds, or other sensory phenomena, or mental events like thoughts and emotions. Although outwardly you may be very still, your internal experience may be very different as you sit back and watch the ever-shifting tides of physical and mental experience.

Together, your body and mind are a single dynamic organism that's constantly in a state of change, with interactions between stimuli from thoughts, emotions, physical sensations, sounds, sights, smells, and tastes. As you practice choiceless awareness, simply observe what's predominant or compelling in the mind and body and be present to it. If nothing is especially prevalent and you're unsure of where to place your attention, you can always go back to the breath, sensations, sounds, or thoughts and emotions as a way to anchor into the here and now.

This practice is analogous to sitting by the edge of a river, just watching whatever goes downstream, and indeed, it is one of the most fluid of meditation practices, as it reflects the unfolding of your direct experience moment by moment. Sometimes there are sounds, sometimes sensations, sometimes thoughts and emotions. Just sit and witness the sea of change in your mind and body. Even if you're experiencing storms of anxiety, pain, sadness, anger, or confusion, know that by giving them space, they will gradually diminish.

Mindfulness FAQ

JEFF BRANTLEY

Isn't meditation something religious? Why is meditation taught in hospitals? In answering questions that he fields on a daily basis, Jeff Brantley, MD, of Duke Integrative Medicine, gives us insight into how mindfulness acts as "self-regulatory practice" that promotes deep relaxation and circumvents harmful reactions to stress.

MANY PEOPLE I encounter in the hospital setting want to know exactly what meditation means. I tell them that meditation refers to intentionally paying attention to a particular object for a particular purpose. Spiritual practitioners and members of many faith traditions have developed meditation practices over countless years of human experience. There are literally thousands of ways to practice meditation. As it has been developed in diverse faith traditions, the purpose of all meditation practice is to awaken us. Meditation is intended to bring about transformation and change through understanding, compassion, and clarity of seeing.

Meditation practices may generally be grouped into two basic categories based on the emphasis placed on where one's attention is directed during practice. First, there are "concentration" practices. In these, the practitioner focuses attention (concentrates) on a narrow field, usually a single object. For example, in the service of spiritual practice, people may repeat a meaningful phrase or prayer over and over, or they may fix their attention on an object or a sacred figure. In these concentration practices, when the attention wanders or is drawn away from the object of attention, practitioners gently return their attention to the object. The object is selected for reasons specific to each person and to his or her particular faith tradition. Done for health purposes, concentration practices may select a more neutral object such as the sensation of the breath or the sensation of the body as it moves.

The second general category of meditation practice includes all forms that emphasize awareness, or "mindfulness." Such activities seek to develop and nourish present-moment awareness. They encourage paying attention so as to be more aware in the present moment of all that is here and of the constantly changing nature of what is here. These mindfulness practices are often described as "being, not doing," because mindfulness itself is the innate quality of human beings, which is bare awareness. Mindfulness can be defined as careful, openhearted, choiceless, present-moment awareness.

Mindfulness benefits from the ability to concentrate attention but is not the same as concentration. It is a quality that human beings already have, but they have usually not been advised that they have it, that it is valuable, or that it can be cultivated. Mindfulness is the awareness that is not thinking but is aware of thinking, as well as of each of the other ways we experience the sensory world; that is, seeing, hearing, tasting, smelling, and feeling through the body. Mindfulness is nonjudgmental and openhearted (friendly and inviting of whatever arises in awareness). It is cultivated by paying attention purposely, deeply, and without judgment to whatever arises in the present moment, either inside or outside of us. By intentionally practicing mindfulness, deliberately paying more careful moment-to-moment attention, individuals can live more fully and less on "automatic pilot," thus being more present in their own lives. Mindfulness meditation practices seek to develop this quality of clear, present-moment awareness in a systematic way so that the practitioner may enjoy these benefits. Being more aware in each moment of life has benefits both to a person doing a specific spiritual practice and to the same person in everyday life.

Why is meditation now offered in health care settings and for stress reduction?
The use of meditation in health care settings and for stress reduction is related to discoveries about the mind-body connection in health and illness that have been made in Western medicine over the last twenty-five to thirty years. In that time, researchers have discovered that the mind and body are

intimately connected. It is now known that thoughts, beliefs, emotions, and stress all have a great impact on health and illness. Meditation is one of a variety of so-called self-regulatory practices people can learn to do for themselves to promote their own health and well-being. Research has shown that individuals who learn and practice these skills are likely to have better health outcomes than those who do not. In particular, research has shown that the ability to concentrate one's attention can promote deep relaxation in the body and that the ability to be more mindful in each situation can help break one's destructive habitual reactions to stress.

Why is daily meditation practice important?

Research has shown that meditation is similar to other lifestyle changes in that it is only effective if you do it. Exercise, dietary changes, or meditation—any lifestyle change requires consistent practice to gain results. In early studies of meditation, Harvard cardiologist Herbert Benson demonstrated that practicing meditation for twenty minutes, twice a day, was sufficient to bring about significant reductions in blood pressure in many people. The exact number of minutes of daily practice necessary to bring benefits for large populations is not well understood, and in truth, it probably varies. Generally, however, we can say that regular daily meditation practice of at least thirty minutes or more is likely to bring benefits to the person who does it.

Do the meditation practices taught in health care settings have anything to do with Eastern religions or cults?

The use of meditation practices here in the West, largely for health benefits and promoted and investigated by the emerging field of mind-body medicine, is only about twenty-five to thirty years old. However, many of the meditation methods now taught in the West for health purposes owe some (or considerable) debt to the instructions and experience detailed by meditation teachers of more ancient traditions.

There is already an enormous body of experience with meditation and yogic practice in different traditions worldwide. The challenge for those working in the emerging field of mind-body medicine in the West has been to identify what is useful and relevant about meditation and yogic practices in those more ancient and diverse contexts and to translate it into something practical for those in the contemporary Western health care culture who wish to utilize that information, be they consumers or providers. Those who have pioneered meditation for health purposes in Western medicine in the past three decades have made deliberate efforts to make the meditation practices they teach nonsectarian and available to people of any and all faith traditions.

I can't meditate. Instead of quieting my mind, all I do is think.

As we practice mindfulness or present-moment awareness, we can expect to experience difficulties. For example, with growing awareness in each moment in each situation of our lives, we begin to be aware of the unpleasant and painful as well as the pleasant. We may become more aware of "neutral" experiences as well, seeing even in these some unpleasant or pleasant aspect that was previously unnoticed. This growing awareness of the unpleasant can be upsetting to the beginning meditator. They can mistakenly believe they are "not doing it right" or are "not cut out to meditate." At this stage, it is vital that the meditator realizes that growing our awareness of any aspect of life is actually progress. Those in a Mindfulness-Based Stress Reduction program might ask, "How does growing awareness of pain and the unpleasant help reduce my stress?" The answer is that to have a chance to reduce our stress and to heal ourselves from the toll stress takes in our lives we must find a way to see clearly all that is here. We must remain aware and present in order to give ourselves the best chance to make the most skillful response to whatever situation life offers us.

So if through the practice of present-moment awareness, we grow in awareness and begin to experience the unpleasant (as well as the pleasant) more deeply, more intensely, this is actually waking up to the reality of our lives. Yet it can be difficult to remain present, to "keep our seat," to continue meditating and continue our practice of present-moment awareness. To support us in remaining present in these difficult moments, it is useful to call upon some other qualities we have within us. These qualities are kindness, compassion, and equanimity. It is important to realize that we are not imagining these qualities or inventing them. Rather, they are already within us, important elements of our deepest nature as human beings. Unfortunately, many people do not realize the depth and power of these qualities within themselves, nor do they know how (or that it is even possible) to bring them forward and cultivate these qualities in their own lives.

As we gain some increasing awareness of our own pain, it is important to notice our reaction. Too often people meet pain in themselves with criticism, meanness, or a sense of failure. They fall into patterns of stressful and destructive self-blame that just add to the misery they already feel. Practicing mindfulness, we can be aware of our own pain, whatever its nature (physical, emotional, and so on). And we can recognize our patterns and habits of judging and blaming ourselves for our own pain. Recognizing these patterns, we can respond with kindness and compassion instead of reacting with blame and meanness. Our challenge thus becomes, "Can we meet and hold our own pain with the same compassion and kindness as we would meet and hold the pain of a loved one?" This holding of ourselves in kindness and compassion is not easy! Most of our lives we have taken a very different attitude toward ourselves and our own pain. For that reason, we have to practice kindness and compassion openly and often toward ourselves. Our growing mindfulness can be a great ally in changing our habits of meanness toward ourselves to habits of kindness and compassion. As we learn to be aware of our own pain and our habitual critical and judgmental reactions about that pain, we have a choice in each moment of taking a different path, the path of compassion and kindness.

How do I bring mindfulness into my daily life?

Have you ever started eating an ice cream cone, taken a lick or two, then noticed all you had was a sticky napkin in your hand? Or been going somewhere and arrived at your destination only to realize you hadn't noticed anything or anyone along the way? Of course you have; we all have. These are common examples of mindlessness, or "going on automatic pilot."

We all fall into habits of inattention that result in our not being present for our lives. The consequences of this inattention can be quite costly. They can result in our missing some really good things and also in our ignoring really important information and messages about our lives, our relationships, and even our own health.

Our reactions to the stressful events of our lives can become so habituated that they occur essentially out of our awareness until, because of physical or emotional or psychological dysfunction, we cannot ignore them any longer. These reactions can include tensing the body; experiencing painful emotional states, even panic and depression; and being prisoners of habits of thinking and self-talk, including obsessional list making and intense, even toxic self-criticism.

An important antidote to this tendency to "tune out," to go on automatic pilot, is to practice mindfulness.

All we have to do is establish attention in the present moment and allow ourselves to rest in the awareness of what is here. To pay attention without trying to change anything, to allow ourselves to become more deeply and completely aware of what it is we are sensing, and to rest in this quality of being in each moment as our life unfolds.

And to the extent we can practice "being" and become more present and more aware of our life and in our life, what we do about all of it will become more informed, more responsive, and less driven by the habits of reaction and inattention.

Make the effort! Whenever you think of it in your day or night, remember that you can be more mindful. See for yourself what it might be like to pay more careful attention and allow yourself to experience directly what is here, especially what is here in your own body, heart, and mind. Change the way you start a new activity. For example, begin a meeting with two minutes of silence and attention on the breath, or take a few mindful breaths before entering a patient's room, or focus on the breath before starting your exercise routine. In the middle of an ongoing situation or process, bring attention to the breath or to the sensations that arise while you are washing dishes, eating a meal, walking the dog, doing a job, and so forth. Or when you are just waiting, in between the things on your schedule, gently bring attention to the breath. If you're at a red light, in a line at the bus stop or grocery store, or waiting for someone to arrive, notice the sounds, sensations, sights, or thoughts that arise.

In these situations, use the sensation of the breath as your anchor for awareness in the present moment. Establish mindfulness on the narrow focus of just-the-breath sensation. Allow yourself to feel the breath as it goes in and out and the pause between in and out. Do not try to control the breath. Simply let it come and go. Bring as much complete and continuous attention as you can to the direct sensation of the breath.

Anytime you feel lost or confused or frustrated, gently narrow the focus and return awareness to the sensation of the breath. You may have to do this frequently. That's okay. Or you may wish to concentrate mainly on the breath, especially if you are new to meditation. That, too, is okay.

The important thing is the quality of awareness you bring to the moment. One moment of mindfulness, one breath when we are truly present, can be quite profound. See for yourself!

Practice for a few breaths at a time, even for a few mindful moments. And if you wish, you can make this a more formal meditation practice by setting aside some time (from a few minutes to an hour or more, as you wish) free from other activity or distraction to devote full attention to simply being present, being mindful of what is present. Over time you may find that the formal practice supports and strengthens your ability to practice mindfulness informally throughout the day in different situations.

My mind is all over the place, and it's just too hard to stay here.

Expect your mind to wander, even if you practice for just a few breaths or a few minutes. Practice kindness and patience with yourself when this happens, and gently return awareness to the breath sensation.

Notice any tendency to be hard on yourself or to feel frustrated or like a failure. See this kind of judgment as just another kind of thinking, and gently return awareness to the breath.

Expect to feel some relaxation, even in short periods of practice. This relaxed feeling is an ally. It helps us to be more present, more mindful. Relaxation alone is not what mindfulness is about, however. It is about being present with awareness.

Expect to become more mindful with practice. Expect to notice more things, including more painful things. This is actually progress! You are not doing anything wrong! Quite the opposite, you are increasing mindfulness for all things. When you begin to notice the painful things, see if you can hold yourself with compassion and kindness, and continue to bring open-hearted awareness to the experience that is unfolding. By practicing staying present, not turning away from what is painful in our lives, we can learn to remain open to all possibilities in each situation. This increases our chances for healing and transformation. It also gives us a way to be with those situations when there is nothing more we can do to get away from the pain, when there is no alternative but to be with it. We can discover that the quality of mindfulness is not destroyed or damaged by contact with pain. It can know and relax with pain as completely and fully as it knows and relaxes with any other experience.

Finally, be careful not to try too hard when practicing mindfulness. Don't try to make anything happen or to achieve any special states or special effects. Simply relax and pay as much attention as you can to just what is here now. Whatever form that takes. Allow yourself to experience life directly as it unfolds, paying careful and openhearted attention.

Mindfulness and Awareness

CHÖGYAM TRUNGPA

What does it really feel like to practice mindfulness meditation? Do we focus intently or do we let the mind hang loose? In this classic piece, renowned meditation master Chögyam Trungpa shares his understanding of how to balance the detailed focus of mindfulness with the spaciousness of awareness.

MEDITATION practice is not a matter of trying to produce a hypnotic state of mind or create a sense of restfulness. Trying to achieve a restful state of mind reflects a mentality of poverty. Seeking a restful state of mind, one is on guard against restlessness. There is a constant sense of paranoia and limitation. We feel a need to be on guard against the sudden fits of passion or aggression that might take us over, make us lose control. This guarding process limits the scope of the mind by not accepting whatever comes.

Instead, meditation should reflect a mentality of richness in the sense of using everything that occurs in the state of mind. Thus, if we provide enough room for restlessness so that it might function within the space, then the energy ceases to be restless because it can trust itself fundamentally. Meditation is giving a huge, luscious meadow to a restless cow. The cow might be restless for a while in its huge meadow, but at some stage, because there is so much space, the restlessness becomes irrelevant. So the cow eats and eats and eats and relaxes and falls asleep.

Acknowledging restlessness, identifying with it, requires *mindfulness,* whereas providing a luscious meadow, a big space for the restless cow, requires *awareness.* So mindfulness and awareness always complement each other. Mindfulness is the process of relating with individual situations directly, precisely, definitely. You communicate or connect with problematic situations or irritating situations in a simple way. There is ignorance, there is restlessness, there is passion, there is aggression. They need not be praised or condemned. They are just regarded as fits. They are responses we have become conditioned to apply in various situations, but they can be seen accurately and precisely by the unconditioned mindfulness. Mindfulness is like a microscope; it is neither an offensive nor a defensive weapon in relation to the germs we observe through it. The function of the microscope is just to present clearly what is there. Mindfulness need not refer to the past or the future; it is fully in the now. At the same time, it is an active mind involved in dualistic perceptions, for it is necessary in the beginning to use that kind of discriminating judgment.

Awareness is seeing the discovery of mindfulness. We do not have to dispose of or keep the contents of mind. The precision of mindfulness could be left as it is because it has its own environment, its own space. We do not have to make decisions to throw it away or keep it as a treasure. Thus awareness is another step toward choicelessness in situations.

The Sanskrit word for awareness is *smriti,* which means "recognition" or "recollection." Recollection, not in the sense of remembering the past, but in the sense of recognizing the product of mindfulness. The mindfulness provides some ground, some room for recognition of aggression, passion, and so on. Mindfulness provides the topic or the terms or the words, and awareness is the grammar that goes around and correctly locates the terms.

Having experienced the precision of mindfulness, we might ask the question of ourselves, "What should I do with that? What can I do next?" And awareness reassures us that we do not really have to do anything with it but can leave it in its own natural place. It is like discovering a beautiful flower in the jungle; shall we pick the flower and bring it home, or shall we let the flower stay in the jungle? Awareness says leave the flower in the jungle, since it is the natural place for that plant to grow. So awareness is the willingness not to cling to the discoveries of mindfulness, and mindfulness is just precision—things are what they are. Mindfulness is the vanguard of awareness. We need not regard life as worth boycotting or indulging in. Life situations are the food of awareness and mindfulness, which work together to bring acceptance of living situations as they are.

Mindfulness for Everyone

NORMAN FISCHER

Norman Fischer—the principal meditation teacher in Google's Search Inside Yourself program for its employees—learned to practice meditation through Zen training. Now, forty years after beginning meditation practice, he sees many ways in which mindfulness practice can help people without reference to any religious affiliation. Aside from basic mindfulness practice, there are simple techniques we can all use throughout our day.

A FEW YEARS AGO I was watching a video of a PBS show called *Healing and the Mind* that featured Jon Kabat-Zinn teaching a Mindfulness-Based Stress Reduction class at the University of Massachusetts (UMass) Medical Center. As everyone knows by now, Jon had invented this vocabulary and technique, an adaptation of Buddhist mindfulness practice, to help hospital patients whose cases had been pronounced hopeless. Since there seemed to be nothing the doctors could do to alleviate their chronic pain and illness, the hospital decided to give Jon, then a medical school faculty member, a shot. His eight-week course turned out to be wildly successful. Over many years, it brought not only relief but also wisdom and happiness to thousands of patients with previously intractable conditions.

As a Zen priest who'd spent most of my adult life in monasteries and temples, I was initially skeptical as I watched that video. For me, Buddhism was a radical religion whose goals and practices were at odds with what people were normally looking for in life. I had been trained to view enlightenment as the goal of Buddhism—total liberation that went far beyond worldly aspirations like health and well-being. In my Soto Zen tradition, the desire to derive any benefit at all from the practice—"a gaining idea," as Suzuki Roshi, our founder in America, had called it—was really bad. Gaining ideas would blunt your sincerity, and sincere effort was the most important thing.

Yet as a religious person, I was sympathetic to the idea of helping people in need. It also thrilled me to think that the esoteric practice I was engaged in might serve larger numbers of them. So it took almost no time for Jon's compassion—his sheer love for the people he was working with and his passion to try to help them—to win me over. All doctrines and notions about what the practice was supposed to be or not be were swept aside by the depth of caring I saw in action in that video. Jon was not trying to sell anybody anything. The claims he made for the practice were honest and encouraging. "Try this, I think it will help. But you have to be patient; you can't hate your illness and be desperate to make it disappear. Be patient and work with your condition, not against it. Then maybe something will change." It was a different way of speaking about meditation practice than I was used to, but one that was clearly authentic. Later I went to the clinic at UMass to witness classes. I met and spent time with Jon, and we quickly became friends. I learned from him that what I'd read in the ancient Buddhist texts was true: the path is available to everyone and must be shared, and to guide others effectively, you must be willing to use whatever comes to hand ("skillful means").

Since news of Jon's work has spread, a host of ways have developed to apply dharma, which as Jon has often said, simply means "universal truth."

Mostly these efforts have used, as Jon has used, the language of mindfulness to describe the method of practice. The Sanskrit words for mindfulness are *sati,* which means "basic awareness," and *smirti,* which includes the idea of remembering to come back to awareness when the mind has strayed from it. Although what we call meditation includes many forms and techniques, meditation is basically mindfulness. Sitting quietly, you establish awareness of the body and of the breathing. When your mind wanders, you bring it back. Once basic awareness of body and breath is established, you can also be aware of bodily sensations, thoughts, feelings, and so on—whatever arises in the field of awareness can be appreciated as long as you let it arise and pass away without too much identification, judgment, or entanglement. In fact, one definition of mindfulness is "nonjudgmental awareness." Just seeing what's there.

In the *Mindfulness Sutra,* the primary Buddhist text on mindfulness practice, the Buddha says that mindfulness is "the only way to deliverance." This is very counterintuitive to our can-do Western mentality. Mindfulness proposes that the more we try to fix or improve things, the more we get stuck in them. But if we are willing to simply be aware, without entanglement, things will slowly come naturally to wise equilibrium.

What we call meditation—sitting quietly without moving—is a particularly focused form of mindfulness. But mindfulness practice goes beyond conventional meditation. Once we have some training in mindfulness meditation, we can extend mindfulness to any other activity until mindfulness eventually becomes a way of life. We become much more aware of what is going on, within and without. When we're angry, we know we're angry; when we're afraid, we know we're afraid. With awareness of our state, we don't react wildly, compelled by unconscious impulses; instead we respond with much more accuracy and kindness. This movement from reactivity to response is the key shift that mindfulness practice aims for. But it comes about organically, with training but without forcing anything.

Mindfulness is easy to explain, but the actual practice is subtle. Since we are always aware to some extent, unless we are asleep, it can be hard to grasp the difference between normal awareness and the more subtle, eyes-wide-open, nonjudgmental awareness of mindfulness practice. But with some training, you do get the hang of it. In the last decade or two, there has been an enormous amount of research corroborating the efficacy of mindfulness in healing and mind training of all sorts. At this point, there is not much doubt that mindfulness practice brings benefits on many fronts: it reduces stress and so promotes basic health; it provides methods to bring healing to difficult illnesses; it improves personal effectiveness in work and personal relationships; it can be a basis for the cultivation of all sorts of positive emotional and attitudinal states, like compassion, loving-kindness, and equanimity.

Jon found himself at UMass Hospital, saw a problem, and had the intuitive sense that the basic mindfulness practice he knew might help. I have tried to do the same. Whenever someone has appeared to ask me to help with an issue that mindfulness practice might address, I have always said yes.

In the 1980s, even before I saw the video of Jon's program, colleagues and I at the San Francisco Zen Center began the Zen Hospice Project. We had noticed that the simple act of mindfully caring for the dying—simply offering a damp towel, a cup of tea, and a smile, with a spirit of acceptance rather than resistance to impermanence—was powerfully healing. Our community had cared for Alan Chadwick, our gardening teacher; for the Buddhist writer Lama Govinda; for the philosopher and anthropologist Gregory Bateson; for our friend and Native American teacher Harry Roberts; and for our own Zen teacher, Suzuki Roshi, who died in 1971. It seemed natural, then, for us to apply dharma in this simple way, especially at the height of the AIDS crisis in San Francisco, when so many of our friends and fellow practitioners were in need. Today the Zen Hospice Project continues to do its caregiving work. It has also spun off another organization, the Metta Institute, that aspires to have an impact on how end-of-life care is delivered in America by training health care professionals who work with the dying in the kind of mindful care we have developed over the years.

I am on the faculty of Metta and have found it interesting to figure out how to teach mindfulness practice in a professional context. Professionals have a lot of knowledge about medical and psychological issues relating to the care of the dying and their families. But what they are not necessarily good at, and where mindfulness practice can help, is the development of a compassionate presence—the ability to evoke an atmosphere of love, forgiveness, and acceptance, so that whatever healing is possible in those last days or weeks can be encouraged to take place. Any time death is imminent, this atmosphere is potentially present. But where there's too much fear and denial or too much pressing for a particular result, things don't go well. Sometimes professional knowledge and experience not only don't help with this, but they can get in the way. Thinking you know what to do, having experienced past cases, can blind you to what is uniquely present now. With careful attention to what is going on deep inside, mindfulness practice can bring you to more awareness of your basic confusion about death, your possibly exaggerated need to help heroically, all your unconscious stumbling blocks. If you can learn to be aware of such things with acceptance and forgiveness, if you can also receive some training in becoming comfortable with silence through intensive meditation training, you will have a deeper capacity to be with the dying in a healing way—and also be better prepared to face one's own death.

I have two old friends, Gary Friedman and Jack Himmelstein, who train professionals in conflict resolution and mediation. After years of talking about how mindfulness meditation could be used in their work, we began to include it in the training. Gary and Jack practice what they call "understanding-based conflict resolution." The goal is to help people in conflict understand one another as a basis for resolving issues rather than to simply act as a broker to bring about a compromise solution, which is generally the method used in mediation. One of Gary and Jack's key concepts is the notion that no conflict is about what it seems to be about. Impasses over money or property are really about deeper concerns that usually do not surface. Any solution that does not address these deeper concerns won't really hold.

For years they have taught a method of dialogue that helps mediators guide parties to a discovery of what lurks beneath the surface of conflict, and they have been successful. But the introduction of ongoing mindfulness practice has taken their work to a new level. When mediators learn to see more deeply into their own motivations and prejudices with a sense of acceptance and curiosity rather than judgment, they are able to make use of their own emotions—and to understand others better. The conventional wisdom in mediation work is that the mediator must keep his or her emotions out of the equation and be a neutral, dispassionate observer. But anyone who has practiced mindfulness knows that there's no way to keep your emotions out of anything, and imagining you are doing so only means you are prey to your emotions rather than guided by them with some wisdom. I remember the aha moment in one of our training sessions, when a mediator realized that she didn't have to pretend she wasn't angry at one of the parties—mindfulness practice had given her the capacity to be aware of her anger without expressing it inappropriately, so she could learn from it and make use of it to help the parties find a solution.

For some years, I have also worked with lawyers under the auspices of the Center for Contemplative Mind in Society, a nonprofit with a mission well described by its name. Contemplative Mind's Law Project sponsors a group of lawyers who meet with me regularly to meditate and engage in dialogue and experimentation. Here the issue is, how can mindfulness practice help to humanize what has become a very stressful and difficult profession? Each year we offer national mindfulness retreats for lawyers to share our explorations with others.

Over a number of years, these lawyers have revolutionized the way they view and carry out their work, moving from what some of them have called the "gladiator model" of zealous advocacy to one in which they see themselves as wise counsel and allies to their clients, trying to bring healing to very difficult human situations rather than simply trying to win cases. The lawyers have often noted that sometimes winning the case with maximum aggression does not actually serve the needs of the client.

Probably the clearest way to understand mindfulness work with lawyers, mediators, and end-of-life care professionals is as training in emotional intelligence (EI). EI is a concept popularized by journalist Daniel Goleman, another Buddhist practitioner motivated by a desire to usefully apply dharma. While it is clear from many studies that emotional intelligence is a key factor in effectiveness in all sorts of spheres, it is not so clear how or if one can develop it. It turns out that—as I have found—mindfulness practice is the most effective way to improve EI. At Google, the enthusiastic and idealistic young engineers are not looking for calmness or healing, but they are interested in developing emotional intelligence for work and for their personal lives. Our six-week course there, called Search Inside Yourself, uses meditation, journaling, mindful dialogue, and a host of other techniques to improve EI.

Many of the practices I use there, and in the other trainings I do, are simple extensions of mindfulness practice. They are readily adaptable by anyone who would like to use them to develop more mindfulness in everyday life. We're using an e-mailing practice, for instance, that incorporates mindfulness. You can try it. Instead of shooting off a hurried e-mail and dealing with the consequences later, take an extra moment. Write the e-mail, then close your eyes and visualize the person who is going to receive it. Remember that he or she is alive, a feeling human being. Now go back and reread the e-mail, changing anything you now feel you want to change before sending it.

We also train people in a communication practice called "looping": when listening to someone, intentionally try to pay close attention to what is being said rather than entertaining your own similar or dissimilar thoughts. When the person is finished talking, say, "Let me make sure I understand what you are saying. I think you said . . ." and then feed back what you heard. This way the person feels truly understood and respected—and has a chance to correct whatever distortions there may have been in your hearing. Looping saves a lot of trouble and misunderstanding, especially when the communication is sensitive or difficult.

There are many more practices like this, simple but powerful techniques to maintain mindfulness throughout the day:

Taking three conscious breaths—just three!—from time to time to interrupt your busy activity with a moment or two of calm awareness.

Keeping mindfulness slogan cards around your office or home to remind you to "Breathe" or "Pay Attention" or "Think Again."

Training yourself through repetition to apply a phrase like "Is that really true?" to develop the habit of questioning your assumptions before you run with them.

Whenever you get up to walk somewhere during the day, practice mindful walking—noticing your weight as it touches the ground with each swing of your leg and footfall.

Instituting the habit of starting your day by returning to your best intention, what you aspire to for yourself and others when you have a benevolent frame of mind.

My mediation training partner, Gary Friedman, practices returning to his best intention by pausing before he sits down to meet his first clients of the day. He silently reminds himself, as he places his hands on the back of his chair, that he is about to participate in a sacred act—the effort to bring peace to conflict. In these and many other ways you can invent, mindfulness can be extended to practically any situation in daily life. And it will make a difference.

I believe the Buddha never intended to create a specialized sphere of life called "religion." In his time, there was no question of secular or sacred, church on Sunday and work during the week. There was only life and life's difficulties, and the possibility that with cultivation one could live with less trouble and strife. Although many of his teachings were given in the context of the monastic community in which he lived, many more were given to laypeople to make their lives more peaceful and successful. The contemporary application of dharma to so many spheres of contemporary life would not, I think, seem strange to the Buddha.

Philip Snyder, former executive director of the Center for Contemplative Mind in Society and an anthropologist, is fond of saying that a thousand years ago our civilization was profoundly altered by the spreading of literacy to the general public from the monasteries where it had been exclusively practiced. Could it now be the case, he wonders, that the practice of mindfulness developed for millennia in monasteries and temples will similarly be released and spread throughout the world with just as large an impact?

Why Mindfulness Matters

Jon Kabat-Zinn

Mindfulness-Based Stress Reduction pioneer and best-selling author Jon Kabat-Zinn, founder of the Center for Mindfulness in Medicine, Health Care, and Society, shares several good reasons for us to make mindfulness part of our lives and our communities.

THE WORD DHARMA refers to both the teachings of the Buddha and also to the way things are, the fundamental lawfulness of the universe. So although the Buddha articulated the Dharma, the Dharma itself can't be Buddhist any more than the law of gravity is English because of Newton or Italian because of Galileo. It is a universal lawfulness. I specifically asked His Holiness the Dalai Lama—at the Mind and Life XIII conference in Washington, D.C., in 2005—whether there was any fundamental difference between Buddhadharma and universal dharma, and he said no.

The central mission of my work and that of my colleagues at the Center for Mindfulness has been to bring universal dharma into the mainstream of human activity for the benefit of as many people as possible. That's a very broad calling, so as a skillful means, I chose very consciously from the beginning to anchor it in medicine and health care. I thought that would be the most fertile ground for introducing meditation and the wisdom and compassion of the dharma in its universal aspect to a wider world, hopefully in an authentic and meaningful way. After all, hospitals function as magnets for suffering in our society, so what better place for the teachings about suffering and the end of suffering to be made available in ways that people might be able to resonate with and adopt as their own?

In 2009, we celebrated the thirtieth anniversary of the founding of the Stress Reduction Clinic at the University of Massachusetts (UMass) Medical Center. The original vision has in some sense come to fruition, because Mindfulness-Based Stress Reduction (MBSR) has indeed spread to hospitals, clinics, and laboratories around the world. It's being researched, offered clinically, and experimented with in ways that were virtually inconceivable thirty years ago. I think that has come about because the world is longing for authentic experience that transcends the usual limitations we impose on ourselves through cultural traditions, ideologies, belief systems, and so forth. People are searching for ways to realize the full spectrum of their humanity.

The ultimate promise of mindfulness is much larger, much more profound, than simply cultivating our attentiveness. It helps us understand that our conventional view of ourselves and even what we mean by "self" is incomplete in some very important ways. Mindfulness helps us to recognize how and why we mistake the actuality of things for some story we create. It then makes it possible for us to chart a path toward greater sanity, well-being, and purpose.

Today, as we bring science together with meditation, we're beginning to find new ways—in language we can all understand—to show the benefits of training oneself to become intimate with the workings of one's own mind in a way that generates greater insight and clarity. The science is showing interesting and important health benefits of mind-body training and practices and is now beginning to elucidate the various pathways through which mindfulness may exert its effects on the brain (emotion regulation, working memory, cognitive control, attention, effects on some of the somatic maps of the body that the brain uses to manage sensory-motor activity of the body, cortical thickening in specific regions) and the body (symptom reduction, greater physical well-being, immune function enhancement, regulation of activity in large numbers and classes of genes). It is also showing that meditation can bring a sense of meaning and purpose to life, based on understanding the nonseparation of self and other. Given the condition we find ourselves in these days on this planet, understanding our interconnectedness is not a spiritual luxury; it's a societal imperative.

Three or four hundred years ago, not so long in the scheme of things, people practicing meditation did so under fairly isolated conditions, mostly in monasteries. Now meditation is being practiced and studied in laboratories, hospitals, and clinics, and it is even finding its way into primary and secondary schools. The people teaching and researching it have, in many cases, been involved with mindfulness for ten, twenty, thirty, or more years by now. They are not just jumping on some new mindfulness bandwagon. And their work has resulted in many professionals being drawn to mindfulness for the first time. That in itself is a wonderful phenomenon, as long as it is understood that mindfulness is not merely a nice "concept" but an orthogonal way of being that requires ongoing practice and cultivation.

Mindfulness work is spilling into areas way beyond medicine and health care and also beyond psychology and neuroscience. It's moving into programs on childbirth and parenting, education, business, athletics and professional sports, the legal profession, criminal justice, even politics. In so many different domains, it's becoming recognized as virtually axiomatic that the mind and body are and always have been on intimate speaking terms, at least biologically. We need to learn to be much more tuned in to the conversation and participate actively if we are going to function effectively and optimize our health and well-being.

The awareness we are speaking of when we use the term *mindfulness* also encompasses the motivations for our actions; for example, the ways we are driven by self-aggrandizement or greed. In the financial crisis of 2008–2009, we saw the effects of greed played out on a massive scale in the banks and insurance companies. Healing that disease is not just a matter of bailouts, stimulus packages, and magically creating greater confidence in the economy. We need to create a different kind of confidence and a new kind of economics, one that's not about mindless spending but more about marshaling resources for the greater good, for one's own being, for society, and for the planet. Mindfulness can help open the door to that by helping us go beyond approaches that are based on conceptual thought alone and that are driven by unbounded and legally sanctioned greed. It seems that we can't simply think our way out of our problems. Even very, very smart people—and there are plenty of them around—are starting to recognize that thinking is only one of many forms of intelligence. If we don't recognize the multiple dimensions of intelligence, we are hampering our ability to find creative solutions and outcomes for problems that don't admit to simple-minded fixes. It's like having a linear view in medicine that sees health care solely as fixing people up—an auto mechanic's model of the body that doesn't understand healing and transformation, doesn't understand what happens when you harmonize mind and body. The element that's missing in that mechanical understanding is awareness.

Genuine awareness can modulate our thinking so that we become less driven by unexamined motivations to put ourselves first, to control things to assuage our fear, to always proffer our brilliant answer. We can create an enormous amount of harm, for example, by not listening to other people who might have different views and insights. Fortunately, we have more of an opportunity these days to balance the cultivation of thinking with the cultivation of awareness. Anyone can restore some degree of balance between thinking and awareness right in this present moment, which is the only moment that any of us ever has anyway. The potential outcomes from purposefully learning to inhabit awareness and bring thought into greater balance are extremely positive and healthy for ourselves and the world at large.

On the other hand, if we continue to dominate the planet the way our species has for the past six or seven thousand years, it could be very unhealthy. Regardless of the beauty that's come out of civilization, we could continue on a path of colossal upheavals that basically come from a human mind that does not make peace with itself—war, genocide, famine, grossly inadequate responses to natural disasters. These upheavals could destroy everything we hold most dear.

All we can do is listen deeply to the calling of our own hearts and of the world and do the best we can. One of the ways that I have tried to bring the healing and transformative potential of the dharma into modern everyday life in the West has been through attempts to develop an American vocabulary, a Western vocabulary, for speaking about things that until now we haven't really had a vocabulary for except within religious traditions. I emphasize the universality of the power of mindfulness and awareness, but I'm not talking about a universal church or a universal religious movement. I'm talking about understanding the nature of what it means to be human. I don't even like to use the word *spiritual.* Can we simply address what it means to be human—from an evolutionary point of view, from a historical point of view? What is available to us in this brief moment when the universe lifts itself up in the form of a human sentient body and being, and we live out our seventy, eighty, or ninety years (if that) and then dissolve back into the undifferentiated ocean of potential? A lot of the time we become so self-absorbed, so preoccupied, that we don't pursue the kind of fundamental inquiry Socrates proposed when he made the comment that "the unexamined life is not worth living."

In addition to developing a universal, nonreligious vocabulary, I have tried to stress the critical importance of the nondual aspect of meditation by emphasizing that it is not about getting anywhere else. This, of course, immediately brings up a lot of bewilderment in people, because almost everything we do seems to be about trying to get somewhere else. Why on earth would you not want to get somewhere else? If you're in a lot of pain or you have some kind of illness or whatever, you always want to get back to where you were or get to some better place in the future. It sounds almost un-American just to settle for what is, but that is a misunderstanding of the potential for living in the present moment. It's not a matter of settling. It's a matter of recognizing that, in some sense, it never gets any better than this.

The future is not here, even though we can create as many illusions about it as we'd like. The past is already over. We have to deal with things as they are in the moment. So it's most effective to deal with them if you don't perpetrate illusions on yourself about the nature of your experience and then fall into wishful thinking or ambition that drives you to create more harm than good.

When we delude ourselves about the true nature of our experience, we not only harm other people, we also harm ourselves, because we don't befriend certain elements of who we are, of our basic connection to others and to our environment. That's very sad and very unsatisfying. Healing and transformation are possible the moment we accept the actuality of things as they are—good, bad, or ugly—and then act on that understanding with imagination, kindness, and intentionality. This is not easy or painless, by any means, but it is both an embodiment of and a path toward wisdom and peace.

In this regard, we are trying to create a way of speaking about mindfulness as a practice, a way of being, and also as the culmination of the practice in any given moment that is so commonsensical that people will say, "Of course, that makes sense. It makes sense to be in the present moment, to be a little less judgmental or at least be aware of how judgmental I am. Why didn't I notice this earlier? It's so obvious."

As human beings, we have a history of great thoughts. Working on our mindfulness, by ourselves and with others, hinges on appreciating the power of awareness to balance thought. There's nothing wrong with thinking. So much that is beautiful comes out of thinking and out of our emotions. But if our thinking is not balanced with awareness, we can end up deluded, perpetually lost in thought, and out of our minds just when we need them the most.

PART TWO

Mindfulness in Daily Life

Mindfulness Makes Us Happy

Thich Nhat Hanh

The Vietnamese Zen monk Thich Nhat Hanh—one of the leading proponents of bringing mindfulness into all aspects of our lives—tells us that we don't have to work hard to be mindful. We find opportunities everywhere we go.

OUR TRUE HOME is not in the past. Our true home is not in the future. Our true home is in the here and the now. Life is available only in the here and the now, and it is our true home.

Mindfulness is the energy that helps us recognize the conditions of happiness that are already present in our lives. You don't have to wait ten years to experience this happiness. It is present in every moment of your daily life. There are those of us who are alive but don't know it. But when you breathe in, and you are aware of your in-breath, you touch the miracle of being alive. That is why mindfulness is a source of happiness and joy.

Most people are forgetful; they are not really here a lot of the time. Their minds are caught in their worries, their fears, their anger, and their regrets, and they are not mindful of being here. That state of being is called forgetfulness—you are here, but you are not here. You are caught in the past or in the future. You are not here in the present moment, living your life deeply. That is forgetfulness.

The opposite of forgetfulness is mindfulness. Mindfulness is when you are truly here, mind and body together. You breathe in and out mindfully, you bring your mind back to your body, and you are here. When your mind is there with your body, you are established in the present moment. Then you can recognize the many conditions of happiness that are in you and around you, and happiness just comes naturally.

Mindfulness practice should be enjoyable, not work or effort. Do you have to make an effort to breathe in? You don't need to make an effort. To breathe in, you just breathe in. Suppose you are with a group of people contemplating a beautiful sunset. Do you have to make an effort to enjoy the beautiful sunset? No, you don't have to make any effort. You just enjoy it.

The same thing is true with your breath. Allow your breath to take place. Become aware of it and enjoy it. Effortlessness. Enjoyment. The same thing is true with walking mindfully. Every step you take is enjoyable. Every step helps you to touch the wonders of life in yourself and around you. Every step is peace. Every step is joy. That is possible.

During the time you are practicing mindfulness, you stop talking—not only the talking outside, but the talking inside. The talking inside is the thinking, the mental discourse that goes on and on and on inside. Real silence is the cessation of talking—of both the mouth and the mind. This is not the kind of silence that oppresses us. It is a very elegant kind of silence, a very powerful kind of silence. It is the silence that heals and nourishes us.

Mindfulness gives birth to joy and happiness. Another source of happiness is concentration. The energy of mindfulness carries within it the energy of concentration. When you are aware of something, such as a flower, and can maintain that awareness, we say that you are concentrated on the flower. When your mindfulness becomes powerful, your concentration becomes powerful, and when you are fully concentrated, you have a chance to make a breakthrough, to achieve insight. If you meditate on a cloud, you can get insight into the nature of the cloud. Or you can meditate on a pebble, and if you have enough mindfulness and concentration, you can see into the nature of the pebble. You can meditate on a person, and if you have enough mindfulness and concentration, you can make a breakthrough and understand the nature of that person. You can meditate on yourself or your anger or your fear or your joy or your peace.

Anything can be the object of your meditation, and with the powerful energy of concentration, you can make a breakthrough and develop insight. It's like a magnifying glass concentrating the light of the sun. If you put the point of concentrated light on a piece of paper, it will burn. Similarly, when your mindfulness and concentration are powerful, your insight will liberate you from fear, anger, and despair and bring you true joy, true peace, and true happiness.

When you contemplate the big, full sunrise, the more mindful and concentrated you are, the more the beauty of the sunrise is revealed to you. Suppose you are offered a cup of tea, very fragrant, very good tea. If your mind is distracted, you cannot really enjoy the tea. You have to be mindful of the tea, you have to be concentrated on it, so it can reveal its fragrance and wonder to you. That is why mindfulness and concentration are such sources of happiness. That's why a good practitioner knows how to create a moment of joy, a feeling of happiness, at any time of the day.

Do Dishes, Rake Leaves

Karen Maezen Miller

If we need inspiration and motivation to practice mindfulness, Karen Maezen Miller—Zen teacher, wife, and mother—says we need look no farther than the backyard, the kitchen, and the laundry basket. Where drudgery lurks, we may also find peace.

I HAVE A GARDEN in my backyard, and even if you don't call it a garden, you do too. In the fall, the broad canopy of giant sycamores in my yard turns faintly yellow and the leaves sail down. First by ones, and then by tons. A part of every autumn day finds me fuming at the sight of falling leaves. Then I pick up a rake.

Tell me, while I'm sweeping leaves till kingdom come, is it getting in the way of my life? Is it interfering with my life? Keeping me from my life? Only my imaginary life, that life of what-ifs and how-comes—the life I'm dreaming of.

At the moment I'm raking leaves, at the moment I'm doing anything, it is my life, it is all of time, and it is all of me.

In the spring, the garden bursts to life, and once again I see what time it is. It is time to weed. When I look up across the endless stretch of the job before me, I surely want to quit. But if I manage to regain my focus on what's at hand, I realize it's just one weed. There's always just one weed to do next. I do it weed by weed, and the weeds always show me how. I never finish.

Looking for greater meaning in life, some people think that house-work is beneath them. Cooking and cleaning are beneath them. I know that feeling well. Sometimes they seem so far beneath me that I can't see the bottom. I can't see the beginning or the end. Is there a point to doing the work that seems pointless? The work with no visible end, no redeem-ing value, and no apparent urgency? Yes. It's the wisdom of the ancient homemakers.

After Buddhism came to China, the Chan school replaced the tradition of traveling and begging for alms with communal living. It was practical, for one thing. And it was practice. Monastic training came to encompass all the work essential to everyday life—cleaning, cooking, and gardening—as well as meditation. For that reason, we could well view the great Chinese masters as our progenitors in mindful homemaking, since many of their teachings point directly to the everyday chores we might rather high-mindedly neglect.

A monk asked Joshu, "All dharmas are reduced to oneness, but what is oneness reduced to?"

Joshu said, "When I was in Seishu, I made a hempen shirt. It weighed seven pounds."

More than a thousand years have passed since Joshu gave that response, originating one of the many classic koans that recount the provocative teachings of this renowned ninth-century Chinese master. Such koans, enigmatic little dialogues and stories, are used to provoke insight in the process of struggling to unravel their meaning. To this day, seekers are still struggling to find a way out of the shirt: *What does it mean? What is he get-ting at? I don't understand!*

We don't just struggle with a shirt in a Zen koan. We struggle with the shirts in our hampers. With the pants, the blouses, the sheets, and the un-derwear. Laundry presents a mountainous practice opportunity because it provokes a never-ending pile of egocentric resistance.

It's not important to me. It's tedious. I don't like to do it!

The monk in the story is like the rest of us, seeking wisdom through intellectual inquiry. If we're not careful, this is how we approach mindful-ness: as an idea, one we rather like, to elevate our lives with special contem-plative consideration, a method for making smarter choices and thereby ensuring better outcomes. The problem is that the life before us is the only life we have. The search for meaning robs our life of meaning, sending us back into our discursive minds while, right in front of us, the laundry piles up.

In his commentary on this koan, the late teacher and translator Katsuki Sekida rinsed Joshu's shirt clear of obfuscation: "Joshu's words remind us of the keen sensibilities of people who lived in the days when things were made by hand. The seven pounds of hemp were woven into cloth and cut and sewn into a shirt. When Joshu put on his hempen shirt, he experienced a sensation that was the direct recognition of the shirt for what it was."

The shirt, you see, is just a shirt. Feel the fabric, the weave, and the weight of seven pounds in your hands. The laundry is just the laundry. Pull it out of the hamper, sort it by color and fabric, read the care instructions, and get on with it. Transcending obstacles and overcoming preferences, we have an intimate encounter with our lives every time we do the wash. It's nothing out of the ordinary, but no one turns their nose up at a clean pair of socks.

With only a change in perspective, the most ordinary things take on inexpressible beauty. When we don't know, we don't judge. And when we don't judge, we see things in a different light. That is the light of our awareness, unfiltered by intellectual understanding, rumination, or evaluation. When we cultivate nondistracted awareness as a formal practice, we call it mindfulness meditation. When we cultivate it in our home life, we call it the laundry, the kitchen, or the yard—all the places and ways we can live mindfully by attending without distraction to whatever appears before us. But it's hard for us to believe that attention is all there is to it, and so we complicate things with our judgment—debasing the ordinary as insignificant and idealizing the spiritual as unattainable—never seeing that the two are one.

A monk said to Joshu, "I have just entered the monastery. Please teach me."

"Have you eaten your rice porridge?" asked Joshu.

"Yes, I have," replied the monk.

"Then you had better wash your bowl," said Joshu.

This famous koan is easy to view as a metaphor. Empty your mind and get rid of your notions of spiritual attainment. But suppose you don't view the bowl as a metaphor? That might change the way you look at the dishes in your kitchen sink and instruct you just as thoroughly.

The kitchen is not only the heart of a home, it can also be the heart of a mindfulness practice. In cooking and cleaning, we move beyond ourselves into compassionate care of everything and everyone around us.

Eating is our sole essential consumption, and cooking is our one common charity, so you'd think its purpose would be obvious. Yet with a critical eye to the value of time and what we judge to be our higher talents, meal preparation may seldom seem worth it. Cooking for two? *Not worth it.* Filling the fridge? *Not worth it.* Sitting down to dine? *Not worth it.* Cleaning up after? *Not worth it.*

Nothing is worth the measure we give it, because worth doesn't really exist. It is a figment of our judging minds, an imaginary yardstick to measure the imaginary value of imaginary distinctions—and one more way we withhold ourselves from the whole enchilada of life that lies before us.

If nothing is worth it, why cook? Why shop and chop, boil and toil, and clean up after? To engage yourself in the marvel of your own being. To see the priceless in the worthless. To find complete fulfillment in being unfilled. And to eat something other than your own inflated self-importance. That's what we empty when we empty the bowl, and a busy kitchen gives us the chance to empty ourselves many times a day.

A monk asked Joshu, "What is the meaning of Bodhidharma's coming to China?"

Joshu said, "The oak tree in the garden."

In this koan, the question about Bodhidharma, the legendary Zen patriarch who is credited with bringing Zen to China, represents our concerns with the deep spiritual questions. Enough about laundry and dishes, we might think: What about the meaning of everything? Why do the great mystics strive so diligently for enlightenment if it has no more depth than what's found in ordinary housework?

See beyond your house, Joshu answers, beyond the delusion of a separate self trapped by the false perception of what is inside and what is outside. This is true mindfulness: not the narrow boundaries of our conceptual abode, but the phenomenal world of the awakened mind. Joshu tells us to open our eyes and awaken in our own backyard.

Once again, Sekida pruned the intellectual interpretation that can obscure our clear sight: "There were many giant oaks in the garden of Joshu's temple. We can well imagine that Joshu himself was personally familiar with every tree, stone, flower, weed, and clump of moss—as intimately acquainted as if they were his own relatives."

Where is the place you know as well as your own family? Indeed, that is as proximate as yourself? It is the place where you are at ease with a full load, fulfilled by an empty sink, tell time by the leaves and weeds—making yourself mindfully at home in the home you never leave.

Wild Raspberries

Bob Howard

Nothing could be more basic, or some would say boring, than dirt. Yet long-time meditator Bob Howard, who taught contemplative gardening at Naropa University in Boulder, Colorado, finds worlds within worlds in what lies under our feet. And he suggests that we find a place to rest the mind and tend our garden in nature's rhythms.

WHEREVER I GO, my first interest is the soil. Even in a parking lot, I admire the diligence that creates soil in the low shelter of wheel-stop curbs. In these protected sanctuaries, the wind lays down fine particles of dust; leaves drift in and stay to slowly decay. In time, weeds spring up to launch a subterranean assault on the asphalt.

On a car trip through the Midwest last summer, I stopped somewhere in Iowa, got out, and walked into a cornfield to see what had become of the fertile plains the pioneers found here. From where I was standing, the land was planted in corn for a day's drive in every direction. At my feet, it glistened with recent rain. I stooped and tried to press a finger into the still-moist earth, but even wet it was too hard, too packed by the wheels of huge machines, to allow my finger to penetrate more than a fraction of an inch. No worms worked air and drainage into this dirt. Modern methods produced large stalks of corn, but for every bushel harvested, they let the rain carry off twice that volume in soil.

Nearby was a woodlot, one of yesteryear's holdovers. In a ditch along its flank, water flowed. The soil here was healthy, alive, laced with the roots of herb and weed. Farther on, under the trees themselves, the mosaic of twig and leaf rustled under my feet, awakening my ear to the presence of others. Birds chattered warnings about the noisy intruder. Squirrels flew to distant branches. Other creatures, unseen, traversed every inch of the woods—microbe, beetle, and cricket moved through the leaves, air, and soil, churning the whole thing like a big, airy compost. In that place, I felt an instinctual sense of belonging, a knowledge that I was home. The cornfield, by contrast, may feed me, but it left me uneasy.

In the Woods

That same summer my wife, Dessie, and I went hiking in an Adirondack wood. The area boasts some forty-six peaks exceeding four thousand feet in altitude; those who climb all of them become "Forty-Sixers." Dessie likes to take me along to carry the pack.

For a while, we hiked along Johns Brook, listening to the water play against the big black boulders in its path. There are boulders like that everywhere in the Adirondacks, hitchhikers dropped off twelve thousand years ago by the great ice sheets that carved out these hills and valleys. Now they lie there, immobile, musing over that ancient journey, slowly vanishing beneath a carpet of gray-green lichen.

Soft, that carpet, but like the weeds in the parking lot, bent on larger ends. Along with the wind, rain, freezing cold, and summer heat, these simple plants (lichens and then mosses) slowly render the giant boulder they cling to into one of earth's most precious treasures: good, rich soil. Slowly they crack their hosts into shards, gravel, and then sand. Always, the searching roots probe deep into the stone, drawing out the precious minerals and transforming them into new life.

In the course of time, lichens are followed by higher plants. Dust blows into the crevices. Mosses grow and die. These early pioneer plants build a loose protosoil. As it thickens, the deeper roots of annual and biennial plants find a home. Its loose organic texture stores moisture well and makes a fine seedbed for new seedlings. The roots of the new plants continue to pry cracks in the stone, dividing mineral from mineral. From spring to fall, from seed to flower, the cycle of growth and decay leads, in time, to a living fertility, a lush memory that the cornfield can only faintly recall.

As each successive cycle lives and flourishes in its strength, so each eventually dies, giving way to natural successors. As one plant dies into the seedbed of its successor, mild acids are released that mingle with other forces of decay. The decaying plant bodies add fiber—humus—to the mineral portion of the soil. In death, lichens and weeds return to the elements. As they decay, their organic compounds are released into solution or stored in the humus, later to be taken up by other living bodies. Nitrogen, potassium, and other elements are continuously recycled, held for a living moment or two, then given back again.

Over countless springs and winters, one plant form gives way to another. Eventually taller, deeper-rooted perennials establish themselves, and from that point on, the annuals' days are numbered. As the perennials flourish, they come to monopolize the light, moisture, and nutrients needed for seed germination and growth. In time, the perennials, too, give way to woody shrubs, which in turn give way to trees. The transitions of plant succession work toward a climax, a species that cannot be challenged further and that can sustain itself indefinitely. In this place I now stand, it is the tall white pines.

They have been here for some time now. We come to an old bridge supported by posts made of their timbers. In our terms, the bridge is old, built a good century ago. Crossing it, Dessie and I continue down the road and then turn off onto a wooded path.

In the shade of the pines, the air is brisk, and my face is soon flushed with the cold. The coming winter is already caressing the slumbering boulders with a cool touch. My black wool sweater holds warmth and wood smoke.

From a gardener's point of view, the soil under a pine forest like this one isn't very good. It's too acid because of all the fallen needles. High acidity and cold temperatures limit the number and activity of soil organisms. Lack of life in a soil means slow conversion of needles and other forest matter into humus. Since there is little humus here, snow and rainfall sink through this soil quickly, leaching nutrients downward to the rock below.

We move along, not talking much. There is a strong scent of pine in the air. Gradually, my eyes adjust to the forest shadows. Little grows in the deep shade—lichens and moss, some groups of fern here and there, bunchberries. All huddle together in small colonies. In the odd sunny spot along the path, wood sorrel spreads its carpet.

The path winds along the brook. Up ahead, a lean-to appears. We reach it quickly. Walking around the campsite, I feel a tentative, furtive curiosity, as if I were poking around in someone's living room. But the gardener in me needs to examine the soil here, so I bend down to dig in it.

Digging gently, I manage to ease up some eight inches of soil. It is fine and crumbly, a rich, light brown. Taking a handful, I squeeze it, making a ball that holds the imprint of my fingers—a good sign, since it tells me that this soil retains water well. Now I run my thumb against the ball, and it breaks up into smaller, irregular lumps, like bread crumbs. Another good sign. Soil that has a malleable crumb structure allows air to circulate around the roots. Soil that is too clayey can be pressed into a ball, but it doesn't crumble freely, if at all. Clay soils don't breathe.

At the other end of the spectrum, soil that is too sandy would crumble and fall apart easily—too easily. It probably wouldn't even hold its shape in the first place. Water runs right through sand, as do air and nutrients. This forest soil in my hand is friable, the good intermediate that gardeners seek. This soil accepts and releases, has a rhythmic circulation, like healthy skin.

The best, most friable soils of all are found under prairies, along river bottoms, and under deciduous—not coniferous—forests. The leaves that fall to earth in a deciduous forest are less acid than pine needles, and the temperatures are normally warmer. More soil microbes and other organisms can live in them to eat, digest, and aerate the soil. Rich in organic material, such soils hold moisture and nutrients well and are superb for farming and gardening. In a forest of oak, for instance, the earth might well attain a rich, deep, chocolate-cake texture. The soil in my hand is better than I expected in an evergreen forest, but still it's too light—more of an angel food.

Living soil breeds life and invites seed germination, root penetration, nutrient manufacture and storage, and the circulation of air and water. Squeezing the ball of soil in my hand once more, I feel the grains of disintegrated rock in it, and images of long nights, cold winds, and misty mornings come to mind. The decaying needles lightly prick my skin. A great deal of time, lots of bacteria, and all the other forces of nature are at work here. In a way, it doesn't matter whether I garden or not, whether I grow one tomato bigger than another. What matters is that I experience nature, that I sense her power.

Breathing the tangy fragrance around us, Dessie and I move on, walking slowly, just glad to be there. Presently my attention is drawn to a break in the shadows up ahead and to a growing light. The air changes, losing some of its pineyness, taking on a hint of something fresher, greener. Just as I sense this, Dessie says in a tone of soft surprise, "I smell berries!" *Berries?* I think. *People don't smell berries in the wild; animals—rabbits, deer—do.*

SURPRISE!

I was wrong. The path bent around another turn; the dark pines gave way to bright-leaved maple and birch; and in a wide, open glade where neither conifer nor deciduous tree ruled was a spreading bramble of red, ripe, delicious raspberries.

According to the logic of plant succession, we shouldn't have found raspberries successfully competing with trees. But fortunately nature isn't always logical, and there they were. Somehow the trees lost their domi nance in this spot, and the raspberries took over.

It wasn't difficult to see why. The key, as always, was under my feet. Beneath the bramble, the woodland floor was littered with decomposing, half-charred branches: there had been a fire here, probably caused by lightning, and it had opened the way for the raspberry rebellion. When the smoke had cleared, sunlight had come streaming in. The seeds got the message and decided it was time to wake up and get to work.

But how did raspberry seeds get here in the first place? Like the soil, the earthworm, and the warbler, raspberry seeds are part of the reserves of the forest. Birds had fed on the berries elsewhere, then airmailed them in. The seeds were indigestible and passed through their bodies. Warmed by the sun, the seeds had sprouted, sending up the first of the long, stickery canes that now make up this wild bramble before me.

That fire was a double blessing, for it also left an added bonus: potash, a valuable source of the nutrient potassium. So these raspberries thrived. Soon their wide-ranging, shallow root system was soaking up the water here, and for a change, it was their leaves that were casting the shadows, holding back their competitors.

Raspberries come off the stalk effortlessly into the hand, rise swiftly to the mouth. *All gardening should be so easy,* I think, popping them down. Now that I know what raspberries like, maybe I'll grow some. They want a humusy soil, slightly acid, and rich in potassium. They want good direct sun and good drainage too. In a garden, the fruit would need protection from birds, a net of some kind. To avoid ending up with a tangled bramble like this, they'd need to be trained to a trellis or along wires. I make a mental note to take a look at a gardening manual when I get home to see how they should be pruned.

Only moments earlier, some subtle shift in nature's light, color, and scent had spoken to Dessie, causing her exclamation. She grew up in these woods, and her experiences as a child, of finding wild raspberries here, has stayed with her. But something else happened as well. The relaxed awareness of our walk made us more perceptive of our world. Without meaning to, we let our usual mental chatter drift away, and we were just here, fresh, composed, receptive to what nature had to say to us.

Let Your Passion Cook

Edward Espe Brown

Cooking a meal can be a wonderful, daily opportunity to practice mindfulness. Edward Espe Brown, chef and author of several cookbooks written from a mindfulness perspective, explains that mindful cooking is not detached or subdued. It's cooking with your whole being—mind, body, and emotions—engaged.

AT A WEEKLONG meditation session one year, I think it was 1968, my teacher Suzuki Roshi lectured about how to practice Zen. "Zen," he said, "is feeling your way along in the dark. You might think it would be better to have more light, to know where you are going, and to get there in a hurry, but Zen is feeling your way along in the dark. Then you are careful and sensitive to what is happening."

Later I asked him (young man that I was), "Hmm, feeling my way along in the dark . . . Now that the program is over, what if we have a party?"

"If you do it with that spirit, it will be perfectly okay," he said.

Wonderful, I thought and started to get up from kneeling in front of him, when his voice brought my movement to an abrupt halt.

"The most important point is," he paused, while I prompted myself to listen intently as the words slowly came out, "to find out what is the most important point."

And I thought he was going to tell me! Only he had—and years later I continue to investigate this.

One of the places where I have studied this is in the kitchen. When we're cooking, what is the most important point? As a meditator, there are many ready-made answers: being mindful, being silent, watching your mind, being calm and peaceful. All well and good. But did anyone say, "Preparing food"? Or "Feeling your way along in the dark"? We do well to study how we do what we are doing and ask ourselves, "What is the most important point?"

"Be mindful in the kitchen while you work," people often say. Perhaps useful, but unfortunately the word is overused, often inaccurately. When people do not pick up after themselves, they are not being mindful. When they are gossiping while cooking, that's not mindful. In other words, when people are not doing what they should, they are not being mindful. So "be mindful" becomes "do it right," the way you are supposed to.

I'm not sure, but I think that being mindful is to experience your experience without judging good or bad, right or wrong. Being mindful in this fashion, you might notice dishes, crumbs, or scraps on what was formerly a clean surface—and this could be followed by choosing how to respond. Saying that the people who left those items were not mindful is another way of saying they are bad, that it is wrong. That does not sound like mindfulness to me, which is to be aware without judging.

Do you want to prepare food or to be mindful? And is there a way to do both? I'd like to offer alternatives to the usual explanation of "being mindful in the kitchen," but I would caution you to feel your way along in the dark and to investigate the most important point. In others words, find out for yourself how to make working in the kitchen a source of awakening.

When I asked Suzuki Roshi for his advice about working in the kitchen, he said, "When you wash the rice, wash the rice. When you cut the carrots, cut the carrots. When you stir the soup, stir the soup." Though very similar, this is not the same as "be mindful in the kitchen," which makes it sound like you always have two things to do: washing and being mindful, cutting and being mindful, stirring and being mindful. What would that mindfulness part look like? Probably a bit stiff, as your impulse would be to move slowly and carefully so that only a moderate amount of energy and emotion arises to meet the circumstances. In other words, most people hear "be mindful" as "keep yourself in check."

Yet what is magnificent and magical is finding out how to manifest the cutting of carrots with your whole body and mind; how to wash the rice with your eyes and your hands, connecting consciousness with the senses and the world—not just going through the motions. This brings me to a pivotal point. When you stop going through the motions and manifest the stirring of soup, alive in the present moment, emotions may surface. While some find this problematic and recommend dispassion, my suggestion is to invite your *passion* to *cook.*

Instead of tying yourself down so that nothing volatile arises, use what is vibrant and volatile—feelings—to energize your presence in the kitchen. Invite them to handle, stir, wash, touch, scrub, scour; invite them to see, smell, taste, and delight in the play. The cook's temperament is a passion for life: give it a field in which to practice—put it to work. If I were to cook only when I was most loving, kind, and benevolent, I would have starved long ago. I am not telling you to act out in the kitchen; I simply encourage you to turn afflictive emotions, as well as enthusiasm and exuberance, into something edible and nourishing—food.

So along with mindfulness, "washing the rice when you wash the rice" puts more emphasis on concentration, focus, attention, and energy. These actions rather blend together: Prepare food! Make it happen! Wash, cut, cook, taste, savor. Gather yourself, as many disparate parts as you can muster. Zero in on the activity and how to do it easily, effectively, effortlessly (do not just go through the motions). Give your attention to observing and perceiving rather than giving out directives and enforcing rules. Let your life force bloom and sparkle. *Interact.* Study how to use your body to do the work of cooking.

This kind of instruction accords with the oneness of practice and realization. When you make food, you are actualizing the fundamental point. You are making food *real.* It's not just talk; it's not just a head trip—you can eat it.

Engage in what you are doing. Zen Master Dogen's advice is to "let things come and abide in your heart. Let your heart return and abide in things. All through the day and night." To engage is to meet and connect and, out of that meeting and connecting, to respond. Responding from the heart, your implicit intention is to bring out the best. This is learning to relate with the things of this world and your own body-mind rather than seeking to hide out in a place where you don't have to relate with anything. There are recipes to follow in order to get it right and gain approval. There are no recipes for telling you what your heart knows and precious little workable advice for trusting your heart rather than your head. You choose to do it and practice finding your way in the dark.

Manufactured products say, "I'm quick. I'm easy. You won't have to relate with me at all. Put me in the microwave, and I'll be there for you, just the way you want me." Recipes say, "Do what I tell you, and everything will be okay—you too can make masterpieces (and if it's not going to be a masterpiece, don't even bother)." To engage with the world is to study what to do with a potato, a carrot, cabbages, and bell peppers. What to do and how to do it. Are you in the dark yet?

Touch with your hands, see with your eyes, smell with your nose, taste with your tongue: let things come and abide in your heart; let your heart return and abide in things. Your capacity for cooking will grow and develop from your devotion to being in the dark, not knowing what to do, but carefully finding your way. You enter the kitchen and become intimate with cooking through cooking. You begin to trust your own aesthetic, and your close experiencing of cooking (and the sometimes uncomfortable feedback from others) starts to inform your aesthetic further.

After a number of months as the cook at Tassajara Zen Center, I went to Suzuki Roshi with another problem: "How do I get my fellow workers to practice the way they should?" I explained to him that I was endeavoring to practice his instruction to "wash the rice," but others in the kitchen often came late to work, disappeared for long bathroom breaks, and when they opened their mouths, their hands stopped moving. "How do I get them to really practice?"

Roshi did not say, "Tell them to be more mindful." He listened attentively, as his nods punctuated my litany with what I took as confirmation: *Yes, I know, it's hard to get good help these days.* He seemed so completely sympathetic. When I finished speaking, he paused for a bit, then startled me by saying, "If you want to see virtue, you'll have to have a calm mind."

"That," I protested to myself, "is not what I asked you." I had something new to study.

How will you survive the kitchen, make it through the fire? One key I found is not to calm my mind first and *then* look for virtue, but simply to look for virtue. There it is. What you look for, you'll get more of. When you look for fault, you'll find it. I started looking for virtue.

Seeing virtue encompasses two aspects: the relative and the absolute. When you taste what you put in your mouth, you may notice sweet or sour, earthy or sunny, and along with these relative characteristics, you can sense something essential, something from beyond. This something is not a thing. Go ahead and taste it—the virtue inherent in your careful, attentive, receptive experiencing of the moment. When your awareness is in the dark, and you are opening your perception, you can also taste your own inherent goodness and the virtue of others working with you. You may meet sincerity, kindness, wholeheartedness, vulnerability, grief, anxiety, determination, stubbornness. And you may meet mind itself: vast and spacious. Awesome!

You can shift your effort, shift your attention. From doing it right, aiming to gain approval, you shift to meeting and working with the ingredients at hand. Looking to see what is available, you dream up what to do with the ingredients while honoring their virtue. Our ordinary effort is to dream up a picture of how we want things to be and endeavor to make it come true. Now, in the dark, you feel your way along, and your wisdom flashes: a salad, a soup—the virtue of spinach, apple, and walnut speaks to you. The body comes alive because you are *doing* something. Yes, it's good to stop and sit and allow the usual impulses for motion an opportunity to move inwardly instead of outwardly—beautiful work there. Yet hands love to be hands. You give them life by allowing them to find out how to do things—how to wash and cut, stir and knead, ladle and mop. Your consciousness comes out of its nest or den in the head and finds its way into activity. These are the hands that have an eye in the middle of the palm that can see and connect with the object of touch. In this connection is health and healing; you are learning to work with the virtue of things and receive the blessings of being human.

Everybody knows that cooking can be stressful. When your awareness becomes overwhelmed, stop for a few moments and make a mental (or even a written) checklist of what needs to be done. Revise your list in accordance with reality: how much time and energy you have and what is the one thing you need to do next, so that you can give that one thing your undivided attention. When you are stressed, *stop* and *check* before proceeding step-by-step.

As Suzuki Roshi mentioned, "When you are in the dark, you don't know where you are going, but when you carefully feel your way along, where you find yourself will be okay." To your health and happiness, joy and well-being, in the kitchen and out. Let's taste the blessings of the moment.

Digital Mindfulness

Steve Silberman

The devices in our pockets, on our desks, and in our cars offer round-the-clock pressures and distractions that can make the virtual world into a mind trap. Steve Silberman—a longtime Wired *magazine writer and editor—shares some tips on how to handle it mindfully and save your sanity.*

THE WEB has become nearly inextricable from the fabric of our lives in a relatively short time. We work and play online, stay in touch with our loved ones, follow the news, track our investments, and plan our journeys in the offline world using Google Maps. As more people use wireless devices like iPhones to tap into the global network, it's getting hard to tell where the virtual world ends and the actual world begins.

I saw a preview of the way we live now on the streets of Helsinki in 1999. Cell phones had not yet become ubiquitous in the United States, but because Finland is the home country of Nokia, nearly everyone I met had a "kanny" in his pocket. It was strange to see Finns ignoring the person beside them in cafés while busily chatting and texting to friends who were someplace else. It was as if everyone lived in two places at once: wherever their bodies happened to be, and where they *really* were in their minds, which could change at the chirp of a ringtone.

We are all Finns now. The channel of distraction that used to be confined to the box on our desk is suddenly all around us, always on, teasing and tempting us with perishable tidbits of information. New-media experts call applications like Twitter, Facebook, and Google Wave the "real-time Web." The social currency of the real-time Web is awareness of news breaking right at this instant. Have you seen that new viral video everyone's talking about? The latest smackdown of you-know-who? Do you realize how much has *happened* in the past ten minutes?

The backlog of bleeping alerts starts accumulating the moment you glance away from the screen. We've been trying to reach you. She tweeted more than an hour ago. I just called and left a message on your phone. Where are you?

We have banished the specter of boredom for the burden of always having something to do. Insomniacs can now find plenty of ways to occupy their buzzing minds at 3 A.M. The whole networked world has become the City That Never Sleeps.

This constant stream of titillating ephemera can pose challenges for people who are trying to live in a more conscious way. The effort of settling the mind in the here and now often requires reducing the amount of input and taking a friendly attitude toward boredom. "The practice of meditation can be described as relating with cool boredom, refreshing boredom, boredom like a mountain stream," wrote Tibetan meditation master Chögyam Trungpa in *The Myth of Freedom.*

Nowadays, we rarely allow ourselves to be refreshed by boredom. Restorative intervals of silence and solitude have become an endangered species of experience. As thankful as I am for the invaluable gifts that the Internet has brought into my life, I also miss the slower pace of the pre-Web era, the spacious, uninterrupted hours spent turning the pages of a novel with snow sifting outside the window. You could lose yourself in a book and come back to earth feeling like you had a chance to make things right.

It's hard not to wonder if all this connection and convenience is driving us crazy.

Henry David Thoreau, who praised the virtues of contemplative life off the grid in *Walden,* would not be surprised that our craving for constant communion has brought us to this point. "Our inventions are wont to be pretty toys, which distract our attention from serious things," the sage of Concord wrote in 1849. "We are in great haste to construct a magnetic telegraph from Maine to Texas; but Maine and Texas, it may be, have nothing important to communicate. . . . We are eager to tunnel under the Atlantic and bring the Old World some weeks nearer to the New; but perchance the first news that will leak through into the broad, flapping American ear will be that the Princess Adelaide has the whooping cough."

Thoreau referred to much-touted technological marvels like the transatlantic cable as "improved means to an unimproved end." Some days it feels like he was right. The Internet, once hailed as a wellspring of information that would reinvigorate public participation in democracy, has turned out to be a font of disinformation and spin. In the din of the 24/7 news cycle, every uninformed opinion and knee-jerk reaction—particularly outrage—gets turned up to "11." Family members on opposite sides of issues like climate change and vaccine safety feel like they're drifting further and further apart into different countries with alternate versions of history.

At the same time, interactions on the Internet can be surprisingly deep and healing. When I first joined an online community called The WELL in the early 1990s, I got to know a young artist and father named Damian who lived a few blocks away. Sadly, shortly after I met him, he was diagnosed with cancer. I encouraged Damian to keep an online journal to record his experiences in treatment. This journal became a sanctuary for those who cared about him and his family, like a little holy place made of text.

"A few years ago, I was reading a book about Suzuki Roshi," Damian wrote one day, referring to the late founder of the San Francisco Zen Center. "The author said that Suzuki referred to his cancer as 'his little friend.' I thought that was just a little *too* Zen for me. Let's just say I've changed my mind. This internal nemesis has become an ally. Every day I feel healthy is a gift. If I can't get to sleep at night, I read a book and am grateful for this new little pocket of time for reading. I see love with all of its flaws heading at me from all directions like a herd of runaway locomotives. I never had a feel for it before. I've had to rebuild my life in a very short time and find it to be an exhilarating experience (most of the time). Meanwhile, I try to kill this nemesis, thanking it all the while."

The Internet has also supported my efforts to become more mindful in ways I couldn't have foreseen, and it's brought painful lessons and joyful discoveries. A few years ago, the loss of a treasured friendship after a hurtful exchange helped me pay attention to how ravaging online words can be when used carelessly. When Eric, a friend I met on Facebook, came for a visit, we meditated by the ocean, timed by a handy iPhone app called Meditator.

Whatever your interest in meditation, we're living in a golden age one author called "the Digital Silk Road." In past centuries, students had to travel long distances and endure hardships to hear great teachers. Now thousands of guided meditations and talks are easily downloadable from sites like Dharma Seed (http://dharmaseed.org). Every day, people all over the world learn how to listen more closely to the state of their health by Googling their way to a Mindfulness-Based Stress Reduction class or performing a "body scan" at home.

One of the first outposts of mindful living on the Web—a collection of texts and essays called "What Do You Think, My Friend?"—was built in 1995 by a twenty-five-year-old software engineer from Singapore named Chade-Meng Tan. These days, Meng works for Google as the company's "Jolly Good Fellow," leading a program called Search Inside Yourself that offers courses in attention training and emotional intelligence. Lately, he has been cooking up a project that will harness the technical and scientific expertise of his resourceful personal network—which includes neuroscientists, fellow programmers, and the Dalai Lama—to investigate the areas of the brain that are activated by meditation practice.

The problem with traditional mindfulness training, Meng says (sounding very much like a Google engineer), is that it's a blind search that takes too long. By mapping the neurological markers of mindfulness practice, he hopes to provide practical milestones for meditators and accelerate the process of achieving deep awareness. "What if, instead of taking forty years to become like the Dalai Lama, it only took four years to become a person of compassion, kindness, and wisdom? That would change the world," he says. "I don't know yet if the technology is possible, but I'm trying to figure it out."

I ask Meng how he manages to stay grounded while working in a high-pressure corporate environment like Google. "Think of the mind as an ocean—very choppy on the surface, but calm and happy just below that," he says. "I call that clarity my 'default mind.' I try to get back to my default mind a couple of times a day." He supplements this practice with another time-tested method for maintaining perspective: "I remind myself that I'm going to die. Given that, how important is this thing bothering me right now?"

Another friend who has embraced technology as a way of exploring the nature of mind is John Tarrant, author of *Bring Me the Rhinoceros* and other Zen books. For years, John has been evaluating various ways of including online life in his students' field of practice. I recently shared with him a concern that the Web could act as a jungle gym for "monkey mind," the restless part of our ego that hops from one potential source of gratification to the next, chattering internally all the while. How is it possible to stay grounded in the face of perpetual distraction?

John observed that it may just be a matter of acquiring new skills. People first learn to meditate while sitting, then while walking. Eventually, they learn to cultivate the mind of awareness while talking or preparing a meal. Why should Web surfing be any different?

At the same time, he said, "The Zen take would be that there isn't a 'right way' to be online. There's a kind of freedom *deeper* than the right way—an awareness that's always happening while all this other stuff is going on. I woke up with a splitting headache the other night, but this awareness knows it wasn't really a problem. It's calm and having a good time, noticing, 'He's got a headache,' or 'He's online now, and he thinks his attention is scattered.' The relationship between this foreground creature that you think you are and this vast background is the question. When there's a relationship, most people feel their experience is more nourishing."

In the 1980s, when few people outside the Pentagon and university computer science departments were even aware of the Internet, Gary Snyder wrote a poem called "Why I Take Good Care of My Macintosh Computer." The choice of subject may have startled some of Snyder's fans, who think of him primarily as a spokesperson for the timeless values of wilderness and tribe—one of Thoreau's heirs, perhaps even a bit of a Luddite.

But Snyder has no inherent distrust of technology. Like any skilled craftsman, he's eager to praise his tools. His books contain odes to ax handles, pickup trucks, and hydraulic backhoes, as well as mountains, rivers, and coyotes. After paying tribute to his Mac as if it were a totemic animal ("it broods under its hood like a perched falcon"), Gary offers gratitude to his elegant machine for reminding him of important truths:

> Because whole worlds of writing can be boldly laid out
> and then highlighted, & vanished in a flash at
> "delete" so it teaches
> of impermanence and pain

In 1844, Ralph Waldo Emerson wrote that the poet's job is to reclaim scattered pieces of the sacred whole by reattaching "even artificial things and violations of nature, to nature, by a deeper insight." This "deeper insight" could be described as simply paying attention to elements of experience that nonpoets usually find unworthy of notice. "Readers of poetry see the factory-village, and the railway, and fancy that the poetry of the landscape is broken up by these, for these works of art are not yet consecrated in their readings," he explained. "But the poet sees them fall within the great Order not less than the beehive, or the spider's geometrical web."

Our job as mindful citizens of this planet is not so different. By paying attention, we rescue orphaned elements of human experience and discover richness in them. The "vast background" described by John Tarrant is equally at work in a spiderweb and the World Wide Web. As members of social networks, our friends' status updates are constantly bringing us news of the universe: births, deaths, celebrations, sorrows, and transitions, as well as signs of the inevitable approach of old age and death.

Being open to this news without feeling overwhelmed and anxious takes practice and can also require making choices. Psychologist and Buddhist teacher Sylvia Boorstein enjoys e-mail and the Web, but she declines invitations to high-traffic networks like Facebook and LinkedIn. "I know they're valuable for many people," she says. "I'm just certain I would not thrive with more contacts than I already have."

Mindfulness of speech also applies to words online. It's so easy to fire off a testy reply or detonate a self-righteous blast in the comments section of a blog. After exchanging more than 300,000 e-mails, I've learned to be thankful for the petulant messages I never sent, the bristling reactions I zapped into the void. When I feel hot anger quickening my fingers at the keys, I try to take a mindful breath (or ten) or even a walk around the block. If my response is so important, it will still seem so when I sit back down at my computer. Not every reactive blip needs to be broadcast to the world.

Strategic use of inspirational reminders can help. Some people install software that chimes at random intervals during the course of a day, prompting them to take a conscious breath. Thich Nhat Hanh wrote a poem to recite silently before logging on. When I visited the Boorsteins at home in Sonoma County two years ago, I noticed a square of paper taped to the edge of Sylvia's monitor with a quote from Cala, one of the first women to take vows in Buddha's order: "I, a nun, trained and self-composed, established mindfulness and entered peace like an arrow." I recently asked Sylvia if she still relies on these dharmic Post-Its. "I have a laptop now, so there's no space for them," she replied. "But if there were, I would use a phrase that my friend Susan puts at the end of all her e-mails: Stay amazed."

Staying amazed and compassionate, even in the face of imminent death, is a worthy goal in any tradition. As the pain and therapeutic demands of Damian's illness increased, he still found time to comfort another member of our online tribe whose father had been diagnosed with cancer. Overjoyed at being the father of a four-year-old girl, Damian wrote not long before he died, "I'm renewed every time I come home and see her running down the hallway shouting out, 'Daaddy!' I'm reborn every time I think of her. I am the luckiest guy in the world."

Your Mind and Your Money

KRISTI NELSON

Few aspects of life are more challenging than money. The very thought of it—whether we have enough of it, how can we make more of it, how much should we spend or give away—can bring instant stress. Financial adviser Kristi Nelson, a veteran MBSR practitioner, offers some insights into how our mindfulness and our money can come together.

MONEY IS A LOADED SUBJECT. No matter where we currently sit on the continuum of "enough," our relationship to money is often burdensome. And for those of us committed to living mindfully, it is no less so.

Mindfulness helps us cultivate qualities of attention so that we can more fully greet and be available for what unfolds in our lives. And yet, when we come face to face with pivotal financial moments—a depleted checkbook, an investment decision, asking for a loan, coveting something we cannot afford, or riding the stock-market roller coaster—mindful attitudes we embody so seamlessly in other moments can disappear. At these times, we can be prone to unconscious emotions and behaviors that lead to suffering.

Fortunately, to the same degree that money is an area of our lives fraught with challenges or neglect, it's also a pathway that can lead us to greater insight, agency, and ease. In the twenty-five years I have guided organizations and individuals toward a more fulfilling and effective relationship to money,

I have learned that despite the vast differences between us, we have much in common in terms of why we struggle with money, and how we can experience greater peace about it.

Look Inside

Each of us has a unique money story we carry around and express to the world in countless ways. These stories—our money baggage—can become the unexamined default settings that control our financial lives. Becoming mindful about money means, first, deconstructing the sources of the stories we tell ourselves. We cannot transcend what we cannot see. Consider the role of these influences:

Your "Inheritance"

We are products of our ancestors and immediate families, as well as our cultural and class backgrounds. Messages, maxims, and myths about money are overtly and subtly conveyed to us. Are there stories and messages you heard repeatedly growing up? What were you told is "true" about money? How much was "enough" in your family? What attitudes about money or class did you inherit? What were you taught about people from other classes? How might you still be paying allegiance to this history?

Your Driven Self

We all have early beliefs about money that we unwittingly adopted. These beliefs can drive our behavior, filtering what we are able to see. A scarcity mentality keeps us from noticing sufficiency in our lives. Feelings of insatiability make us vulnerable to intoxicating dreams and promises of abundance. Deprivation can result in closeted forms of gluttony. How have desire and aversion played out in your relationship with money? Have you mistaken some of your drivers as your identity?

Your Hidden Self

What are you hiding about money? What judgment do you fear? Wealthy people often hide their riches, just as those who struggle with money hide their debt. When we hide whatever is true, we become "class impostors." How, in both small and large ways, might you misrepresent the truth about money in your life? How does this keep you from having authentic relationships?

Our money stories are powerful; they can either keep us arrested in illusion or direct us to insight. Let these unconscious places percolate up to your awareness. Once you understand the factors influencing you, you can begin to act with greater discernment. Wonder gently. We all sometimes mistake our story for who we are. Stories are meant to be convincing.

LOOK OUTSIDE

Our internal conditions create a field of vulnerability that Western societies have set themselves up to "solve." It's hard not to be susceptible to the myriad financial remedies and prescriptions that bombard us from the outside. But these "solutions" can narrowly define us and reinforce the status quo rather than encourage us to question the assumptions behind them.

Your Plans

Traditional money mavens counsel us to set ambitious goals, create elaborate budgets, and develop long-term financial plans. Their guidance is heavily weighted toward trading away the present moment to prepare for—and protect against—an unknown future, and is based in assumptions: we *must* all want to be wealthy, retire early, and have lots of luxuries . . . with no taxes. To be mature means having a long list of goals focused on "more." Ends trump means. Security is measured as purely financial. Even some of the most "enlightened" advice owes its roots to these assumptions.

Your Spending

In our culture, few habits are as deeply ingrained as the desire to acquire, and few delights rival having scored a bargain, indulged successfully, or invested wisely. Our identities and pleasures become inextricably linked with where we put our money and what this says about us. We develop tastes that need to be expressed and fulfilled, and we reveal our unique fingerprint to the world through the choices we make, including our investments. Even yoga, meditation, and simplicity have been commercialized. We need to stay very mindful; consumerism is a favored domain of mindlessness.

Your Earning

We are not what we earn. Just because we can charge $100 per hour doesn't mean we should, and just because it might be difficult for us to charge $100 an hour doesn't mean we shouldn't. If asked by a prospective employer for our required salary range, where do we place the bottom? Doesn't a range imply a ceiling? Do you have a ceiling of "enough"? Money has become falsely bound up with success, worth, and entitlement. From this entangled place, we can rarely think clearly about what we truly need and value.

It takes very focused work to untangle the places where our thinking and behavior related to money have become convoluted. We may know, intellectually, that security is not "material," that we are not what we own, and that our lives are not equal to what we earn. But this conditioning goes deep and is reinforced almost everywhere. We are under the weight of tremendous social pressures about money, and getting free requires an equally tremendous commitment.

Look at the Whole Picture

Money is a form of currency—as are time, energy, and love. What we do with these precious resources tells the hard truth about who we are and what matters to us. We claim and reclaim ourselves in the allocation of our currencies. Our clear intentions can form a touchstone for our financial freedom, just as the breath moving in and out of our bodies can be the touchstone for mindfulness practice.

Your Values

Much as our bodies align around the spine, our financial lives need to align with the template of our values. We must consistently explore, define, and check our values.

What do you truly stand for? What principles and beliefs do you want to express with your life? What commitments do you want to advance?

How much is *your* enough point? What difference do you want to make? What is the real cost of more/less than enough to your life, relationships, and the world?

Articulating our core values is not an idle exercise. It is powerful and humbling, and plants us on the cushion of self-responsibility and accountability. The work of our values is to be alive—how we do and don't bring our values to life is *our* work.

Your Money

Choose to look very clearly at how money comes into your life and where it goes. The raw truth of our money trail tells an important story. Details matter. Hold every allocation against your values template and examine the degree to which it contradicts or advances what matters to you. How do your values show up in your income? How don't they? Do you hold on to money out of fear? Do you give away more than you can truly afford? Do you have more than you need? Less than you need? Notice. Honestly.

Ultimately, the antidote to being susceptible to the pull of our internal stories and the lure of society's money messages may rest in unequivocally knowing what we stand for, and aspiring to embody that in every single financial decision we make. As Cheri Huber, author of *Transform Your Life: A Year of Awareness Practice,* says, "How you do anything is how you do everything." Everything is a chance at freedom.

Your Choice

Prominently display some of your values: write them on your checkbook, computer screen, wallet, and credit cards. Remind yourself what you stand for. Try bringing *balance* to your checkbook every month. Be *generous*— give something meaningful away. Start a *sufficiency* conversation every day. Express *gratitude* for all the ways you are rich. Be *transparent* with a friend. Nourish *community*. Express *compassion* by making a thoughtful donation. What else can you do to start a mindful money movement in your life?

If we commit to a mindful relationship to money as a portal to learning, we can befriend what we have been ignoring, release myths we've been harboring, and live more fully the life we want . . . and the world needs.

Allowing money to be front and center in our attention, we can take a deep breath each time we face a pivotal financial moment, and explore new possibilities for having money illustrate what we truly want to embody in our lives.

At Work, Be a Don't-Know-It-All

Michael Carroll

"I don't know what I'm doing." Is there a worse thing to say when we are at work? And yet, consultant and business coach Michael Carroll says not-knowing is one of the best places to be. Rather than feeling we have to make things happen, we can let things happen—a key outgrowth of mindfulness.

ALL OF US WANT to have a purpose at work, and we want to feel that we know how to perform our jobs. If we are dishing up ice cream, we want to scoop the correct portions and serve it attractively. If we are repairing the space shuttle, we want to engineer effective protective shields to withstand extreme temperatures. In the most basic way, knowing how to do things at work is what it's all about.

On the other hand, *not knowing* what we are doing at work seems downright unacceptable. If we were to say to our boss or a customer, "I don't know what I'm doing. I'm not sure I have a handle on the situation," the other person could lose confidence in our abilities and might begin to doubt that we are right for the job. If we don't know what we are doing, things could get out of control. Problems of all kinds could arise.

In order to avoid the appearance of such disasters, we generally keep our work-related quandaries to ourselves. Because it is unacceptable to not know, we may at times need to pretend we know what we are doing when in fact we don't. Wall Street is great for such charades. On Wall Street, *appearing* to be an expert by talking the part is half the game: matched maturities, on-balance volume, jobbers, continuous net settlement, rising bottoms—the more financial jargon you throw around, the more others assume you know what you're doing. Of course, Wall Street is not the only place where people hide behind jargon. We all, to some degree, feel uncertain at work and try to mask it—to project an image of confidence and knowledge.

The fact is that we cannot avoid "not-knowing"; we simply don't know a lot of the time. Because work is messy and full of surprises, we are constantly presented with not knowing what is going on or about to happen. Since this feels uncomfortable and uncertain, we grasp for answers in order to feel sure of ourselves. But being uncomfortable and uncertain need not be seen as a weakness or problem that needs an immediate answer. If we pause and examine closely, we might take the advice offered in the classic Zen teaching "Only don't know" and discover that not knowing is a tremendous resource for being effective and innovative at work.

Cultivating not-knowing does not mean that as bus drivers we forget which route to take or to pick up our customers at the bus stop. Nor is it an excuse for being incompetent: "Gee, I don't know how to put paper in the copier; I guess I'll just skip it and find a copier that works." Nor is not-knowing a kind of fog where we sit back and vaguely say to ourselves, "What the hell is going on around here?" Rather, not-knowing means being willing to slow down, drop our preconceptions, and be interested and present to our work situation as it unfolds. Not-knowing in this sense is an exercise in balancing effort—actively and intelligently *being* somewhere in the process of *getting* somewhere.

Not-knowing starts by giving ourselves a break from constantly seeking to accomplish. We shift from the feeling of *making* something happen to *letting* something happen. We relax with our bodies and minds and take a good look at our environment. We no longer cling to what we know and instead become excited about what we don't know. We ease up on the race to get our jobs done and permit ourselves to notice things we don't normally notice. We let our curiosity have a free rein. The family pictures hanging in our colleague's cubicle no longer fade into the background but are colorful and inviting. Our subordinate's frequent use of "Excuse me, I'm sorry but . . ." no longer goes routinely by, simply overlooked as a worn-out phrase. Our client's lawyer's habit of looking at her watch becomes intriguing. The crack in a metal beam, the joy in a voice, the incorrect date on a form letter all become available and potentially of interest.

Not-knowing is highly inquisitive, an energetic curiosity that inspects and questions without being rude or disrespectful. Here, we are not curious in order to prove a point or place blame or fix a problem; rather, there is a feeling that our work situation is inviting and crisp—maybe even vast and profound—and worthy of our attention. By not knowing, we give ourselves permission to wander and observe, becoming interested in seeming incidentals that could yield helpful insights.

In the eighties, Wall Street firms measured everything: percent of trades settled in twenty-four hours, average turnaround time for stock swaps, percent of margin calls settled on time—the list was infinite. Management "knew" what was going on, sometimes up to the second. Despite such attention to detail, or maybe because of it, some vital issues were overlooked.

One of my consulting assignments at the time required that I interview employees in a 120-person "reorg department" to find out why people were going over to the competition in droves—there was a 50 percent annual turnover rate. During an informal tour of the floor, everything seemed routine; people were busy and generally amiable. The department was full of activity but quite focused. I noticed a middle-aged woman off in the corner who, at first glance, blended in perfectly with the setting, but her desk seemed a bit too neat and her composure too relaxed. I asked to interview her and was told that she was "just the department secretary," who had been with the company for thirty-one years, had little to do with the daily function of the department, and really wasn't at risk of leaving. There were more critical managers and employees to interview.

As I got to know people in the department a bit, I found that one of the conditions they complained about most bitterly was the lack of water. Summertime in many older Wall Street buildings could be brutal. Air-conditioning was often not available on the large, open operations floors, and fans kept air circulating in eighty- to eighty-five-degree temperatures. The only "perk" was cooled springwater: each department had its water-cooler, but this department's cooler had been removed. Other items, such as desk fans, calculators, even pencils and yellow pads, were virtually impossible to get—for "budget reasons," people were told. Many considered such conditions a signal to move on to another job.

When I brought this issue to management's attention, they were floored. Budgets were tight, sure, but denying people water and pencils? The managers were beside themselves and wanted to know who had authorized such controls. Her name was Sarah, and she was "just the department secretary," who after thirty-one loyal years with the company blended in with a desk that was just a bit too neat—and had a deep desire to control.

In a very real sense, the problem was not Sarah but management's inability to not know about the conditions in the department. As far as management was concerned, 95 percent of the trades were being settled in less than twenty-four hours, so they knew the department was fine. Ironically, this knowing had blinded them. People were leaving, not because they didn't have water or pencils, but because the managers, by thinking they knew what was going on, were in fact out of touch, announcing loud and clear, "We are neglecting you; you are not valued." The managers would not have overlooked such a message if they had permitted themselves to not know on occasion. They might have paid closer attention to the expense reports they were signing, authored by Sarah, who was doing such a great job at controlling costs and depriving employees of water.

The reminder "Do not know" encourages us to ease up on our speed to constantly be experts at our jobs, to shift from making something happen to letting something happen. We can permit our work settings to become available to us, allowing our intelligence and natural curiosity to have free rein. Rather than resisting not-knowing, we can relax with it as a natural and necessary part of work. We can allow ourselves the opportunity to appreciate, listen, and observe and to be curious about the incidentals, routines, surprises, and even irritations of our work rather than taking them for granted or being put off by them. We can afford to listen for the unspoken messages, often sent unintentionally and even more often misunderstood. By not knowing, we open up, and so does the world around us, offering an untapped wealth of insight and guidance.

Mindfulness, Photography, and Living an Artistic Life

ANDY KARR AND MICHAEL WOOD

In any creative endeavor, there are so many ways the mind can get in the way—and yet so many opportunities to know better how the mind actually works. The authors of this selection explain how mindfulness can help aspiring artists to see the world with fresh eyes. Though they are writing primarily for photographers, their insights can be applied to any art form.

THIS ORDINARY, workaday world is rich and good. It might not seem that way at six in the morning when you are rushing to prepare your coffee or tea and get out the door to go to work, or when you are tired and irritated after dinner and have to take out the garbage. Instead, ordinary life might seem hassled, repetitive, and boring. When you are impatient, resentful, or uninterested in daily life, you will be blind to the potential for living cheerfully and creatively.

Life seems repetitive and boring when you don't notice the uniqueness of each moment and the constant, subtle changes that are going on all around you. For example, you might have the same thing for breakfast every morning and not notice that it tastes different each day because of natural fluctuations in your body and mind, as well as small variations in the details of your meal.

Even though things usually seem solid and enduring, nothing really lasts a second moment. Our experiences are always in the process of disintegrating and transforming. As photographers, we can know this intimately. Photographers are always working with light, and light is always changing. The brightness changes; the angle changes; the color changes; the diffuseness changes. Not only does the light change, whatever is illuminated changes with the light. As Mies van der Rohe, one of the great pioneers of modern architecture and design, famously observed, "God is in the details."

Ordinary experience is the raw material of our photographic art. As the photographer, writer, and curator Beaumont Newhall wrote, "We are not interested in the unusual, but in the usual seen unusually." When we separate our artistic activity from daily life, we cut ourselves off from our most valuable resource. We divide the world into the worthwhile and the unimportant, the meaningful and the merely functional. Instead of appreciating what we have, we look for something better, something more beautiful, more entertaining. Seeking extraordinary perceptions and special artistic experiences leads us to overlook the riches that surround us. We might dream of being successful artists, living in the south of France or northern California, while ignoring the golden glow of sunlight on the kitchen sink. Instead of looking elsewhere for nourishment, we can live artistic, elegant lives, appreciating the details of our ordinary existence.

We should be clear about what we mean by living an artistic life. It does *not* mean surrounding yourself with beautiful things and banishing everything that is ugly: choosing only to look at fresh flowers and rejecting dead leaves ignores the deep beauty that both share when you open your eyes to them. Labeling things "beautiful" and "ugly" masks what they *really* look like. When you pick and choose in this way, all you really see are the masks, which are your own mental fabrications. Living artistically means appreciating things just as they are, in an intimate, unbiased way.

Living artistically also doesn't mean cultivating an artistic persona. You don't need to create elaborate rituals so that preparing dinner and doing the dishes become "Art." Trying to live an exceptional, beautiful life will only alienate you from the ordinary. Instead, the way to live artistically is to conduct ordinary activities in a relaxed and attentive way.

Finally, artistic living is not something you can go out and buy, like an extreme makeover. It arises from within.

Living artistically means seeing and caring for the details of your world. You can always take a moment to uplift your situation, no matter how basic it is. Just wiping the bathroom counter after you brush your teeth will remove the stains of resentment and carelessness. What matters isn't how luxurious your surroundings are, but how much you can appreciate the richness and freshness of your experience.

REVEALING NATURAL ARTISTRY

Strangely enough, you don't need to learn how to be artistic. It is as natural as breathing and the beating of your heart. Nevertheless, natural artistry is often inaccessible because it is concealed by preoccupation or resentment. A good analogy for this is the way the sun constantly radiates light even though you can't always see it. The sun is *always* shining, even when clouds cover the sky. No one has to make the sun shine. Sunshine becomes visible when the wind removes the clouds. Similarly, artistry arises from the mind's natural wakefulness, creativity, and humor when the obstacles that obscure it are cleared away. This is the main point of what we call "contemplative photography" (or any creative endeavor): you don't need to learn how to fabricate creativity; you need to learn to remove the clouds that prevent it from expressing itself.

Before you can learn to remove the clouds, you need to understand their nature. We have briefly mentioned the way preoccupation and resentment obscure our vision. Judgmental, cynical, and angry states of mind separate us from the richness of our world and cover over natural artistry. An angry mind may *seem* sharp, but it is a sharpness that is bewildering, lacking both insight and intelligence. Anger produces crudeness rather than artistry. An angry person is fixated on the object of their anger and blind to the details of their experience and the environment. Anger overwhelms subtlety.

Possessiveness, craving, ambition, and other forms of desire cut us off from artistry, because they are bound up with projections about objects of desire and possibilities of fulfillment. Being fettered in this way, we are unavailable to ordinary perceptions, and there is no room for the dance of creativity. Thus, even the desire to be artistic and creative can become an obstacle when we fixate on it. This is not to say that passion is necessarily a problem. The basic energy of passion, when it is not bound up with projections, brings out and energizes inquisitiveness and natural creativity.

Ignoring experience, however we go about it (dreaminess, dullness, laziness), is the emotional equivalent of putting out the Do Not Disturb sign. No fresh perceptions or inspirations are welcome. Needless to say, ignorance is an obstacle.

These various types of emotionality are like billowing clouds that block the sunlight. Sometimes they erupt in damaging storms. Other times they are like long spells of wet, gray weather.

A different type of obstacle is the ongoing internal narrative that accompanies us from the moment we wake up in the morning until the moment we fall asleep at night (even reappearing in our dreams). Sometimes this narrative is a monologue, sometimes an inner dialogue. The "voice" always *seems* to be the observer, looking out at the world. But what this discursiveness really does is fill up space, leaving little room for creativity and shutting out most of the light. Contrary to the way it seems, the inner narrator is more like a talkative blind person than a skillful observer. Occasionally, there is a break in the discursive flow, and a fresh perception gets in, but whenever this happens, the inner narrator quickly jumps in and smothers that perception, wrapping it in commentary until all freshness is lost.

Struggling with these various emotional and discursive clouds is a losing proposition. It only adds to their energy and solidity. There is also really no way to suppress them. Surprisingly, the best way to deal with these obstacles is to recognize whatever they are and let them be. A light touch of awareness, repeatedly applied, cuts the momentum of emotions and discursiveness. Trying to get rid of them just leads to more struggle.

You can become skillful at developing this light touch of awareness, and this is a key to living artistically. Another key is learning to recognize naturally occurring breaks in the clouds, moments when the light naturally shines through. The more you cultivate these gaps, the longer they will last and the more opportunity you will have to settle into your experience and creatively engage with the world.

There are things you should cultivate to enhance these experiences. The most important is an inquisitive mind. You can be inquisitive about your confusion, as well as what lies beyond confusion—the world of ordinary, fresh perceptions. The more curiosity you have, the more you will be available to your experience and the more you will see. Cultivating patience will also be a great help, since unraveling the layers of confusion that have accumulated over a lifetime is a gradual process. Finally, nurturing a sense of humor is essential. Our emotionality plays games within games to perpetuate itself. You can't help but get sucked in. If you take the whole thing too seriously, you'll be dragged down into the maelstrom. However, just one moment of seeing the irony of that situation brings you back to the surface. Phew!

Art in Everyday Life, and Everyday Life in Art

Seeing the ordinary world clearly is a source of raw material and inspiration when you work with your camera. If art is life experience expressed through creative technique, photography is one method for concentrating those experiences into images. You don't need a lot of craft or technique to produce fine photographs. When you experience your world clearly and shoot what you see, the results will be artistic.

Training in artistic living will enhance your photography, and training in contemplative photography will deepen your ability to live a creative, artistic life. As the wonderful photographer Dorothea Lange said, "The camera is an instrument that teaches people how to see without a camera." The practice of contemplative photography will definitely increase your appreciation of the world around you, which is infinitely richer than you could ever imagine.

Making Music

Madeline Bruser

All of us need to perform in front of others from time to time, whether we do it for a living or not. Concert pianist and teacher Madeline Bruser offers advice on unlocking our natural musicality and shows us how to overcome the fear of being in front of others and bring mindfulness to practicing and performing.

IN MAKING MUSIC, we mix passion with discipline. Our love for a piece of music motivates us to become intimate with it by producing the sound ourselves, with our instrument and our own body. This intimacy grows through countless hours of practice, as we face the physical, mental, and emotional challenges that the piece presents. Often, these challenges are extreme; in fact, scientists have stated that playing a musical instrument is the most complex neuromuscular activity known to mankind. In the process of executing highly refined movements, we must also respond to a myriad of sounds and develop an intellectual grasp of the structure of the piece we are playing. As we try to meet all of these demands, we continually come up against our habits of being tense or distracted or of distorting the composer's emotional intentions, and we must get past these habits in order to master the piece. When, on top of all this, we come to perform the piece, we add the element of stage fright to the mix, pushing our capacities to the limit.

Meditation gives us space to breathe in the midst of these extreme challenges and can help us discover new ways of practicing our instruments. As our mind settles through meditation, we begin to notice our habits of pushing ourselves too hard or tightening our muscles in an effort to express ourselves. We can learn to stop trying so hard and to simply open to the music and our physical sensations—to be less active and more receptive. This shift toward greater receptivity unlocks our natural musicality and coordination.

PEACEFUL EFFORT

You can practice such receptivity by using a simple listening technique with a phrase of music: place your attention on each individual sound as you play or sing it, and notice how it affects you. The following story about a musician I worked with describes this technique and how powerful it can be.

David came to the Meditation for Musicians Retreat in Vermont hoping to rediscover the joy he used to feel in playing the viola. Twenty years old and highly gifted, he attended an extremely competitive conservatory and grew up with a father who encouraged him to practice by constantly pushing him to work hard, play fast, and excel. Although David appreciated his father's support, he longed to feel more independent of his influence. At his first workshop with me, he revealed to the group that his father had become very ill during the last year and could no longer provide support as he used to, that he might even die within a few years. David felt torn. As much as he wanted to feel free of his father's input, he also wanted desperately to make his father happy by practicing extremely hard. The conflict between these opposing desires had often paralyzed his inspiration, causing him to stop practicing for weeks at a time.

After listening to David's story, I asked him to stand solidly upright, holding his viola in one hand, and to notice how his body felt from head to toe. He took a few moments to scan his body and feel his own presence in this way. I then asked him to place his viola in position and to play only the first note of his piece, noticing how that single sound affected him. He drew the bow across the string for several seconds, extending the note until he felt the power of that sound. His face showed great concentration, and the sound soon became intensely resonant and expressive. He went on in this manner, slowly playing each successive note. Gradually, he picked up speed while visibly maintaining intense concentration, rootedness to the ground, and connectedness to the viola. His sound was rich and vibrant, and his playing was full of longing, joy, and beauty. When he finished, his face broke into a radiant smile, and I had to brush away tears before I could speak. I turned and saw others crying too. David's breakthrough had moved everyone in the room.

David found his creative power simply by opening to the energy within himself, bringing that energy into the playing of each note, and noticing how each sound affected him. Revealing his personal story and feelings in a friendly environment helped him relax. Taking the time to sense the living quality of his solid, still, physical presence and to focus on the sensations within him enabled him to gather his deep emotional and visceral energy and to use it to play. His playing was informed by the fullness of his being.

The effort David made to play in this powerful way can be described as "peaceful effort." Rather than battling with himself to pick up his instrument and practice, or struggling to "get it right" or make it expressive, he simply tuned in to his body, his sensations, and the sound he was making and let the music flow from within him.

TRANSCENDING STAGE FRIGHT

Once we make a piece our own, we may have the opportunity to perform it. Whether we are playing on the stage of Carnegie Hall or in a small room, our awareness of ourselves and of our environment becomes heightened. When others are listening to and looking at us, we feel on the spot and may look at ourselves with more doubt than usual. Even if we have prepared very well, we don't know how our performance will go, and we may imagine the worst and start to panic.

In order to become confident onstage, we need to make a basic shift in focus: instead of worrying, "What do they think of me?" we can learn to think, "I want to give them something."

Although this may seem like a difficult shift to make, you can actually accomplish it through a short contemplative practice I've created for musicians. It has helped people in other fields as well to cut through fear, doubt, and confusion and to reconnect with their communicative power. At a program in New York called Meditation for Actors, participants find that this contemplative exercise opens them up to greater spontaneity and expressive freedom in performance.

I adapted this contemplation from a practice in my particular meditation tradition, in which we take a moment at the beginning of each day to contemplate the lineage of teachers who have passed down the practice of meditation to us, from one generation to the next, for our benefit. Because we naturally feel grateful toward those who have helped us in this way, this practice opens our heart. The practice I designed for musicians includes a similar contemplation. Those who have tried it have found it very powerful in transforming stage fright into confidence.

Lineage

We begin this practice by closing our eyes and reflecting for a moment on what we've inherited as musicians. When we were first attracted to music and decided to learn to play an instrument, it came from a place deep within us that is indestructible. We call this place many things: inspiration, motivation, talent, musicality, passion, love, appreciation, connection. It's part of who we are, and no one can take it away. From that starting place, we sought out a teacher. And hopefully we had people in our family, such as our parents, who appreciated our longing to make music and who helped to find us a teacher. The music, our parents, and our teachers are all part of our inheritance.

Many of us have had experiences with parents, teachers, and others that have been less than ideal and, in some cases, very destructive to our confidence. Nevertheless, it's important to reflect on the people who have helped us to pursue music in some way, to acknowledge that they did give us something. And we can also reflect on music itself—on certain composers and performers who have inspired us. We have inherited a phenomenal treasure.

I remember getting out of school to go to concerts at the San Francisco Opera House when I was a child. I heard Leon Fleisher perform there when I was seven years old, and it had a huge impact on me—to sit in the darkened auditorium and watch him walk into the light onstage, sit down at the piano, and create magic. That experience connected me to the Western musical tradition in a powerful way. I instinctively sensed that I belonged in it.

As musicians, we talk about our lineage often: "I studied with so-and-so, and they studied with so-and-so, who studied with so-and-so." We can trace our lineage back several generations. When I was seventeen, I began studying at Indiana University with Menahem Pressler, who had a profound impact on me. He introduced me to what it is to be an artist; not only a pianist, but an artist.

Recently, I was reading a book about him called *Menahem Pressler: Artistry in Piano Teaching*. In the back of the book, I discovered a lineage tree—like a family tree—of Pressler's teachers and their teachers extending back several generations. Over the course of his youth, he had teachers in Germany, Israel, France, New York, and California. As I looked at this chart, I saw some great names on the smaller branches of the tree that I had already known were part of my lineage, including Busoni and even Beethoven. Then all of a sudden, as I was following three particular branches, I saw the name Frederic Chopin. I burst into tears.

As most pianists know, Chopin was not only an amazing composer for the piano, but he was a consummate pianist and a great teacher of the instrument. Although we don't have any recordings of his playing, there are many accounts of it—as well as descriptions of his teaching—that were recorded by his students and other musicians of his time and later put into a book. So I was stunned to see that he had taught someone whose descendants taught my own teacher. I instantly realized that Chopin is part of my pianistic lineage too. I could hardly believe that I could be so fortunate.

When you do this contemplation, reflect on whatever comes up for you in your particular lineage—people and experiences that have inspired, encouraged, and supported you in your journey as a musician from the beginning until now. Reflect on all of it, on the people and situations that really mean something to you. Take a couple of minutes to appreciate what you've been given.

Your Own Goodness

The second part of the contemplation is to reflect on your own goodness, that you are able to receive this great inheritance. You have a natural and unique place in the tradition, and you have disciplined yourself for a long time to develop your abilities. Like all musicians, you have practiced countless hours, day after day, from the first day of studying your instrument. So not only were you born into this tradition by virtue of your talent, but you have also earned your place in the tradition and become part of it. Take a couple of minutes to appreciate that.

The Goodness of Your Audience

The last part of the practice is to reflect on the goodness of your audience, including every audience you will ever have extending into the future. These people come to be uplifted or consoled by your performances. They come from many different backgrounds, but they are all human beings like you, and your job is to connect with them. They may be distracted when they arrive to hear you and may need time to settle down. You have the ability and the opportunity to give them a moment to relax and then to give them what you've received—to give music to whoever is there. You are part of a continuous stream called lineage, and it is a living lineage.

I spoke once with a dancer who performed for thirteen years with the Joffrey Ballet. He often had to perform a particular ballet hundreds of times, many times for children's matinees. But he made a practice of telling himself, "Maybe there's one person out there who's never seen dance before or who's never seen this work before. I'm going to do it for them." Twenty years later, he was standing in the lobby during the intermission of a performance he was attending, and a nineteen-year-old man came up to him and said, "Mr. Holder?" When he turned around, the young man said, "You don't know me, but when I was four years old, I was at the kiddie matinee and saw you dance. And it's because of you that I became a dancer."

We never know what our performance will do for people.

Anna's Story

Anna was an amateur pianist in her early fifties. Like the other participants in the Meditation for Musicians Retreat, she was invited to perform in the concert that would take place on the last night of the weeklong program. She declined the invitation, however, saying she had never had confidence in her playing or any desire to play for others. She was just doing it for herself, and it was even hard for her to play in the workshops at the retreat. During the week, she had spoken several times about how deprived she had been studying music as a child, with "bad teachers and bad pianos," and she seemed sad and even somewhat bitter about her experiences.

The day before the concert, however, Anna had a change of heart. We had just spent a few minutes doing the contemplation practice I've described, and Anna was one of the people who spoke with tears of the amazing effect it had. She said she realized that she didn't have to keep complaining about her disadvantaged childhood and that she felt gratitude toward her parents for doing their best. They were very poor, and ten dollars a week for her piano lessons had been a lot for them, a sacrifice they willingly made so that she could learn to play. As she thought of them, of her teachers, and of everything she had received in her life as a musician, she was filled for the first time with a desire to "give something back" by playing for others. The next evening at the concert, she walked with dignity toward the grand piano, bowed to her audience, and played more expressively and confidently than I had heard her play before.

I am still grateful to Anna for her generosity and bravery in that performance. She took the practice I gave her and turned it into a gift for all of us.

Senior Moment, Wonderful Moment

SUE MOON

Mindfulness is often defined as the opposite of forgetfulness, but as we get old, and our memories decline along with our other systems, what we need to remember is not every last little thing, but how to laugh at ourselves.

I CALLED MY FRIEND CORNELIA, a fellow grandmother, to ask if I could borrow a crib for my granddaughter's upcoming visit. When she answered the phone, I said, "Hi, Cornelia. It's Sue," and then my mind went blank. I paused hopefully, but no more words came out of my mouth.

"Morning," she said. "What's up?"

She was a good enough friend that I didn't have to fake it, but still, it was unsettling. "Ummm," I said, waiting for the old neurons to start firing up again. I asked myself if it had to do with our weekly walking date. Nooo . . . Was it about her son's article on stream conservation? Nooo . . . Outside the window, a squirrel was running along the porch railing with a walnut in his mouth. "I'm having a senior moment," I said finally. "Do *you* happen to know why I called?"

She laughed. "You must have known that I have some plums to give you from my tree." The squirrel was now sitting on the railing, peeling the outer shell off the walnut and spitting it on the ground. I'd never noticed before how the long fur of their tails waves back and forth like grass when they flick them.

By the time I went over to Cornelia's house to pick up the plums, I had remembered about the crib, and I got that too.

The Buddhist teacher Thich Nhat Hanh helps me appreciate my senior moments. In his book *Present Moment Wonderful Moment,* he writes, "The real miracle is to be awake in the present moment." I'm confident he would agree that a senior moment, a moment of forgetting what day it is or where you are going, can be a moment of deep understanding.

For example, standing in the kitchen wondering why I have a pair of scissors in my hand, I notice the sunlight glinting off its metal blades and dancing on the wall, and I repeat Thich Nhat Hanh's sentence to myself, "The real miracle is to be awake in the present moment!" Younger people can also experience such transcendent moments of deep immersion in the infinite present, but they have to go to much greater lengths to do so, meditating for days at a time, for example, or hang gliding. I have only to carry a pair of scissors from one room to another.

I started out on a hike with friends, and when the path turned steeply and unexpectedly upward, I had to send them on without me, knowing my knees would not be able to bring me back down. I sat on a rock before returning to the lodge. This was not what we usually think of as a senior moment, but I speak of it here because it was another occasion when the frailty of age dropped me into a gap in time. I listened to my friends' voices, to their twig-snapping and leaf-rustling, until I could hear them no longer. I was cross at my knees for making me miss the companionship, though I knew they hadn't done it on purpose. I watched a yellow leaf twist its way down to the ground, and I heard it land on another leaf. Have you ever heard a leaf land on another leaf? Okay, it wasn't the most exciting moment of my life, but it was good enough, and I wasn't missing it.

I say, "I'm having a senior moment" when I blow it, hoping to fend off the irritation of others with humor. But the next time the blankness comes over me, I'll try to be bold and move beyond self-deprecation. I'll say, "Senior moment, wonderful moment!" in order to remind the people around me of the wisdom that is to be found in these little coffee breaks of the brain.

A friend of mine takes another tack. He tells me he memorizes a stock phrase and keeps it handy to fill the gaps. So if he's saying to an acquaintance over lunch, "Have you ever noticed that . . ." and suddenly forgets the rest of the sentence, he brings out his all-purpose phrase: "It's incredibly hard to get the wrapper off a new CD." Or if he sees two old friends who don't know each other at a party, and their names vanish into the yawning void when the moment comes to introduce them, he shakes hands enthusiastically and says it again: "It's incredibly hard to get the wrapper off a new CD!" Like a pebble striking bamboo in an old Zen koan, his shocking statement offers his listeners a wake-up call to be here now.

It's not my fault when I have a senior moment any more than it was my fault when my hair turned gray. I'm just a human being, after all. I've had a lifetime of junior moments, when one word follows another in logical— and boring—succession, when each action leads to the next appropriate action. For countless years, I have remembered to bring the pencil with me when I go downstairs to use the pencil sharpener. I think I've earned the right to break free from the imprisonment of sequential thinking.

A senior moment is a stop sign on the road of life. It could even be a leg up toward enlightenment. So I stay calm, let the engine idle, and enjoy the scenery. What happens next will be revealed in due course.

PART THREE

Mindfulness, Health, and Healing

Paying Attention to Our Own Mind and Body

ELLEN LANGER

Harvard psychologist Ellen Langer's approach to mindfulness is distinct from that of most other scholar-researchers. She does not rely on meditation practice in her research, and she does not derive her understanding of mindfulness from Buddhism or Eastern philosophy. Instead, she began studying mindfulness out of an interest in mindlessness, or automaticity, as it is known in Western psychology. She defines mindfulness as simply "noticing something new," and her work suggests that this small shift in attention can cause big changes in how we look at "medical conditions" and how to treat them.

EVERYTHING IS THE SAME until it is not. Tightly woven ideas and theories may be fabrications that make it hard to see how things could be otherwise. Scientists elaborate on theory with a series of concatenated probabilities to the point that it becomes very difficult to take accepted truth apart in the face of so much "supporting" data.

For example, while we all have a pretty good picture of what dinosaurs looked like, clearly no one has ever actually seen one. At first, a few bones were found, and a picture of dinosaurs was constructed based on someone's view of how they fit together. Then more bones were found, and it was easier to put together the picture of other dinosaurs once we had a starting point. Now imagine that a new and different set of bones were found and scientists began creating a picture of what would become a googliasaurus, where the bones made a reasonably complete image. After it was finished, imagine that a new bone was found that didn't fit the prior conception of the googliasaurus. How many new, previously missing pieces that don't fit would have to be found before we entirely remade our conception of a googliasaurus?

We might "know," for instance, that certain brain injuries create "irreversible" brain damage and accept that as fact. But if we asked how we could reverse "irreversible" brain damage, we would seek out information different from what we now examine when we take such labels as hard-and-fast truths and merely test existing theories. And so our medical conditions appear more and more to us as they have been defined by the research behind them.

ATTENDING TO VARIABILITY

In 1961, Yale psychologist Neal Miller suggested that the autonomous nervous system, which controls blood pressure and heart rate, could be trained just like the voluntary system, which allows us to raise or lower our arm and other deliberated acts.[1] His suggestion was met with a great deal of skepticism. Everyone knew that the autonomous system was just that, autonomous and beyond our control. Yet his subsequent work on biofeedback, which makes autonomic processes such as heart rate visible by hooking people up to monitors, found that people could be taught to control these processes. If we recognize that we can control the unseen, controlling the visible can seem a more doable task. Once we learn to pay attention to variability—that is, to notice change—we are in a better position to ask what the reason for the changes we observe might be and to ask what we can do to control the change.

Laura Delizonna, Ryan Williams, and I recently conducted research to see if people could be taught to regulate their heart rate after focusing their attention on how it varies.[2] We asked participants to record their heart rate by taking their pulse over the course of the day for a week, although we set different conditions for each of the four groups. People in what we called the "stability group" measured their heart rate upon going to sleep and at first awakening every day. We expected that members of this group would be likely to see their heart rate as reasonably stable, with little change from one measurement to the next. A "moderate attention to variability group" was asked to measure their heart rate twice a day, at different times that we designated for them each day. We expected that they would see a greater degree of variation in their rate.

The "high attention to variability group" was told to measure their heart rate every three hours, which would most likely ensure a great deal of variability in the recorded numbers. In addition, we instructed this group to record the activity they were engaged in at the time of the reading and to pay attention to the degree to which their heart rate differed from previous measurements as a way of getting them to be more mindful of the variability. Finally, a control group of participants did not monitor their heart rate; they were simply asked to monitor their activities for the week.

Before the study began, all the participants completed a brief questionnaire about one's ability to control one's heart rate and a test of their mindfulness, then were sent home. They returned to the lab after a week of monitoring, and after gathering their data, we gave them a surprise task of first raising and then lowering their heart rate. No one was instructed on how to control their heart rate; they were just asked to use their mind to change their heart rate without changing their muscle tension or breathing.

Both the stability group and the moderate attention to variability group weren't very good at increasing their heart rate, but the high attention to variability group, the more mindful group, did significantly better. The difference was small but meaningful. The control group, interestingly, tended to decrease their heart rate even as they were attempting to increase it. Those who scored highest on the mindfulness scale, regardless of the group to which they were assigned, were more successful at raising their heart rate and exercised greater control over heart-rate regulation. We don't know exactly how they did it, but our concern was with whether mindful awareness would enable them to find a way.

Instructing people to notice variability and biofeedback both provoke mindfulness. While they are similar, there are important ways attention to variability is different. Biofeedback assists a person to gain control over autonomous processes by employing an external device, such as a heart rate monitor, to make the process accessible. Biofeedback is a very important tool that deserves to be more fully explored, but attention to variability need not rely on external devices or be focused on solely biological phenomena. The effects of our attention to variability can be very general, bringing physiological response, emotions, and behaviors within our control. Probably the most important difference between the two is that in biofeedback experiments, people are instructed in how to change bodily processes. In our study, the high attention to variability group, which was told to notice change, was simply exposed to conditions that would foster such learning.

The Illusion of Stability

If attention to variability can be effective in such an "uncontrollable" process as heart rate, it may be effective in situations where our control is even more apparent if we choose to notice, as in a disease such as asthma. Although we lead ourselves to believe that chronic conditions such as asthma become "manageable" as we learn to approach them in a consistent, predictable fashion, all diseases and the symptoms they present vary to some degree day by day, if not minute by minute. An asthmatic's first task should be to recognize that the most stable thing about her disease is her mind-set about it. The shortness of breath she experiences is never really the same as it was the last time or the time before that, although the differences too often go unnoticed.

Medical devices such as inhalers foster this illusion of stability. The inhaler doles out much the same amount of medication regardless of our need; it is not calibrated to lead us to consider how much we actually need at this particular moment. If an asthmatic notices that his current episode is not as bad as—or is worse than—the last, it likely occurs to him to ask why this is so. It might be that when he has an episode while visiting Jane, he doesn't need the inhaler, but he needs an extra dose at Stephen's house.

With that information, he begins to figure out what tends to trigger his asthma and how to control these episodes better. Perhaps he shouldn't spend time at Stephen's anymore, or he might investigate what is different about each environment. Recognizing that there are distinct external circumstances that give rise to symptoms is itself empowering, and using that information sends us on a self-rewarding, mindful journey in search of a solution.

All types of diseases and psychological processes are just as open to our attention. Consider depression. Typically, when we are depressed, we have little or no desire for the company of others or interest in looking for activities that might break the spell of depression. We tend to feel that no person and no distraction can help and that engaging with the world might even make us feel worse. Our answer is to retreat even further and avoid a change in circumstance, lest it worsen our condition. Familiarity is comforting, and we cling to the familiar to avoid the possibility of stress. When we're depressed, we take comfort in holding our routines still, even as they induce and reinforce our disengagement. The mind-set of depression is such that we often believe that we are always depressed, that our depression is a constant factor in our lives.

There is a different approach. When we grow depressed, we tend to imagine that we are falling back into a familiar and even necessary condition, one no different from the other episodes of depression we've experienced. We don't consider that there are surely differences in our present circumstances or look to identify them. Our first experience of anything will be different from the tenth if we consider it clearly. One instance of depression may have needed a significant provocation; the next time, perhaps all we needed was a subtle cue to bring it on. If we notice the differences between these bouts of depression, we have a chance to cope in a more successful way. One reason we come to see being depressed as a constant condition is that when we are content, we don't check in with ourselves to see how we feel. We simply feel fine and go about living without gathering evidence about our feelings. When we grow depressed, we tend to ask why we are unhappy and gather evidence to support our depression. Thus, when we are depressed, we ask why, and when we're happy, we don't. As a result, when we become depressed, we don't have complete information about our mental state, and we have little evidence to support our happiness, which allows us to imagine we're always depressed.

What would happen if we were encouraged to notice how our depression right now was different from the way it felt yesterday? We would become more mindful about our mental state. When we use a single attribution *depressed* for our feelings, we are retreating into that term's familiar and mindless meaning. We feel less than alive, in part or whole, because we are not living. We're only existing. Now imagine if science led us to understand that there isn't a single kind of depression but rather five or more similar but distinct kinds of depression and that it is our job to figure out which kind we have. Let's say that we were told by doctors that we might experience more than one of them and that we might have one kind of depression in the morning and another one in the evening, or we might even vacillate among a few of them throughout the day. Now, instead of a single-minded, mindless focus on ourselves—the hallmark, I believe, of depression—we would be mindfully focused. The result of this search, ironically, might actually reduce our depression.

CONFRONTING STABILITY

There are several reasons that we cling to the illusion of stability to the extent that we do. First, although we recognize on some level that the world around us is always changing, we are oblivious to the fact that we mindlessly hold it still. When we are mindful, we notice. When we are mindless, we are "not there" to notice that we are not there.

Second, from the moment we are born we are presented with absolute facts rather than facts in context. We aren't taught that distinctions such as "young" and "old" or "healthy" and "unhealthy" are social constructs and that their meaning depends on context. We are conditioned to learn about and see the world as a set of facts, such as $1 + 1 = 2$. The world is far more subtle than such facts allow, and we should have learned that $1 + 1 = 2$ only if we are using the base 10 number system, but $1 + 1 = 10$ if the number system is base 2, and $1 + 1 = 1$ if we are adding one wad of chewing gum to one wad of chewing gum.

The educational system forgoes that more nuanced approach in favor of certainty. It simplifies and makes the world seem more predictable than it is. And so we educate ourselves into mindlessness. As psychologist Silvan Tomkins often noted, some of us believe the world is to be discovered, while others believe it is to be invented.[3] There are great rewards to be had by "discovering" the "truth" and knowing these "truths" that provide incentives for us to cling to the illusion of stability. The stable, consistent world we accept mindlessly isn't the one we live in. One person's depression is different from another's and different from itself on different occasions whether we choose to notice these differences or not. Searching out the nature of our depression would be engaging, and that engagement may be mutually exclusive with feeling depressed.

We should take an interpersonal view of our health care whenever possible. You help me notice the external factors that seem to correlate with my symptoms, and I notice them for you. Ultimately, the responsibility is still the individual's, but just as therapists can point these things out to us, so too can our physicians, significant others, close friends, or relatives. Consider what would happen with an elderly parent in this regard. Adult children often feel helpless when trying to deal with their aging parents. Not infrequently, they infantilize them and overprotect them. For example, we often forget that whether or not a parent wants to wear a hearing aid is still her choice, not ours. Some older people may not want to hear what their children or nurses have to say. I have a friend whose liberal-Democrat great-aunt would turn off her hearing aid when she and her arch-Republican husband set off from Boston to drive to the town where they voted. More important, hearing, like most everything else, is not likely to go away all at once, nor is our ability to hear the same for all types of sounds and in all types of environments. A lack of interest may masquerade as hearing loss. If we were to notice the distinctions in our parents' ability to hear—the times and conditions when their loss is particularly great and when it is not—two things would happen. First, we would feel useful. Second, our parent might find the information useful. But most of us don't make these distinctions. Instead, we see older people as experiencing a general loss, make unhelpful comments about their inability to hear, and shout when we may not have to.

Noticing differences is the essence of mindfulness. Don't imagine, however, that all this noticing needs to be exhausting and leave little time for anything else. Mindfulness is actually energizing, not enervating.

NOTES

1. N. E. Miller, "Analytical Studies of Drive and Reward," *American Psychologist* 16 (1961), 739–54.

2. L. Delizonna, R. Williams, and E. Langer, "The Effect of Mindfulness on Heart Rate Control," *Journal of Adult Development and Aging* (forthcoming).

3. As quoted by Robert Abelson in personal conversation.

This Is Your Brain on Mindfulness

Matthieu Ricard

People say that meditation is good for your brain, but can it be proved? A long-time monk, meditator, philosopher, and sometime scientist, Matthieu Ricard reports on studies that show the benefits of meditation for the brain. Since he himself was a laboratory subject in one of these major scientific studies, he has a unique vantage point from which to describe the historic encounter between science and meditation.

TWENTY YEARS AGO, almost all neuroscientists believed that the adult brain had very little margin for change and could not generate new neurons. There could only be some limited reinforcement or deactivation of synaptic connections, combined with a slow decline of the brain through aging. It was thought that major changes would wreak havoc in the unbelievably complex brain functions that had been gradually built up in early life. Today, ideas have changed considerably, and neuroscientists are talking more and more about *neuroplasticity*—the concept that the brain is continually evolving in response to our experience through the establishment of new neuronal connections, the strengthening of existing ones, or the creation of new neurons.

In a seminal research project, Fred Gage and his colleagues at the Salk Institute in California studied the response of mice to an "enriched environment." The rodents were transferred from a bland box to a large cage with toys, exercise wheels, tunnels to explore, and plenty of play-mates. The results were striking: in just forty-five days, the number of neu-rons in the hippocampus—a brain structure associated with processing novel experiences and dispatching them for storage in other areas of the brain—grew by 15 percent, even in older mice.[1]

Does this apply to human beings? In Sweden, Peter Ericksson was able to study the formation of new neurons in cancer patients. When those el-derly patients died, their brains were autopsied and it was found that, just as with the rodents, new neurons had been formed in the hippocampus.[2]

It has become clear that neurogenesis in the brain is possible through-out life. As Daniel Goleman writes in *Destructive Emotions,* "Musical train-ing, where a musician practices an instrument every day for years, offers an apt model for neuroplasticity. MRI studies find that in a violinist, for ex-ample, the areas of the brain that control finger movements in the hand that does the fingering grow in size. Those who start their training earlier in life and practice longer show bigger changes in the brain."[3]

Studies of chess players and Olympic athletes have also found profound changes in the cognitive capacities involved in their pursuits. The question we can now ask is, "Can a voluntary inner enrichment, such as the long-term practice of meditation, even when carried out in the neutral environ-ment of a hermitage, induce important and lasting changes in the workings of the brain?"

That is precisely what Richie Davidson and his team set out to study in the W. M. Keck Laboratory for Functional Brain Imaging and Behavior at the University of Wisconsin–Madison (now known as the Waisman Labo-ratory for Brain Imaging and Behavior).

AN EXTRAORDINARY ENCOUNTER

It all began half a world away, in the foothills of the Himalayas in India, in a small village where the Dalai Lama located his government-in-exile fol-lowing the Chinese invasion of Tibet. In the fall of 2000, a small group of some of the leading neuroscientists and psychologists of our time—Fran-cisco Varela, Paul Ekman, Richard Davidson, and others—gathered for five days of dialogue with the Dalai Lama. This was the tenth session in a series of memorable encounters between the Dalai Lama and eminent scientists that had been organized since 1985 by the Mind and Life Institute at the initiative of the late Francisco Varela, a groundbreaking researcher in the cognitive sciences, and former businessman Adam Engle.

The topic was "destructive emotions," and I had the daunting task of presenting the Buddhist view in the presence of the Dalai Lama, a test that reminded me of sitting for school exams. Following that remarkable meeting, which has been endearingly recounted by Daniel Goleman in *Destructive Emotions,* several research programs were launched to study individuals who had devoted themselves for twenty years or more to the systematic development of compassion, altruism, and inner peace.

Four years later, in November 2004, the prestigious scientific journal *Proceedings of the National Academy of Sciences* published the first of an ongoing series of papers about what can arguably be described as the first serious study of the impact of long-term meditation on the brain.[4] Meditation states have traditionally been described in terms of the first-person experience, but they now began to be translated into a scientific language.

To date, twelve experienced meditators in the Tibetan Buddhist tradition (eight Asians and four Europeans, comprising both monks and lay practitioners) have been examined by Richard Davidson and Antoine Lutz, a student of Francisco Varela's who joined the Madison laboratory. These accomplished practitioners, who have completed an estimated ten thousand to forty thousand hours of meditation over fifteen to forty years, were compared, as a control, with twelve age-matched volunteers who were given meditation instructions and practiced for a week.

MEDITATORS IN THE LAB

I happened to be the first "guinea pig." A protocol was developed whereby the meditator alternated between neutral states of mind and specific states of meditation. Among the various states that were initially tested, four were chosen as the objects of further research: the meditations on altruistic love and compassion, on focused attention, on open presence, and on the visualization of mental images.

There are methods in Buddhist practice devoted to cultivating loving-kindness and compassion. Here, the meditators try to generate an all-pervading sense of benevolence, a state in which love and compassion permeate the entire mind. They let pure love and compassion—intense, deep, and without any limit or exclusion—be the only object of their thoughts. Although not immediately focusing on particular people, altruistic love and compassion include a total readiness and unconditional availability to benefit others.

Focused attention, or concentration, requires focusing all one's attention upon one chosen object and calling one's mind back each time it wanders. Ideally, this one-pointed concentration should be clear, calm, and stable. It should avoid sinking into dullness or being carried away by mental agitation.

Open presence is a clear, open, vast, and alert state of mind that is free from mental constructs. It is not actively focused on anything, yet it is not distracted. The mind simply remains at ease, perfectly present in a state of pure awareness. When thoughts intrude, the meditator does not attempt to interfere with them but allows the thoughts to vanish naturally.

Visualization consists of reconstituting a complex mental image, such as the representation of a Buddhist deity, in the mind's eye. The meditator begins by visualizing as clearly as possible every detail of the face, the clothes, the posture, and so on, inspecting them one by one. Lastly, he visualizes the entire deity and stabilizes that visualization.

These various meditations are among the many spiritual exercises that a practicing Buddhist cultivates over the course of many years, during which they become ever more stable and clear.

In the lab, there are two main ways to test the meditators. Electroencephalograms (EEGs) allow changes in the brain's electrical activity to be recorded with a very accurate time resolution, while functional magnetic resonance imaging (fMRI) measures blood flow in various areas of the brain and provides an extremely precise localization of cerebral activity.

The meditator alternates thirty-second neutral periods with ninety-second periods in which he generates one of the meditative states. The process is repeated many times for each mental state. In this instance, the instrument measuring the meditators was equipped with 256 sensors. The electrodes detected striking differences between novices and expert meditators. During meditation on compassion, most of the experienced meditators showed a dramatic increase in the high-frequency brain activity called gamma waves "of a sort that has never been reported before in the neuroscience literature," says Davidson.[5]

It was also found that movement of the waves through the brain was far better coordinated, or synchronized, than in the control group, whose members showed only a slight increase in gamma wave activity while meditating. This seems to demonstrate that "the brain is capable of being trained and physically modified in ways few people can imagine" and that the meditators are able to regulate their cerebral activity deliberately.[6] By comparison, most inexperienced subjects who are assigned a mental exercise—focusing on an object or an occurrence, visualizing an image, and so on—are generally incapable of limiting their mental activity to that one task.

One of the most interesting findings is that the monks who had spent the most years meditating generated the highest levels of gamma waves. This led Davidson to speculate that "meditation not only changes the workings of the brain in the short term, but also quite possibly produces permanent changes.[7]

"We can't rule out the possibility that there was a preexisting difference in brain function between monks and novices," he says, "but the fact that monks with the most hours of meditation showed the greatest brain changes gives us confidence that the changes are actually produced by mental training."[8] Further supporting this was the fact that the practitioners also had considerably higher gamma activity than the controls while resting in a neutral state, even before they started meditating. As science writer Sharon Begley comments, "That opens up the tantalizing possibility that the brain, like the rest of the body, can be altered intentionally. Just as aerobics sculpt the muscles, so mental training sculpts the gray matter in ways scientists are only beginning to fathom."[9]

THE STARTLE RESPONSE

The startle response, one of the most primitive reflexes in the human body's repertoire of responses, involves a series of very rapid muscular spasms in reaction to a sudden noise or an unexpected and disturbing sight. In all people, the same five facial muscles contract instantaneously, notably around the eyes. The entire thing lasts a mere third of a second.

Like all reflexes, this one responds to activity in the brain stem, the most primitive part of that organ, and is usually not subject to voluntary control. As far as science is aware, no intentional act can alter the mechanism that controls it.

The intensity of the startle response is known to reflect the predominance of the negative emotions to which someone is subject—fear, anger, sadness, and disgust. The stronger a person's flinch, the more he is inclined to experience negative emotions.

To test the first meditator's startle reflex, Paul Ekman, a psychologist who has been a pioneer in the study of emotions, brought him to the Berkeley Psychophysiology Laboratory run by his longtime colleague Robert Levenson. The meditator's body movements, pulse, perspiration, and skin temperature were measured. His facial expressions were filmed to capture his physiological reactions to a sudden noise. The experimenters opted for the maximal threshold of human tolerance—a very powerful detonation, equivalent to a gunshot going off beside the ear.

The subject was told that within a five-minute period he would hear a loud explosion. He was asked to try to neutralize the inevitable strong reaction to the extent of making it imperceptible, if possible. Some people are better than others at this exercise, but no one is able to suppress it entirely—far from it—even with the most intense effort to restrain the muscular spasms. Among the hundreds of subjects whom Ekman and Levenson had tested, none had ever managed it. Prior research had found that even elite police sharpshooters, who fire guns every day, cannot stop themselves from flinching. But the meditator was able to.

As Ekman explained, "When he tries to repress the startle, it almost disappears. We've never found anyone who can do that. Nor have any other researchers. This is a spectacular accomplishment. We don't have any idea of the anatomy that would allow him to suppress the startle reflex."

During these tests, the meditator had practiced two types of meditation: single-pointed concentration and open presence, both of which had been studied by fMRI in Madison. He found that the best effect was obtained with the open presence meditation. "In that state," he said, "I was not actively trying to control the startle, but the detonation seemed weaker, as if I were hearing it from a distance." Ekman described how, while some changes had been effected in the meditator's physiology, not one muscle in his face had moved. As the subject explained, "In the distracted state, the explosion suddenly brings you back to the present moment and causes you to jump out of surprise. But while in open presence, you are resting in the present moment, and the bang simply occurs and causes only a little disturbance, like a bird crossing the sky."

Although none of the meditator's facial muscles had quivered when he was practicing open presence, his physiological parameters (pulse, perspiration, blood pressure) had risen in the way usually associated with the startle reflex. This tells us that the body reacted, registering all the effects of the detonation, but that the bang had no emotional impact on the mind. The meditator's performance suggests remarkable emotional equanimity—precisely the same kind of equanimity that the ancient Buddhist texts describe as one of the fruits of meditative practice.

WHAT TO MAKE OF IT ALL

The research, writes Goleman,

> seeks to map . . . the extent to which the brain can be trained to dwell in a constructive range: contentment instead of craving, calm rather than agitation, compassion in place of hatred. Medicines are the leading modality in the West for addressing disturbing emotions, and for better or for worse, there is no doubt that mood-altering pills have brought solace to millions. But one compelling question the research with meditators raises is whether a person, through his or her own efforts, can bring about lasting positive changes in brain function that are even more far-reaching than medication in their impact on emotions.[10]

As far as the cognitive scientists are concerned, the point of this research is not simply to demonstrate the remarkable abilities of a few isolated meditators, but to make us rethink our assumptions about the potential impact of mental training on the development of constructive emotions. "What we found is that the trained mind, or brain, is physically different from the untrained one. In time, we will be able to understand the potential importance of mind training and increase the likelihood that it will be taken seriously," says Davidson.[11] The important thing is to find out whether that process of mental training is available to anyone with enough determination.

We may wonder how much practice is necessary for the brain to effect such changes, especially in an exercise as subtle as meditation. For example, by the time they have reached the competition for admission to national music conservatories, violinists have logged an average of ten thousand hours of practice. Most of the meditators now being studied by Lutz and Davidson have gone way beyond the equivalent ten thousand hours of meditation. The major portion of their training has been undertaken during intensive retreats, in addition to their years of daily practice.

Ten thousand hours may seem daunting, if not entirely out of reach, to the vast majority of us. Yet there is some comforting news. A study that Davidson published with Jon Kabat-Zinn and others has shown that three months of meditation training with highly active employees of a biotech company in Madison showed increased activation in the left prefrontal cortex. Work carried out principally by Davidson and his colleagues in the last twenty years has found that when people report feeling joy, altruism, interest, or enthusiasm, and when they manifest high energy and vivaciousness, they present significant cerebral activity in the left prefrontal cortex. The immune system of these apprentice meditators was also boosted, and the flu vaccine they received in the fall, at the end of the training, was 20 percent more effective than in the control group.[12]

If it is possible for meditators to train their minds to make their destructive emotions vanish, certain practical elements of that meditative training could be valuably incorporated into the education of children and help adults to achieve better quality of life. If such meditation techniques are valid and address the deepest mechanisms of the human mind, their value is universal and they don't have to be labeled Buddhist, even though they are the fruit of more than twenty centuries of Buddhist contemplatives' investigation of the mind. In essence, the current collaboration between scientists and contemplatives could awaken people's interest to the immense value of mind training. If happiness and emotional balance are skills, we cannot underestimate the power of the transformation of the mind and must give due importance to the profound methods that allow us to become better human beings.

NOTES

1. G. Kemperman, H. G. Kuhn, and F. Gage, "More Hippocampal Neurons in Adult Mice Living in an Enriched Environment," *Nature* 286 (April 3, 1997): 493–95. For a general review, see Gerd Kem-

perman and Fred Gage, "New Nerve Cells for the Adult Brain," *Scientific American,* May 1999.

2. P. S. Ericksson, et al., "Neurogenesis in the Adult Human Hippocampus," *Nature Medicine* 4, no. 11 (November 1998): 1313–17.

3. Daniel Goleman, *Destructive Emotions: How Can We Overcome Them?* (New York: Bantam, 2003).

4. A. Lutz, L. L. Greischar, N. B. Rawlings, M. Ricard, and R. J. Davidson, "Long-Term Meditators Self-Induce High-Amplitude Gamma Synchrony During Mental Practice," *PNAS* 101, no. 46 (Nov. 16, 2004).

5. Davidson interviewed by Sharon Begley in "Scans of Monks' Brains Show Meditation Alters Structure, Functioning," *Wall Street Journal,* November 5, 2004, B1.

6. Davidson interviewed by Mark Kaufman in "Meditation Gives Brain a Charge, Study Finds," *Washington Post,* January 3, 2005, A5.

7. Ibid.

8. Begley, "Scans of Monks' Brains."

9. Ibid.

10. Ibid.

11. Kaufman, "Meditation Gives Brain Charge."

12. R. J. Davidson, J. Kabat-Zinn, et al., "Alterations in Brain and Immune Function Produced by Mindfulness Meditation," *Psychosomatic Medicine* 65 (2003): 564–70.

The Proven Benefits of Mindfulness

Daniel Siegel

Psychiatrist Daniel Siegel, a pioneer in the emerging field of interpersonal neurobiology, reports on the state of research into the effectiveness of mindfulness-based interventions in health care.

THE PRACTICE OF INTENTIONAL, nonjudgmental awareness of moment-to-moment experience has been practiced since ancient times in both the East and the West. Wisdom traditions have, for thousands of years, recommended mindfulness practice in a variety of forms to cultivate well-being in an individual's life. Now science is confirming these benefits. Here, we'll explore the common elements of these practices and review the research findings that affirm that daily mindful practice is good for your health.

Mindful awareness practices include yoga, tai chi, qigong, centering prayer, chanting, and mindfulness meditation derived from Buddhist tradition. The science of mindfulness could have delved into any of the practices of intentionally focusing on the present moment without judgment, but through the impact of Mindfulness-Based Stress Reduction (MBSR), much of our in-depth research on the impact of mindful awareness on brain and immune function—as well as psychological and interpersonal changes—has emerged from the study of mindfulness meditation.

Jon Kabat-Zinn, a microbiology PhD then teaching at the University of Massachusetts Medical Center, was inspired in the late 1970s to apply the basic principles of mindfulness meditation to patients in a medical setting. His work developing the MBSR program proved effective in helping to alleviate the suffering of chronic and previously debilitating medical conditions such as chronic pain. It also served as fertile ground for a systematic set of research investigations in collaboration with one of the founders of the field of affective neuroscience, Richard Davidson of the University of Wisconsin–Madison.

Kabat-Zinn repeatedly clarifies in his writings and teachings that MBSR, despite its Buddhist roots, is a secular application of mindfulness, which is a practice of carefully focusing attention, not a form of religion. Indeed, each of the mindfulness practices mentioned earlier share common, secular elements: cultivating an awareness of awareness and paying attention to intention.

Studies show that the ways we intentionally shape our internal focus of attention in mindfulness practice induces a state of brain activation during the practice. With repetition, an intentionally created state can become an enduring trait of the individual, as reflected in long-term changes in brain function and structure. This is a fundamental property of *neuroplasticity*— how the brain changes in response to experience. Here, the experience is the focus of attention in a particular manner.

A question that is raised regarding the specific features of MBSR is what the "active ingredient" is in its powerful effects. Naturally, the experiences of joining with others to reflect on life's stresses, listen to poetry, and do yoga may each contribute to the program's scientifically proven effectiveness. But what specific role does meditation itself play in the positive outcomes of the MBSR program? One clue is that those practicing mindfulness meditation during light treatment for psoriasis experienced four times the usual speed of healing for the chronic skin condition. And in other studies, long-term improvements were seen and maintained in proportion to the formal reflective meditation time carried out at home in patients' daily practice.

Further research will be needed to verify the repeated studies affirming that long-term improvements are correlated with mindfulness practice and not just the effect of gathering in a reflective way as a group. Sara Lazar and her colleagues at Massachusetts General Hospital have found that people who have been mindfulness meditators for several decades have structural features in their brains that are proportional to the number of hours they've practiced. But this finding too, along with studies of "adepts" (those who have spent often tens of thousands of hours meditating), need to be interpreted with caution as to cause and effect. Are people with differing brain activity and structure simply those who've chosen to meditate, or has the meditation actually changed their brains? These questions remain open and in need of further study.

MBSR has proven an excellent source of insight into these questions because it enables novices to engage in new practices that can then be identified as the variables that induce the positive changes that follow. What are these changes, whatever their specific causes? Studies of MBSR have consistently found several key developments that demonstrate its effectiveness as a health-promoting activity. These may be key to the "science of mindfulness."

First, a "left-shift" has been noted, in which the left frontal activity of the brain is enhanced following MBSR training. This electrical change in brain function is thought to reflect the cultivation of an "approach state" in which people move toward, rather than away from, a challenging external situation or internal mental function such as a thought, feeling, or memory. Naturally, such an approach state can be seen as the neural basis for resilience.

Second, the degree of this left-shift is proportional to the improvement seen in immune function. The mind not only finds resilience, but the body's ability to fight infection is improved. At the University of California–Los Angeles (UCLA), David Cresswell and his colleagues have found that MBSR improves immune function even in patients with HIV. Improved immune system function may help explain the increase in healing found in the psoriasis treatment studies that incorporate mindful reflection during treatment.

Third, MBSR studies reveal that patients feel an internal sense of stability and clarity. Using a modified version of the general MBSR approach in our own pilot study at the UCLA Mindfulness Awareness Research Center, we've found that adults and adolescents with attentional problems achieved more executive function improvements (such as sustaining attention and diminishing distractibility) than are accomplished with medications for this condition. Other researchers (for example, Alan Wallace, Richie Davidson, Amishi Jha) have also found significant improvements in attentional regulation in patients who have had mindfulness meditation training; these include enhanced focus as revealed in the reduction of the "attentional blink," times when new information is not seen because of prolonged attention on the prior stimulus. Some of these studies have been done during three-month retreats whose primary focus was on isolated meditative practice rather than group discussions.

Fourth, researchers in a wide array of mental health situations have found that adding mindfulness as a fundamental part of their treatment strategies has proven to be essential in treating conditions such as obsessive-compulsive disorder, borderline personality disorder, and drug addiction; it is also helpful in the prevention of chronically relapsing depression.

Some insight into the possible core mechanisms that enable application to the treatment of a wide range of mental disorders was offered in a recent study by Norman Farb and colleagues in Toronto. After the eight-week MBSR program, subjects were able to alter their brain function in a way that confirmed they could distinguish "narrative chatter" (often called discursive thinking) from the ongoing sensory flow of here-and-now experience. This ability to develop discernment—to differentiate our unique streams of awareness—may be a crucial step in disentangling the mind from ruminative thoughts, repetitive destructive emotions, and impulsive and addictive behaviors.

Living Well with Chronic Pain

VIDYAMALA BURCH

Mindfulness can help us to see how the mind can turn the sensation of pain into a deeper and more troubling form of suffering. According to mindfulness trainer Vidyamala Burch, we can learn to work with chronic pain with precision and care, learning to neither block out nor drown in the pain.

NO ONE WANTS TO SUFFER, yet, in reality, everyone experiences some degree of pain at one time or another. The Buddha suggested that rather than being driven solely by the desire to eliminate or avoid suffering, the wise person learns to change his or her relationship with it. Of course, some pain can be eased, and it's sensible to do so—eating when you're hungry or taking a painkiller to relieve a headache, for example. But chronic, intractable pain or a terminal illness (like the existential pain that is also part of the human condition) cannot be removed easily, and the wise person knows a deeper solution is needed.

The Buddhist tradition offers practical guidance in changing your relationship with pain in the story of the two arrows. Asked to describe the difference between the response of a wise person and that of an ordinary person to pain, the Buddha used the analogy of being pierced by an arrow:

> When an ordinary person experiences a painful bodily feeling, they worry, agonize, and feel distraught. Then they feel two types of

pain—one physical and one mental. It's as if this person was pierced by an arrow and then, immediately afterward, by a second arrow, and they experience the pain of two arrows.

This image describes my own experience of pain. I have an unpleasant feeling in my body—in my case, it's back pain. This is the first arrow. But after I feel it, it seems that I'm assailed by fear, sorrow, anger, anxiety, and similar distressing emotions. This is the second arrow, and it means that on top of the physical pain, I now experience a mass of additional suffering. In fact, it frequently feels as if a whole volley of second arrows assails me! Grief and sorrow are often appropriate responses to pain, but even these healthy emotional responses become more complex and problematic if they dominate you. They become not only a response to pain, but causes of additional pain in themselves, as the Buddha explains:

> Having been touched by that painful feeling, [ordinary people] resist and resent it. They harbor aversion to it, and this underlying tendency of resistance and resentment toward that painful feeling comes to obsess the mind.

It seems the human mind has been following the same well-worn grooves for millennia. The second arrow comes because you respond by trying to push away the first arrow—the physical pain. Paradoxically, the effort of resisting pain means your energy gets tied up with it until the "underlying tendency of resistance" becomes a habit that you revert to again and again without knowing why. In my own experience, and from what I've learned from others who have attended the Breathworks course I teach, this resistance to pain is the major cause of suffering and distress. It's what causes you to be pierced by the second arrow, and the same is true of any intractable difficulty, be it physical or mental.

The Buddha goes into more detail about how this resistance makes us behave:

> Touched by that painful feeling, the ordinary person delights in compulsive distraction, often through seeking pleasure. Why is that? Because compulsive distraction is the only way they know to escape from painful feeling. This underlying tendency of craving for distraction comes to obsess the mind.

When I first heard this, I didn't agree, as my main response to pain is to push things away rather than to seek pleasure to replace it. Instead of reaching for the chocolates, I'm more likely to pick a fight. But on deeper reflection, I realized I was picking fights because, perverse though it might be, I found having an argument more enjoyable than experiencing the pain. When I revert to distraction in this way, whatever form it takes, I erect a barrier that separates me from unpleasant experience. It seems sensible at the time, but it creates more and more layers of resistance, as if I think I can escape my own shadow if I run away from myself fast enough.

If you look at your own experience, you'll probably find favorite versions of compulsive distraction that you revert to whenever you try to escape from painful feelings—obvious "pleasures" such as cigarettes, chocolate, recreational drugs, alcohol, and shopping, as well as more subtle ones like arguing or obsessively engaging in activities such as cleaning or tidying.

It's important to realize the Buddha isn't suggesting that all pleasure is bad. With mindfulness and awareness, life actually becomes lighter, freer, more fun, and much more satisfying. Indeed, mindful or aware "distraction"—consciously taking your mind off things—can sometimes be a useful strategy when living with pain. When the Buddha mentions pleasure-seeking, he means the blind and driven ways we compulsively look for distraction and thus entrench habits of unawareness and avoidance. Just as resistance quickly becomes a habit, compulsive distraction soon turns into obsession.

I have many habitual ways of distracting myself from my back pain. In addition to arguing, I find myself restlessly surfing the Internet, wandering around the house like a caged animal, making endless cups of tea, and surveying the contents of the fridge without quite knowing how I got there. All these states are accompanied by tension and strain, and it can be a tremendous effort to stop whatever I'm doing and come back to a more whole and aware sense of myself. As the Buddha explains, these compulsive habits of avoidance are stressful:

> Being overwhelmed and dominated by pain (through resistance and compulsive distraction), the ordinary person is joined with suffering and stress.

The battle with pain, which is lived out through resistance, aversion, and obsession, compounds suffering and stress. I become "joined with" my pain and my reactions to it, even fettered to it. A fetter is a chain fastened round the ankle, and when I'm compulsively reacting to my pain—through either avoidance or obsession—I really do feel as if I'm chained. Before I know it, my whole experience seems like a dense web of conflicting pulls and tendencies. To summarize:

- First comes the experience of pain, the basic unpleasant sensations. This is what the Buddha called the first arrow and what I have termed "primary suffering." Then you respond to the pain with aversion, resistance, and resentment.

- Next, you seek to escape from pain by getting caught up in compulsive distractions and avoidance strategies.

- Ironically, in your attempts to escape the pain, you become stuck in a troubled state until you're finally joined with or fettered to suffering and stress, and this dominates your life and obsesses your mind. It is what the Buddha called the second arrow and what I describe as "secondary suffering."

BLOCKING AND DROWNING

When I examine my own experience in more detail and talk to others with chronic pain, I see recurring patterns in how I live out my resistance in my day-to-day behavior. These patterns can be grouped into the two tendencies of blocking and drowning. I think you'll find your own particular recipe of avoidance strategies fits into one of these categories.

Blocking: Obvious Resistance and Avoidance

When you run away from something you don't like, you can feel restless, brittle, and driven, as if you can't stop; you get caught up in addictions as you attempt to block out the pain—alcohol, cigarettes, recreational drugs, shopping, chocolate, work, talking, sleeping, and so on. Every time the pain breaks back into your experience, you reach for more of your chosen addiction, and before you know it, you're spinning on the hamster wheel of avoidance, anxiety, and panic.

Drowning: Obsession and Feeling Overwhelmed

Alternatively, you may feel preoccupied and overwhelmed by your pain. You lose perspective and feel as if you're drowning in it, that it's the only thing in your experience. You may also feel exhausted and depressed and find it hard to function. It may not be obvious that a sense of being dominated by pain is a form of resistance to it, but as with blocking, a drowning reaction grows from an underlying desire for your experience to be different from the way it really is.

One common pattern is to run away from the pain, hectically pursuing avoidance strategies to block it out. You can keep this up for a while, but there's a cost: it's very tiring, and eventually your capacity to continue running is used up. Your defenses are breached, you feel exhausted, and the pain comes crashing back into your awareness, often with a ferocious intensity. Now you tend to swing to the other extreme and collapse, feeling overwhelmed. As the pain dominates your experience, you'll probably lose perspective and forget there's anything in life apart from pain; it can almost feel as if you have become your pain. After a time, your resources and energy recover a little, and you become more active again. For a while, you manage to feel more balanced, but before you know it, you're back into patterns of avoidance and compulsive distraction, accompanied by the familiar whirring of the hamster wheel. And so it goes on in a depressingly familiar cycle.

These tendencies express themselves differently in different people. Most of us living with chronic health problems flip-flop between blocking and drowning. You might go through a cycle with big extremes over a long period, or you may experience the two poles within shorter cycles that happen several times a day, even within moments.

THE WISE RESPONSE

According to the Buddha, there's an alternative response to painful bodily feelings, which is that of a wise person:

When a wise person experiences a painful bodily feeling, they don't worry, agonize, or feel distraught, and they feel physical pain but not mental pain. It's as if this person was pierced by an arrow, but a second arrow didn't follow this, so they only experience the pain of a single arrow.

Even a wise person, at peace with himself or herself and living in harmony with the human condition, still experiences the first arrow. Suffering is an inescapable part of experience: if it isn't outright physical pain, it might be the ache of separation from people dear to you, finding yourself in situations that are unpleasant for you, or the difficulties that come with age. A friend recently told me that when his children were babies, he felt huge love for them, but he also experienced the pain of knowing that life would throw difficulties in their way. Their newborn perfection would be knocked about, and there was nothing he could do to prevent it beyond providing care and shelter. I'm sure every parent knows this aching, painful love; there's no way to protect your children from the first arrow.

The inevitability of suffering is obvious when you think about it, but it's surprising how deeply we resist this fact. For many years, I saw my back pain as a sign of failure and tried unrealistically to find cures instead of taking responsibility for my reactions to the pain. When I saw that pain was a natural part of life, I felt relief. I realized my lack of acceptance was far more painful than the back pain itself.

The difference in a wise person's response to suffering, the Buddha says, is that he or she doesn't try to escape painful feelings by resisting them and feeling aversion or by compulsively seeking distraction:

The wise person is not joined with suffering and stress. This is the difference between the wise person and the ordinary person.

The Buddha suggests that we can move toward acceptance of primary suffering and avoid secondary suffering by being like the wise person who "discerns and understands" his or her feelings "as they are actually present." In other words, we must pay attention to our experience as it really is, without trying to block it out or feeling overwhelmed.

HOW MINDFULNESS HELPS

Cultivating this wise response may sound daunting or even unrealistic if you're living with pain. It's easy to get locked into aversion and distraction, to relate to pain as a fixed and hard "thing"—a monster lurking in the shadows that dominates your life because you fear it. That's where mindfulness comes in. The awareness you can develop through mindfulness is steady, calm, and kind, and it's subtle and precise enough for you to notice the different elements of an experience. Paying attention to a painful sensation, for example, allows you to investigate it, to explore its texture, and to see it for what it is rather than what you imagine it to be. You can make surprising discoveries, such as finding that the sensations you identify as "my pain" are continually changing; there may even be pleasant sensations or feelings alongside them. You may also notice that in addition to the painful sensations, you experience physical tension, distressing and angry thoughts about your pain, or escapist fantasies and restlessness; you may feel irritable, frustrated, or upset.

If you can catch this resistance before it overwhelms you, you have the chance to relax into a broader awareness. The key is to allow the feelings to arise and pass away, moment by moment, with an attitude of receptivity and openness. This creates an opening in the dense web of habits, a moment of choice that offers a tiny chance to make a new beginning in each moment by interrupting the usual cascade of reactions. This is the battleground of awareness, because habitual impulses can be compelling, and it takes courage to resist them, but it's also the point of freedom in which you can find a key to living with joy, confidence, and creativity.

Following a car accident, Alan had severe leg pain. When he first attended a Breathworks course, he was overwhelmed by the pain and felt it had destroyed his life. But when he investigated his pain directly, he experienced it as a wave of sensations flowing up his leg that were continually changing and not nearly as bad as he'd feared. He also noticed pleasant elements alongside the pain, such as the softness of his breath and the warmth of his hands. His face lit up as he told the class that, for the first time in years, he felt some freedom in how he related to his pain.

Breaking the Cycle

Mindfulness is also the key to breaking the cycle of blocking and drowning. It means you can catch yourself whenever you find you are tipping into either extreme and choose to behave differently. If you're blocking, you are able to soften the resistance and include the pain in your field of awareness; if you're drowning, you can broaden your perspective to encompass elements of your experience other than the pain.

I've realized that I can maintain the blocking part of the cycle for months at a time. As such, I become more and more hardened to the pain in my body and more and more brittle and driven in my interactions, as if a powerful force is pushing me to avoid relaxing. At such times, I genuinely believe my pain isn't so bad and I'm coping, even though my friends tell me I'm not very pleasant to be around! Eventually, I reach a state of exhaustion; common sense prevails, and I'm forced to rest my weary body. At this point, I sometimes experience a flare-up of pain as I feel the consequences of being harsh toward my body. It's sobering to realize that I've been bullying it through the day.

When I finally recover my energy and emerge from this state of collapse, I often experience a beautiful softness and openness, as if my perceptions have been cleansed and I can balance living a rich, full life with treating my body with care and consideration. This is the point of greatest potential and greatest danger—when I feel an urgent motivation to change, but my habits are waiting to pounce. It's the moment to be mindful! If I'm able to stay with this broad, deep, kindly, yet proactive sense of myself, I can avoid the second arrow. But if I don't take care, I quickly tip back into blocking and drowning.

As my mindfulness practice has deepened over the years, the extremes of my pain reactions have become smaller. Although I still alternate between blocking and drowning, I catch the tipping points much earlier. This is entirely because I practice mindfulness. I'm not claiming to have mastered my reactions to my chronic pain completely, but I've learned that every moment contains an opportunity for choice as long as I remain aware, notice my unhelpful habits, and stand firm against them. Gradually, I am finding that it's possible to experience a sense of creativity and freedom within the struggles of everyday life while living with pain.

Although turning your attention toward your pain may seem scary, people in our courses often say that it's a tremendous relief. For those of us with chronic conditions, changing our relationship with them is the very best medicine. Being locked in a battle with your pain is exhausting, and it reinforces the sense that something is deeply wrong in your life. Letting go of resistance and learning to stay with what's actually happening can be a homecoming for the heart. This attitude of acceptance is well expressed by the Christian serenity prayer, which echoes the lesson of the two arrows:

> Lord, give me the serenity to accept the things I cannot change [the first arrow], the courage to change the things I can [the second arrow], and the wisdom [mindfulness] to know the difference.

Sickness Is Like the Weather

TONI BERNHARD

An accomplished law professor at the University of California–Davis and mother of two grown children, Toni Bernhard was struck down with a "flu" during a cherished vacation in Paris with her husband, Tony. She never recovered from this illness and has been using mindfulness-based practices to make peace with the severe limitations of being chronically fatigued.

THE MOVIE *THE WEATHER MAN* stars Nicolas Cage playing a character named Dave Spritz, a man who is adrift in life, even though he has a steady job as the weatherman for a Chicago TV station. In reality, he's just a "weather reader," dependent on a meteorologist to tell him what to say. When the meteorologist gives him a forecast with an eighteen-degree variance, Dave complains that he needs something more concrete. The meteorologist responds, "Dave, it's random. We do our best." One day, the meteorologist preps Dave for his TV spot by saying, "We might see some snow, but it might shift south and miss us." When Dave protests that the viewers will want a more certain forecast than that, the meteorologist tells him that predicting the weather is a guess. "It's wind, man," he says. "It blows all over the place."

I found this inspiring and very useful. When life's uncertainty and unpredictability throw me for a loop, I like to say to my husband, Tony, "Here

it is again, life and the weather. Just wind, man, blowing all over the place."
I remind myself that the wind that's blowing the bitterest cold at me may be
setting the stage for something joyful to follow.

I work on treating thoughts and moods as wind, blowing into the mind
and blowing out. We can't control what thoughts arise in the mind. (Telling yourself not to think about whether you'll feel well enough to join the
family for dinner is no guarantee that it's not exactly what you *will* think
about!) And moods are as uncontrollable as thoughts. Blue moods arise
uninvited, as does fear or anxiety. By working with this wind metaphor, I
can hold painful thoughts and blue moods more lightly, knowing they'll
blow on through soon—after all, that's what they do.

One night, I felt so sick I wanted to throw out all the work I'd done on
a book I was writing. Dark thoughts. A blue mood. My eyes welled up with
tears. But instead of those tears turning into sobs, I took a deep breath and
began the weather practice, remembering that thoughts and moods blow
all over the place and that if I just waited, these particular ones would blow
on through. And they did.

When it became clear that my "Parisian flu" had settled into a chronic
illness, Tony and I began to consider if it was feasible for him to go away on
retreat for an entire month, during which he'd be out of contact with me
unless I called with an emergency. I badly wanted him to go, because I saw
it as a way I could feel like a caregiver for him. He went for the first time in
2005 and each February thereafter. The retreat became a major annual
event for him. The preparations he made ahead of time were like those
made by people who are in the path of a coming hurricane. He brought a
month's worth of supplies into the house. He filled the freezer with food
he'd cooked ahead of time. He set up people in town for me to contact if I
needed help. My promise to him was to be extra careful in everything I did
and to call him home if I needed him.

The forecast inside our house for February 2009 called for calm weather
despite my illness. But at 9 A.M., two days after Tony left, things changed in
a split second. One moment I was at the top of the two steps that lead down
to our bedroom; the next moment I was writhing in pain on the bedroom
floor, having slipped down the steps and landed on my right ankle.

When the pain began to subside, I pulled myself up on the bed and
went straight to my laptop to research the only question on my mind: Was
I going to have to go to the doctor? Medical appointments can be an ordeal

for the chronically ill—the roundtrip drive, the possibility of a long wait, the energy it takes to communicate effectively with the doctor. It's so much easier to have a caregiver along. When I go to the doctor, Tony drives me, stands in line to check in for me, and accompanies me to the examining room. I never schedule medical appointments during February.

Despite the rapidly increasing swelling and discoloration on my ankle, my Internet research convinced me that I only needed to go to the doctor if I still couldn't put weight on it in twenty-four hours. So I waited. And when I needed to go somewhere off the bed, I crawled. Our dog, Rusty, was delighted to see this. He acted like I'd finally seen the light and was joining his species. This appeared to be a cause for great celebration on his part, so my challenge became to make sure that, in his exuberance, he didn't step on my right foot.

That first day, as I lay in pain on the bed, I thought of the meteorologist's comment to Dave, the weather reader: "Dave, it's random. We do our best." Tony and I had indeed done our best to prepare for a calm February, but as we all discover again and again, anything can happen at any time. We can take precautions, but predicting the future is as futile as predicting which way the wind will blow.

The next morning, when I still couldn't put weight on my right foot, our friend Richard took me to the doctor. Diagnosis: fractured fibula. The forecast: no weight on it for several weeks; a cast so heavy that it took all my energy to move my leg; crutches and crawling to get around. I toughed it out for one more day. Even with people offering to help, the injury on top of the illness proved to be too much. One or the other I could have handled alone, but not both. I knew I needed to call Tony home when, before going to sleep for the night, it took me ten minutes to make the roundtrip to a bathroom that's only footsteps from the bed. As I lay back on the bed in exhaustion, I realized that the light over the bathroom sink was still on—a light that shines right in my eyes. I had no choice but to start the process of getting to the bathroom all over again.

So Tony came home four days into his treasured monthlong retreat and, for a month, traded his caregiver role for that of nursemaid. Life and the weather—one moment it's calm, and the next moment a nasty storm has blown in.

Weather practice is a powerful reminder of the fleeting nature of experience, how each moment arises and passes as quickly as a weather pattern.

A week after I fell, I went to see an orthopedic surgeon. My regular doctor arranged the consult in case I needed surgery to insert a plate and pins. A resident came into the examining room first. Looking at the X-rays, he said that, given the nature of the break and the damage to the ligaments, I might very well need surgery to stabilize the area. He left the room to report his findings to the orthopedic surgeon, and dark storm clouds gathered as Tony and I contemplated the effect on my illness if I had to go through surgery. We expected heavy rain to accompany the surgeon into the room. He walked in and immediately said, "Surgery? No, no, no! The area is stable. You just need to stay off the ankle as long as it hurts and get physical therapy to regain your range of motion." In a flash, the sun had burst through the clouds. Tony and I were elated.

But a half hour later, as I lay on the bed trying to nap, a cold, dense fog settled in as I thought, "What does it matter that the surgeon gave us such good news. Even when I can walk normally again, I'll still be sick and bedbound most of the day, and Tony, despite all this extra care he's giving me, still won't have my company out there in the world." In a little over an hour, I'd experienced dark storm clouds, the threat of rain, the sun bursting through instead, and now a cold, dense fog. Recognizing the fleeting nature of each moment, I was able to smile, and the final verse of the *Diamond Sutra* came to mind:

> Thus shall you think of all this fleeting world:
> A star at dawn, a bubble in a stream;
> A flash of lightning in a summer cloud,
> A flickering lamp, a phantom, and a dream.

Healing Trauma

Claude Anshin Thomas

Claude Anshin Thomas is a Vietnam combat veteran and Zen teacher who studied mindfulness and meditation with the renowned Zen teachers Thich Nhat Hanh and Bernie Glassman. Today he leads meditation retreats for combat veterans who are struggling with the aftereffects of their military service, including young men and women who have recently returned from the wars in Iraq and Afghanistan. Even in the most trying circumstances, he tells us, we can hear the bell of mindfulness.

IMAGINE FOR A MOMENT that you are standing outside in the rain. What do you typically think and feel as rain falls around you? For me, every time it rains, I walk through war.

At the age of seventeen I enlisted in the U.S. Army and volunteered for service in Vietnam. For two rainy seasons there, I experienced heavy combat. During the monsoons in Vietnam, the tremendous volume of water leaves everything wet and muddy. Now when it rains, I am still walking through fields of young men screaming and dying. I still see tree lines disintegrating from napalm. I still hear seventeen-year-old boys crying for their mothers, fathers, and girlfriends. Only after reexperiencing all of that can I come to the awareness that, right now, it's just raining.

Let's call these events "flashbacks." I can be in a grocery store, reaching up to take a can of vegetables off the shelf, when I'm suddenly overwhelmed by fear because I think the can might be booby-trapped. Rationally, I know this isn't true, but for one year—my tour of duty in Vietnam—I lived in an environment where this was a realistic fear—and to this day, I am unable to process that wartime experience.

But this is not just my story. This happens every day all over the world. Every day there are people reliving war—reliving their own experiences of violence, calamity, or trauma. Everyone has their Vietnam. Everyone has their war. I've found that mindfulness practice can help all of us to heal from these wars and transform our lives.

In Vietnam, I was a crew chief for the 116th Assault Helicopter Company. I crewed slick ships (the helicopters that carried soldiers into battle and did medical evacuations and resupplies) and gunships (helicopters that were used to provide close fire support for the soldiers on the ground). One of the many decorations I received was the Air Medal. To get this medal, you must fly twenty-five combat missions and twenty-five combat hours. By the end of my tour, I had been awarded more than twenty-five Air Medals, which amounts to somewhere in the neighborhood of 625 combat hours and combat missions. All of those combat missions killed people, but I never saw them as people.

On one occasion, the infantry unit that our company supported began to receive heavy automatic-weapons fire from a village, so they radioed us and asked for help. We flew in, opened fire, and destroyed the entire village without thought. We destroyed everything. The killing was complete madness. There was nothing there that was not the enemy. We killed everything that moved: men, women, children, water buffalo, dogs, chickens. Without any feeling, without any thought. Simply out of this madness.

We destroyed buildings, trees, wagons, baskets, everything. All that remained when we were finished were dead bodies, fire, and smoke. It was all like a dream; it didn't feel real. Yet every act that I was committing was very real. By the time I was two or three months into my tour, I had been directly responsible for the deaths of several hundred people. And today, each day, I can still see their faces.

When I got home from the war, I reported to Ireland Army Hospital at Fort Knox, Kentucky. I was there to have my shoulder repaired, because it had been seriously damaged in a helicopter accident. I spent the next nine months in the hospital and in physical therapy. When I got out of the hospital, I found myself unable to socialize or reintegrate back into my own culture. The war was ever present in my thoughts. Everything I touched reminded me of it. I was unable to sleep. When I tried to talk to people about the war, they would just say to me, "All that's over now; you should forget it. You survived. Get on with your life." But I wasn't able to do that. So I started using drugs to cover my pain and loneliness; to cover my rejection; to dull the memories; to hide from the sounds, the faces, the smells that clung to me like skunk spray.

During a medical leave from the hospital, I went back to my hometown with my upper body in a cast. While at home, I went to a football game. I was standing near one of the goals, watching the game, when someone lit a firecracker. My immediate reaction was to dive to the ground. The people standing around me all laughed. Because my body was in a cast from my waist to my neck, I struggled to get up. Finally on my feet, in panic and embarrassment, I started to run. I ran and I ran, trying to run away from my feelings, run to safety. I didn't stop running until 1983. My running took many different forms. I ran by using drugs, alcohol, cigarettes, sex; by moving from place to place. I never lived in one place for more than six months because I could not stand to have anyone get close to me, get to know me, because I thought that if anyone really knew me, they would hate me. And the message was clear; it was given to me daily: because I was a soldier from Vietnam, I was not worth anything.

There was no "after the war" for me. My life, as a survivor of Vietnam, was an ongoing war. I isolated myself more and more from other people, took more and more drugs, and lived more and more on the fringes of society. From the time I came home from Vietnam until about a month before I went into a drug and alcohol rehabilitation program in 1983, I carried a gun everywhere. I slept with one, I ate with one, I went to school with one, I had one in my car. My sense of safety was completely dependent on this gun.

One night in 1978, I found myself sitting on the steps of my house with an unloaded shotgun under my chin, pulling the trigger—click, click, click— screaming and crying because my pain was so overwhelming. All I wanted was to die; but at the same time, I didn't really want to die. I just didn't know how to live with all this pain. I kept looking outside myself for something to help me, to fix me, to make it better. But nothing was working.

When I entered a rehabilitation center for drug addiction in 1983, I was able to stop using drugs, stop drinking. Now there were fewer places to hide from the reality of Vietnam. All my feelings about the war had been tightly repressed until then, and now they were coming to the surface. I couldn't push them away any longer.

In 1990, I was living in Concord, Massachusetts, and I was in counseling with a social worker who was a wonderful, generous woman. At a certain point, she told me about a Buddhist monk who had worked with Vietnam veterans and had some success in helping them become more at peace with themselves. Six months later, someone else handed me a catalog from the Omega Institute in Rhinebeck, New York. When I opened it, I saw a photo of the Vietnamese Buddhist monk Thich Nhat Hanh (the same person my therapist had told me about) and an announcement that he was leading a meditation retreat for Vietnam veterans.

I had made the commitment to go to any length to heal, so despite intense fears and doubts, I signed up for this program. At the retreat, Thich Nhat Hanh said to us, "You veterans are the light at the tip of the candle. You burn hot and bright. You understand deeply the nature of suffering." He told us that the only way to heal, to transform suffering, is to stand face-to-face with suffering, to realize the intimate details of suffering and how our life in the present is affected by it. He encouraged us to talk about our experiences and told us that we deserved to be listened to, deserved to be understood. He said we represented a powerful force for healing in the world.

My encounter with Buddhism introduced me to conscious living, paying attention to the smallest detail of thought, feeling, and perception; the term that defines this way of living is *mindfulness.* As a way of living, mindfulness helps me to wake up to and move out of cycles of destructiveness and suffering. Living mindfully, with more awareness, is not a new approach; this teaching has existed for more than twenty-five hundred years. It is not a specifically Buddhist teaching, although it was taught explicitly by the Buddha. Mindfulness expresses the heart of all spiritual teachings, and the heart of all spiritual teachings is mindfulness.

Mindfulness is simply being completely in the present moment, here, now. It is recognizing that there is nothing else but this moment. It is so easy to get lost in the past or the future. That's what was happening to me when I was caught up in my war experiences. I was caught in memories and caught in the fear that these events would happen again. I was trapped in a state of constant replay. I couldn't live in the present moment. I didn't know how. All I could do was run from the past and hide from the future.

One of the tools that I have been given to help me to live in the present moment is breath awareness—to just breathe and be aware that I am breathing. If I am completely aware of my breath, I cannot be in any other place except in the present.

You can see and experience this for yourself. Try it right now: Sit comfortably and place your hand on your abdomen. As you breathe in, feel your abdomen rise. As you breathe out, feel your abdomen contract. In . . . out . . . Move your center of activity from your thought process to your breath. Just be present with your breath. If your mind starts to wander, allow the act of wandering to be like a soft, gentle bell ringing, inviting you back to your breath; just come back to your breath. With each conscious breath, know that you are living in the present moment, that you are developing your ability to live in mindfulness.

Mindfulness, a more profound awareness, is not something that we can direct, that we can create with our thinking self. Mindfulness is a state of existence that arises as we become more aware of our habitual impulses, our patterns of thought and behavior, and begin to stop allowing these habits to dictate how we respond to the world.

Mindfulness does not automatically make me feel less invaded by thoughts and memories, but it helps me to live in a more harmonious relationship with them. By placing my awareness on my breath, I come to see that thoughts are just thoughts, that they shift and change, coming and going like passing clouds. We can easily become so caught up in our thoughts, trapped in the illusion that they are reality. By focusing on the breath, I become the observer of my thoughts, feelings, and perceptions, neither attaching to them nor rejecting them. This is the practice of mindfulness. This is the practice that leads to liberation and peace.

There are still times when my experiences of the war are right here in the present moment. As these thoughts, feelings, and perceptions enter strongly into my consciousness, I concentrate on neither attaching to what comes up nor rejecting it. Instead, I focus on just breathing and, at the same time, on working to establish a different relationship, a more harmonious relationship with this suffering. This does not mean that these thoughts, feelings, and perceptions go away, because they do not. Healing is not the absence of suffering. What happens is that through this process of being more present to my own life, I stop attempting to reject suffering. This is healing and transformation. Mindfulness meditation practice supports me in becoming present to the reality of my life without judgment.

To live in the present moment and find peace in our lives, we need to be mindful in all that we do, in every action that we take: the way we open the door, the way we put the dish on the shelf, the way we do our work, the way we talk to another person, the way we tie our shoes, take a step, stand up, sit down, brush our teeth, drive the car. It is not always easy. We are easily distracted by our thoughts, images of the past and the future, our dreams, our hopes, our regrets. I lived for a time in Thich Nhat Hanh's Buddhist community in France called Plum Village. There, I learned the practice of using a bell to remind me to come back to my breath, a bell of mindfulness. During the abbot's talks and retreats, a bell rings from time to time. When we hear the bell, it is an invitation to come back to our breath.

The bell of mindfulness is not only a Buddhist tradition. In the Middle Ages, it was a Christian tradition: when the church bell rang, it was an invitation to stop work and reflect for a moment on the gifts one had received and on the nature of one's life.

I can get so lost in the past or the future that sometimes I carry a bell with me, and I use it many times when I am giving talks to let everyone stop and breathe and simply be in the present. But it isn't necessary to carry a literal bell. If we want to, we can find bells of mindfulness everywhere. If we listen carefully, the bell of mindfulness rings constantly around us. Perhaps church bells still ring regularly in your city. The telephone can also be a bell of mindfulness. The movement and sound of a car going down the street can be a bell of mindfulness, inviting me to return to my breathing. When the traffic light turns red, it is an invitation for me to stop the hectic rush and return to my breath. When I hear a dog barking, it is an invitation to stop and breathe. All these things can be bells of mindfulness for us. They bring us back to our breath in the present moment, which is all there is.

Mindfulness and Addiction Recovery

LAWRENCE PELTZ

A growing body of research suggests that mindfulness is effective in helping recovering drug and alcohol addicts to remain sober. Addiction psychiatrist Lawrence Peltz explains why mindfulness is such a useful skill and an important complement to conventional treatment for addiction.

JIM WORKS for the electric company and does a lot of overtime in order to support his family. He gets home late to find his wife, Karen, asleep after her day of working and caring for the kids. Jim is tired and depleted, and he wants contact with Karen but is not willing to wake her. He needs to be up again in seven or eight hours but needs some time to recover and experience some pleasure without any demands. So he turns on the TV, has a beer, eats too much, and stays up too late. Jim wakes up exhausted and repeats the process the next day and the next.

This may sound familiar. Our attempts to be successful, earn enough money, and be good partners, parents, and caregivers all take time and energy. We have homes to take care of, errands, medical appointments. All of our efforts may fulfill our role requirements, but they often neglect our well-being. Once we slow down, the body calls out to be comforted, relaxed, satiated. Like Jim, we have all used food, sex, work, exercise, or substances at some point to feel better. Is that a problem? Not necessarily.

The problem begins when we think we have found a strategy to repeatedly control or escape from difficult experiences whenever we want. We turn to alcohol and drugs because they provide a (false) source of power or protection, at least in the short term.

Addiction is a pervasive pattern of attachment to these short-term benefits. There is a saying that "if the only tool you have is a hammer, everything starts looking like a nail." At different times, Jim feels sad, anxious, resentful, or lonely when he gets home. A beer might take the edge off, so why not have two or three? He is only going to sleep. If he is feeling upbeat, what better way to sustain that feeling? Eventually, Jim looks forward to that drink as his refuge from stress and inner turmoil. This is a discovery that works for him, and he can do it on his own. It is a reward and an escape.

We can see that Jim is on a slippery slope, but he cannot. Alcohol seems to help him. Jim also has a few beers when he is around the house with the family or working in the yard. Initially, this is to deal with the little annoyances of family life; later it becomes a habit. He is now glad to come home to find his wife asleep, and in a largely imperceptible way, he begins to withdraw from her and the kids. Jim tells himself they have enough problems, so why worry them with his? There is also a guilty sense of relief in hiding his fear that he is not measuring up as a provider, husband, and father. Karen is genuinely concerned and tries to have an exchange, but Jim angrily fends her off. He is particularly irritated if she raises his drinking as an issue.

Jim can glimpse what is going on. He is sad and ashamed but often drinks to keep those feelings at bay. In fact, his capacity for dealing with his emotions and the simple stressors of life is beginning to diminish. Jim hates what he is doing to himself and his family but feels at a loss as to what to do about it. His strategy for relaxation has created a vicious cycle of stress, drinking, relief, shame, more drinking, shutting down, self-hatred, more drinking, and so on. His health, work, and relationships will all begin to deteriorate, with predictable outcomes, if he does not seek help.

It is likely that Jim will need to go into the hospital for alcohol detox or intensive outpatient treatment to prevent an alcohol-withdrawal seizure. To sustain his sobriety, it will be a good idea for him to go to Alcoholics Anonymous and to have a therapist with whom he can discuss his personal issues and concerns. He may need medicine for depression or anxiety. This course of action will give Jim a chance to recover from alcoholism, but it will not be easy. As we know, many people relapse repeatedly. Each year approximately 100,000 people die in this country of alcohol-related illnesses. Many who are involved in auto accidents, violent crime, and suicide have likely been drinking as well, but this goes unreported. Alcoholism is a disease—and a deadly one.

Mindfulness practice is a powerful accompaniment to the recovery, psychotherapy, and medicine an alcoholic or addict needs. In essence, mindfulness is the quality of awareness that sees without judgment, shining a light on each moment, just as it is. This awareness includes physical sensations, feelings, thoughts, and the continually shifting and changing nature of our experience. With practice, it is a skill that anyone can develop.

With any problem, we must see it clearly before we can solve it. Mindfulness is an investigative technique that can help illuminate a difficulty, helping us to look into it. Once there is some interest in the problem and the obstacles to recovery, a new path is created, and if that path is more interesting than escaping in the usual ways, it likely will be pursued.

Mindfulness skills help addicts to take a greater interest in their well-being than in avoiding their experience. So much of addiction is like living in a tunnel, screening out a great deal of life in the quest for relief or escape. Mindfulness gives us the capacity to open up the field of experience and to do it at our own pace. Greater vision leads to greater choice and the ability to deal with problems we previously thought were unapproachable.

Is it possible to recover from addiction, take charge of one's life, and become an adult without practicing mindfulness? Yes, it is. But a life-threatening problem in a complex life requires a number of tools, and many people have benefited from the simplicity of being aware of their breathing or their feet on the ground in the midst of a challenging moment or situation. It may be obvious that these skills are not only for addicts but for all of us. In treatment groups, it often feels like we are all growing up together, learning how to assume authority over our lives. Many people have said, "Thank God I'm an alcoholic, because otherwise I would never have discovered who I really was." For those struggling with addiction, mindfulness practice can open up new possibilities for contentment, joy, self-efficacy, growth, and compassion. Many have been encouraged just by glimpsing this potential.

I am a psychiatrist at a day-treatment program for addiction. When new patients first come in to meet me, they are understandably nervous and uncertain. They are walking into a doctor's office in an unfamiliar setting, entering a portal that may change their lives—lives that are clearly not working, but ones they have come to know.

Michael is a forty-five-year-old man who arrives with his wife, Patricia, following a medical hospitalization that included a week in the intensive care unit on a ventilator. They sit down, a strong bond apparent between them. He is a bit tense but appears to be reasonably healthy and open to being there. She is clearly concerned and loving but quite worn.

When I first meet with patients, I ask a simple question: "What's bringing you here?" When I ask Michael, he says, "Alcohol." Patricia gives the same answer. It is not an uncommon response, but in this case, I am moved to tell them that alcohol is actually not the problem, that it has never, to my knowledge, flown out of the bottle into someone's mouth. They laugh at my less-than-subtle point, and our subsequent conversation confirms that Michael is here to take responsibility for a pattern of behavior that threatens the integrity of his family. It has also threatened his life.

At one level, Michael's story is not very complicated. This is a regular guy, someone you might sit next to at the ballpark, who has been drinking since the age of fourteen. In retrospect, Michael felt he had a problem immediately but did not acknowledge this to himself until his late twenties, when he realized he could not control when he stopped drinking. He also developed peptic ulcer disease, which is exacerbated by alcohol, but this was not enough to motivate him to seek help. Prior to his recent hospitalization, he had never been admitted for alcohol detoxification. He has worked in maintenance at a local university for twenty years and has been honored for his excellent service. Patricia is unhappy with Michael's drinking, but she sees him as mostly a good provider, husband, and father, and is clear she would never leave him.

Michael grew up in a family of four kids (the youngest of three boys) and particularly loved to play football with his dad and brothers. His father, however, was a heavy drinker, prone to intermittent bouts of verbal abuse and violent outbursts. By the time Michael was twelve, the current age of his son, his father had stopped playing ball with his kids and had, to a large extent, removed himself from the emotional life of his family. This was a huge loss for Michael, a sadness that never found expression and, because his brothers just seemed to move on, a sadness he bore alone.

Roughly a year later, Michael was raped while on a camping trip with the Boy Scouts, an experience he also kept to himself. A link between this event, the loss of connection with his father, and his subsequent drinking had not occurred to him. However, in his adult life, Michael's dad had not shown up to see him receive an award at work, and he recalls drinking to manage his disappointment.

The elephant in the room is grief, and his choice is to face it in some way or to continue drinking, progressively leave his family, and die young. Patricia's dilemma is also clear: How could she leave such a decent man who has already borne so much pain? She has complained about Michael's drinking, bargained and cajoled, but has never directly told him that it is unacceptable and must change. This is because she has not allowed herself to see how it has affected her own body and well-being.

It's important to realize that alcoholics and drug addicts do not come to treatment for personal growth but out of total desperation. Michael needed to nearly die, and Patricia had to be totally exhausted and at her wit's end, before they were willing to sit down in my office. Twelve or even six months ago, looking into the problem this way was not a serious consideration. They were doing the best they could day to day with the many challenges couples face while earning a living, parenting, and enjoying some well-deserved pleasure and relaxation. For many years, it was easier to deny or rationalize problems so they could just get on with their lives.

I often tell our day-treatment patients that they are a select group. They may feel sick and that their lives are going nowhere, but at least they are stopping for a moment to admit that. There are many addicts out there whom we will never see, who will never address their stuck condition, fear, or grief. Asking for help is like getting out of bed on a cold winter morning: a part of us just does not want to do it.

As the legend goes, God parted the Red Sea after one man took the first step. The first step of Alcoholics Anonymous states, "We admitted we were powerless over our addiction, that our lives had become unmanageable." Once that step is taken, everything changes. Somehow we get out of bed, feel the cold air, walk to the bathroom, pee, splash water on our faces, stretch, drink coffee. Then we are able to move to the next activity and the next. We are almost invariably glad we got out of bed. Even if something terrible happens, from the point of view of someone who is out of bed, staying in bed to avoid life is not a viable option. However, addicts are staying in a cocoon or fantasy refuge in order to avoid that blast of cold air, too fearful to emerge.

After Michael's evaluation, we review the problems presented. His alcohol dependence is related to a genetic vulnerability that became a problem in the context of adolescent grief and trauma. He likely has a component of depression or anxiety, but he has never directly experienced either since he has self-medicated all feelings, pleasant or unpleasant, for as long as he can remember. This makes sense since he has been totally alone with a problem he has not understood and has been doing the best he could to be a decent person, albeit at major cost to his family and his own well-being.

Patricia, for her part, knows she has been "enabling" Michael to drink, though it becomes clear that, for her own reasons, she is terrified of abandoning him or of being abandoned by him. We discuss the problem of codependency as a manifestation of an alcoholic system, a relationship addiction in which the addict balances himself or herself by caring for others. Patricia also has been trying to do the right thing for Michael and her son, but she has been denying her own physical and emotional health in the process. If she does not begin to do something different fairly soon, she will likely break down, an outcome that would help no one.

Once they have some understanding of the problem, I discuss what the treatment will entail: recovery work, psychotherapy, medicine, and mindfulness practice. I ask them to try a mindfulness exercise right away, having them direct their attention to their feet on the floor, their butts in the chairs, their hands. I ask them to just notice the points of contact. Now we follow a few breaths into the belly or chest, wherever they feel them. This takes about thirty seconds. I ask them what they notice. Michael is able to see how much tension he holds in his shoulders and some anxiety in his stomach. Patricia feels "relaxed" but could also feel some fatigue around her eyes. Both are surprised. They have not been in their bodies at all, and it is a new experience. It is also, I point out, a valuable source of information they have not been accessing. For example, in the discussion of medicine, it is not clear whether Michael would benefit from medication for anxiety, reactivity, or depression. He cannot say if he has any of those symptoms, and Patricia has a bias against medication. "Well, here is the potential for actual data that could guide our decision," I explain. "A decision based not on any of our ideas about medicine or how alcoholics should be treated, but on what is actually experienced."

The couple feels relieved and encouraged. If they pursue treatment as we have outlined it, their lives will change for the better. Not much has happened, but they are able to glimpse that their chaotic, confusing, overwhelming experience can be transformed. By staying in the present moment—more in the body, less in the head—they will be better able to identify their experience and reactions and respond more effectively as partners and parents. Mindfulness practice provides us with a technology to learn from our experience, develop self-acceptance, and move forward with openness and compassion one moment at a time.

Mindfully Shy

STEVE FLOWERS

When we start to practice mindfulness, one of the first things we notice about our internal dialogue is how much judgment and criticism runs through our heads—often including strong doses of self-criticism. Becoming more aware of this self-criticizing mind can be very helpful in dealing with a range of social anxiety problems, from a case of unpleasant shyness to a full-blown disorder.

BEING THE SON of a military pilot, I was often the new kid at many different schools in different neighborhoods, states, and even countries. I never seemed to fit in. It didn't help to have a last name like Flowers and to be so fair and thin with a head of blond curls that my mother loved and therefore insisted on. It was like someone had painted a target on my back, and every new school brought another bully to tease me. "Flower girl! Weeds! Pansy!" My name seemed like a curse. One particularly mean and huge sixth-grader would regularly chase me home when I was in fifth grade. I became a fast runner and could outrun the other kids, but I could never outrun the specter of my own fearfulness or my shame for being such a coward. And the faster and farther I ran, the more my anxious identity stuck to me.

Because of my fear and shame, I became increasingly disconnected from other kids and feared their judgments as much as I feared the bullies. Avoiding the other kids made me feel safer, but I couldn't escape from the shaming words and feelings in my inner world. As a boy, I learned why people use the phrase "painfully shy." It's painful to feel anxious and unsafe in the world and to think there's something wrong with you. You don't want others to see this private pain, because then they too will think there's something wrong with you. You can end up hiding how you feel from everyone and living in a world in which no one really knows you. My family eventually moved to Japan, and I left that bully on the other side of the world, but my sense of inadequacy and social anxiety followed me everywhere. I kept these feelings of inadequacy and shame for a long time. In fact, they stayed with me into adulthood as I made avoiding other people a way of life.

If you are shy or socially anxious, you can probably relate to some of these experiences. Fearing the judgment and rejection of others, you avoid them and find yourself principally in a relationship with your own thoughts and feelings. Unfortunately, this often isn't such a great relationship. In fact, you've probably noticed that you can say critical things to yourself that you would never say to anyone else—or tolerate from anyone else for that matter. It's a predicament. You can't outrun your own thoughts and feelings, so your meanest critic can follow you anywhere and often does.

As you read this, you may recognize an important and fundamental truth: that the pain of shyness and social anxiety is not only created by these self-critical thoughts and feelings, it's exacerbated into personal suffering by our efforts to avoid or escape those thoughts and feelings.

It's only natural that you should try to use the same escape and avoidance strategy with thoughts and feelings as you've used with external threats; it's what most people do. Unfortunately, the very effort to escape thoughts, or even suppress or control them, usually intensifies them. As a result, this way of trying to deal with mental and emotional difficulties can lead to entrenched patterns that create a confusing mess and more suffering in our lives.

Suppose you don't have to try to avoid or control painful thoughts and feelings to reduce their power and influence in your life. What if there's a way to let them be and instead put your energy into what you value in life? What if you don't have to seek out personality flaws and fix them in order to have fulfilling interpersonal relationships? What if being flawed has nothing to do with deep and satisfying relationships with other people anyway? (You've got to know it doesn't, otherwise satisfying relationships would be impossible for everyone.) In fact, you have a powerful internal resource, mindfulness, that can help you find a healthier relationship with painful thoughts and feelings and help you come home to being who and where you are.

Mindfulness is the awareness that grows from being present in the unfolding moments of our lives without judging or trying to change anything we experience. It's a friendly and curious awareness that we all have, though we may not experience it very often because we are so rarely present with and accepting of things as they are. Problematic shyness and social anxiety are inherently self-critical and rejecting, whereas the nature of mindful awareness is compassionate and accepting. Learning to look at yourself with awareness rather than criticism is an enormous change that will allow you to begin to see the habits of mind and behavior that exacerbate the pain of shyness. This new awareness can loosen the grip of your old habits and reduce their power to influence you.

The principal effort of a mindfulness-based approach to working with shyness is therefore to grow in awareness and self-compassion and learn how to bring this awareness into your life whenever you can. I want to underscore an important distinction: the work isn't to get rid of shyness or change any of your thoughts and feelings; it's about cultivating compassionate awareness. Shyness can become just another facet of the many aspects of yourself. You can quit struggling with it and just let it be; instead, you attend to the facets of yourself that you would like to see grow.

Being shy doesn't mean there's something wrong with you. You can be shy and also be happy and deeply connected with other people and realize your highest values. This is because shyness itself isn't the cause of suffering; how you relate to it is. Mindfulness makes it possible to work with your relationship to your shyness to greatly reduce or eliminate the painful influence it has on your life. The mental and behavioral habits of shyness that cause suffering operate unconsciously and automatically, whereas the intentions of mindfulness are conscious and deliberate. As you make the shift from unconscious to conscious and from reacting to responding, your self-concept and habits of mind will seem less substantial and set in stone.

Any one of us can become identified with some concept of who we are and then perpetuate this self-concept with our thoughts and actions. We may identify with a profession, a family or social role, a particular personality trait like shyness, or any number of other aspects of ourselves. Once we arrive at this self-concept, we tend to remain there and believe that's who we are. We then live consistently with this identity and rarely notice anything to the contrary. For example, if you're giving a presentation, you can prove to yourself that no one likes it by focusing on the faces in the audience that are frowning instead of those that are smiling or captivated.

As long as you identify your entire self with thoughts, emotions, and behaviors related to your shyness or social anxiety, you'll remain locked into that identity. And the longer you remain there, the more you'll come to believe that it is who you are. By centering yourself in mindful awareness, you will come to see that this identity is just a collection of mental habits and therefore can be changed. By observing these mental and emotional habits and letting them be, you become more than your constructed identity; you become the awareness that is observing that constructed identity with compassion and acceptance. You are no longer centered within that identity or defined by it.

How a Mindfulness-Based Approach Works

A mindfulness-based approach to healing recognizes the power of thoughts to shape our lives in the same way as other forms of treatment, such as cognitive therapy. But mindfulness attends to thoughts with acceptance and compassion and works with them by exploring them in awareness. It isn't always necessary to try to change thoughts if you recognize that you aren't defined by them. Mindfulness is a practice of investigation that enables you to become more sensitive and attentive to thoughts and emotions from a center of awareness that is separate from them and therefore able to witness them as discrete events. Mindfulness practice enables you to separate yourself from your thoughts, and this alone is an extremely powerful skill for reducing the power and influence of difficult thoughts and emotions. As you learn to trust your compassionate observer self, you can return to it more often and more easily. In time, it will feel more like home than like a new vantage point.

The essential components of mindfulness are antithetical to the components of shyness that create suffering:

- As mindfulness is nonjudgmental, you can be accepting of yourself rather than self-critical.

- As mindfulness is a moment-to-moment, here-and-now awareness, you can actually be here rather than in some imagined future you feel anxious about.

- As mindfulness is turning toward and being with, you can stop avoiding the thoughts and feelings that scare you and stop generating the self-criticism and shame that can be fueled by avoidance.

- As mindfulness is compassionate and openhearted awareness, you can extend compassion to yourself rather than condemnation.

- As mindfulness is awakening to the fullness of being, you can stop identifying with a false and limiting sense of self.

- As mindfulness is kind and warm, you can free yourself from the prison of self-consciousness and extend the same generosity of spirit to others that you extend to yourself.

Mindfulness has no agenda. It's a way of being rather than a means to an end. Shifting into the perspective of mindful awareness, you simply are where you are, as you are. You can discover a place here, within yourself, that isn't governed by the nagging critic and the ever-striving but always insufficient performer in your head. When centered in this place of wholeness, you can make mindful choices and experience greater freedom. However, these benefits don't come overnight or all at once; they are generally discovered along the way rather than achieved at some specific point in time. It can take a long time to discover your wholeness and completeness, even though it's been your essential nature all along. Be patient. There is much to be discovered at every step along the way. In fact, the mindful path is really each moment and every step you take along the way.

A MINDFUL COMPASS

Sometimes we just show up—we find ourselves being mindful without an explicit intention to do so. It's usually surprising when this happens. We accidentally slip out of the world of our thoughts and suddenly see, hear, and discover things we didn't notice before. These experiences may not always be accessible entirely by choice, but they can be promoted by mindfulness practices. Mindfulness involves inclining ourselves or leaning into the immediacy of our moment-to-moment experience rather than into mental commentaries or interpretations about what's happening now. It requires a certain amount of faith that being fully present is beneficial and a certain amount of intention to return to the present moment when you notice you've left it. Your awareness will help you see and hear things more vividly and help you recognize how your thoughts and emotions are influencing your experience of the here and now. Consider this to be consulting your mindful compass—a compass that has always been with you, even if it has been obscured by thoughts, feelings, and avoidance behaviors.

Let's establish that there are four primary readings to take on this compass: your thoughts, emotions, sensations, and behaviors. When you consult this compass, you might simply acknowledge what you're experiencing and label it pleasant, unpleasant, or neutral. It's easy to see how this applies to thoughts, emotions, and sensations, but what about behavior? Extending compassion to yourself or others is a pleasant behavior; criticizing yourself or others is generally unpleasant. Let's also say that there's a little dial on this compass that you can use to set your primary heading. Set it to "self-compassion." This may not be the direction you've traveled in so far, but if your usual approach were working, you wouldn't be interested in mindfulness practice. Self-compassion will give you a greater ease of being in the world, particularly in the scary and often complicated world of interpersonal relationships.

Because mindfulness enables you to see where you are in any given moment, it can help you choose what direction you need to take. Learning to read and follow this simple but profoundly helpful compass will help you through problematic shyness, social anxiety, and beyond. Though the idea of attending to painful thoughts and feelings may be daunting, your journey into mindfulness will also reveal much that is right with you and the world and bring you to a place of peace, well-being, and greater lightness of spirit. Mindfulness can reveal that you are whole and complete right now, just as you are, and that you can be happy in this life, just as it is.

The Difference between Fear and Anxiety

Fear stems from an immediate threat that you experience with your senses; for example, you turn a corner and see a large, growling dog charging toward you. Anxiety, on the other hand, stems from a mental event. For example, it may come from thinking about the possibility of a large, menacing dog around the next corner. Sometimes an element of anxiety (an internal mental event) can be triggered by an external physical event through a mechanism known as *apperception*. This happens when we perceive new experiences through the lens of unremembered past experience and then react to a relatively benign physical event as though it were a threat. In our example, you may experience any dog as threatening even if you can't remember a traumatic event with a dog. Despite these distinctions, it's important to note that the body doesn't distinguish between fear and anxiety. For the person with a phobia about dogs, the body responds to the thought of a charging dog just as it would to an actual charging dog.

During an illness a few years ago, I experienced anaphylactic shock. My throat seized up so that I couldn't breathe, and my body surged with fear. Fortunately, the episode passed in less than a minute, but even once I could take a breath, my heart still pounded and my body trembled with the chemicals and hormones that flooded it to meet this life-threatening event. It took about fifteen minutes before my body began to settle down and return to its steady state.

Later that night as I was about to fall asleep, I had the thought, "What if that happens while I'm asleep? I could suffocate in my sleep!" Instantly, my body was shot through with the same intensity of alarm as when I couldn't breathe. My heart began to pound, and I felt myself begin to breathe faster and higher in my chest. As I sat up, it occurred to me that this reaction was caused, not by a real event, but by a thought about what might happen. I got up for a few minutes to reflect on what had just occurred. I realized that earlier in the day I had been too much in shock to really feel and acknowledge what had happened to me. I could have died! My heart cracked open, and I cried for the terror I had experienced.

When I lay back down, I felt much more connected to my aching heart and my very tired body. My breathing had slowed and deepened, and I felt it rising and falling from somewhere deep in my belly. I followed it into sleep. Sometimes your heart calls to you and needs you to respond to it with kindness and compassion. As you shift your attention from thoughts about the future or the past to your immediate experience of what's happening now, you may experience a great wave of sadness. However, as you find your way back into your body and back into the present moment, you'll find that the here and now provides a refuge from the perils of imagination.

The Fear Body

Complex and intricate systems in our bodies regulate our physiological state when we're afraid, and if we're often fearful and anxious, these bodily states become habituated and form what Jeffrey Brantley, MD, calls the "fear body." Neuroscientist and author Candace Pert speaks of a learned intelligence in the brain and body that runs all of our bodily systems and stimulates behavior. In her research, she's found that we become addicted to substances like marijuana and heroin because our bodies have receptor sites for these chemicals. This led to her remarkable discovery that we can also become addicted to emotional states because our bodies have receptor sites for certain chemicals (peptides) that emotions create. She calls these peptides the "molecules of emotion" and has surmised that we become habituated to emotional states like fear and anxiety; we need to act out the same thoughts and emotions again and again to give the body the peptides it has become used to.

The fear body can be activated by thoughts, perceptions, or memories. When it is, you're likely to identify with it completely and, in effect, become the habits of mind and behavior that comprise it. At these times, you will feel the compelling tug of the fight, flight, or freeze response. If you are shy, you probably know flight intimately and also have found yourself in freeze mode from time to time. The freeze reaction is an effort not to be seen, and creatures like deer and cats and shy folks do this quite often when they're afraid.

Everyone has a fear body, and when it's activated, powerful chemicals and hormones are pumped into the bloodstream. The arousal we feel helps us deal with the threat, so it's a good thing. We can run faster, hit harder, and accomplish amazing feats of strength. We see, hear, and smell better and are more alert. The heart beats faster to provide more blood to the muscles. The blood drains from the peripheral areas of the circulatory system so that if we get injured, we won't bleed as much, but our hands and feet feel cold. The blood also drains from the digestive tract to serve more vital purposes, and that may cause nausea or a woozy feeling in the belly. The breath moves high into the chest and becomes shallower and faster. As you can see, this evolutionary adaptive response also creates the sensations we experience when we become charged up with fear or anxiety.

Our bodies also have a built-in, essentially unconscious, self-calming system. It has exquisitely sensitive neural networks that immediately calm us when, say, we come upon the same coiled rope that we mistook for a snake yesterday. We don't even have to think about it; it does this automatically. This self-calming system provides what Herbert Benson, MD, called the "relaxation response." If the fear body is overstimulated and has become self-perpetuating as the body craves fear-based molecules of emotion, we can cultivate a more healthful balance by practicing mindfulness and acceptance, which promote the body's self-calming system. Our bodies can become more accustomed to calm states than alarm states with time and practice. However, these changes don't happen overnight; our bodies and minds change with the time we invest in ourselves. And even with practice, it can still take fifteen or twenty minutes for this self-calming system to bring the body back into balance.

Social anxiety is a normal emotional reaction that most people experience at least occasionally. It isn't some weird anomaly that only a few of us have been cursed with. Like any other kind of anxiety, it actually provides us with an important service; in this case, stimulating our minds and bodies to meet potential social challenges, just like fear provides an important service when we face immediate physical challenges. The fact is, if you no longer felt social anxiety, you would be just as vulnerable and at risk in this world as if you no longer felt pain or fear.

THE CAUSES DON'T MATTER

A mindfulness-based approach to shyness involves bringing an enormous amount of awareness and compassion to your direct and immediate experience of shyness or social anxiety rather than trying to investigate its sources in your personal history. Mindfulness attends to what's happening right now as opposed to trying to understand what happened back then. Mindfulness practice asks you to place your attention on the bare experience of what's happening here and now rather than examining how or why you became shy in the first place. You don't have to know the origins of your shyness to learn how to work with it differently. The things that are important for you to know will come up on their own as you do the work of opening to and being with shy thoughts and feelings. As you practice mindfulness, memories from both your recent history and your early child-hood will arise and enter your awareness. Some of these will bring impor-tant revelations; others won't. From the point of view of mindfulness, the invitation is to feel whatever memories do arise and receive and acknowl-edge whatever messages they offer you. You weren't looking for these memories, but they have come to you and will elicit feelings that are hap-pening in the present moment and may very well help you illuminate your mindful path through shyness. Meet them with compassion, and make them a conscious part of you.

What has happened to you only plays a bit part in your shyness equa-tion; what's currently happening with you plays the leading role. This shifts your focus from how you became shy to how you remain shy. This is where the rubber meets the road: What are you doing in your life right now to keep yourself stuck in the pain of shyness? This is an important consider-ation, as it casts problematic shyness as something you *do* rather than something you *are*. This means that the most troublesome components of shyness are things you can work with: thoughts, emotions, sensations, and behaviors that are impermanent, malleable, and within your personal ca-pacity to change.

The mindful path involves becoming better acquainted with anxiety and learning how to work with it more consciously. With this shift from avoidance to acceptance, anxiety becomes more peripheral and utilitarian, and less central and problematic, in your personality—a part of you, but not all of you. For example, when anxiety comes, you might learn to ac-knowledge it, label it "anxiety," investigate it for a few moments to see what it's about, then give it a lot of space and let it be as you return to the im-mediacy of whatever you were engaged in.

When you accept the reality and place of social anxiety in your life, you can start working with it in a more deliberate way. You can start pay-ing better attention to your thoughts and emotions and consider what is true and not true, known and not known. You can recognize whether what you fear is an immediate, real threat or just a catastrophic projection into the future. With this increased awareness, you'll be in a good position to learn to reset and better regulate the self-protection systems of your fear body. Through compassionate awareness and acceptance, you can take the cascade of automatic thoughts, emotions, and reactions off automatic pilot and begin accessing some of the self-calming and self-soothing resources of your mind and body.

PRACTICE

Mindful Breathing

For five or ten minutes (or longer if you like), practice mindful breathing. Use this time to just be here and now with each breath and the sensation of your breath as your belly rises and falls. You can also place your awareness on the sensation of your breath going through your nostrils. This isn't a time for reflection; instead, use the felt sense of your breath as your way to be present.

If any thoughts or emotions arise for you, turn toward them for a moment with openness and curiosity. Notice if they affect your body in any way and then redirect your attention back to your breath.

The next time you feel anxious, give mindful breathing a try. As soon as you notice feelings of anxiety, notice where your breath is. If it's high in the chest, redirect it into your belly and see if you can allow it to settle there and come and go on its own. After a few minutes, you may notice that the rhythm of your breath becomes more and more natural and easy. Stay with the physical sensations of your breath in your belly as much as possible, and return to them when your mind wanders. In a little while, check in on your mood state. You may discover, as many other people have, that feelings of anxiety begin to subside and diminish as you settle into this simple experience of being present with your breath moving in your belly.

Mindful Eating

JAN CHOZEN BAYS

Our struggles with food can cause tremendous distress and suffering. Whether we have a tendency to overeat or undereat, or we just feel conflicted about eating, the practice of mindfulness can help us to rediscover a healthy and joyful relationship with food.

MINDFUL EATING is not directed by charts, tables, pyramids, or scales. It is not dictated by an expert. It is directed by your own inner experiences moment by moment. Your experience is unique. Therefore, you are the expert. In the process of learning to eat mindfully, you replace self-criticism with self-nurturing, anxiety with curiosity, and shame with respect for your own inner wisdom.

Mindful eating is an experience that engages all parts of us—body, heart, and mind—in choosing, preparing, and eating food. It immerses us in the colors, textures, scents, tastes, and even sounds of drinking and eating. Mindfulness allows us to be curious and even playful as we investigate our responses to food and our inner cues to hunger and satisfaction.

As an example, let's take a typical experience. On the way home from work, Sally thinks with dread about the talk she needs to work on for a big conference. She has to get it done in the next few days to meet the deadline. Before starting to work on the speech, however, she decides to relax and watch a few minutes of TV when she gets home. She sits down with a bag of chips beside her chair. At first she eats only a few, but as the show gets more dramatic, she eats faster and faster. When the show ends, she looks down and realizes that she's eaten the entire bag of chips. She scolds herself for wasting time and for eating junk food. "Too much salt and fat! No dinner for you!" Engrossed in the drama on the screen, covering up her anxiety about procrastinating, she ignored what was happening in her mind, heart, mouth, and stomach. She ate unconsciously. She ate to go unconscious. She goes to bed unnourished in body or heart and with her mind still anxious about the talk.

The next time this happens, she decides to eat chips again, but this time she tries eating them mindfully. First she checks in with her mind. She finds that her mind is worried about an article she promised to write. Her mind says that she needs to get started on it tonight. She checks in with her heart and finds that she is feeling a little lonely because her husband is out of town. She checks in with her stomach and body and discovers that she is both hungry and tired. She needs some nurturing. The only one at home to do it is herself.

She decides to treat herself to a small chip party. (Mindful eating gives us permission to play with our food.) She takes twenty chips out of the bag and arranges them on a plate. She looks at their color and shape. She eats one chip, savoring its flavor. She pauses, then eats another. There is no judgment, no right or wrong. She is simply seeing the shades of tan and brown on each curved surface, tasting the tang of salt, hearing the crunch of each bite, feeling the crisp texture melt into softness. She ponders how these chips arrived on her plate, aware of the sun, the soil, the rain, the potato farmer, the workers at the chip factory, the delivery truck driver, the grocer who stocked the shelves and sold them to her.

With little pauses between each chip, it takes ten minutes for the chip party. When she finishes the chips, she checks in with her body to find out if any part of it is still hungry.

She finds that her mouth and cells are thirsty, so she gets a drink of orange juice. Her body is also saying that it needs some protein and something green, so she makes a cheese omelet and a spinach salad. After eating, she checks in again with her mind, body, and heart. The heart and body feel nourished, but the mind is still tired. She decides to go to bed and work on the talk first thing in the morning, when the mind and body will be rested. She is still feeling lonely, although less so within the awareness of all the beings whose life energy brought her the chips, eggs, cheese, and greens. She decides to call her husband to say good night. She goes to bed with body, mind, and heart at ease and sleeps soundly.

Mindful eating is a way to rediscover one of the most pleasurable things we do as human beings. It is also a path to uncovering many wonderful activities that are going on right under our noses and within our own bodies. Mindful eating has the unexpected benefit of helping us tap into the body's natural wisdom and the heart's natural capacity for openness and gratitude.

In the Zen tradition, we practice bringing skillful attention, curiosity, and inquiry to all of our activities, including the activities of tasting and eating. The Zen teachings encourage us to explore the present moment fully, asking ourselves questions like these:

Am I hungry?

Where do I feel hunger?

What do I really crave?

What am I tasting just now?

These are very simple questions, but we seldom pose them.

Mindfulness Is the Best Flavoring

As I write this, I am eating a lemon tart that a friend gave me. He knows how much I love lemon tarts, and he occasionally brings them to me from a special bakery. After writing for a few hours, I am ready to reward myself with a tart. The first bite is delicious. Creamy, sweet-sour, melting. When I take the second bite, I begin to think about what to write next. The flavor in my mouth decreases. I take another bite and get up to sharpen a pencil. As I walk, I notice that I am chewing, but there is almost no lemon flavor in this third bite. I sit down, get to work, and wait a few minutes.

Then I take a fourth bite, fully focused on the smells, tastes, and touch sensations in my mouth. Delicious again! I discover all over again (I'm a slow learner) that the only way to keep that "first bite" experience, to honor the gift my friend gave me, is to eat slowly, with long pauses between bites. If I do anything else while I'm eating, if I talk, walk, write, or even think, the flavor diminishes or disappears. The life is drained from my beautiful tart. I could be eating the cardboard box.

Here's the humorous part. I stopped tasting the lemon tart because I was thinking. What was I thinking about? Mindful eating! Discovering that, I have to grin. To be a human being is both pitiful and funny.

Why can't I think, walk, and be fully aware of the taste of the tart at the same time? I can't do all these things at once because the mind has two distinct functions: thinking and awareness. When the thinking function is turned up, the awareness function is turned down. When the thinking function is going full throttle, we can eat an entire meal, an entire cake, an entire carton of ice cream, and not taste more than a bite or two. When we don't taste what we eat, we can end up stuffed to the gills but feeling completely unsatisfied. This is because the mind and mouth weren't present, weren't tasting or enjoying, as we ate. The stomach became full, but the mind and mouth were unfulfilled and continued calling for us to eat.

If we don't feel satisfied, we'll begin to look around for something more or something different to eat. Everyone has had the experience of roaming the kitchen, opening cupboards and doors, looking vainly for something, anything, to satisfy them. The only thing that will cure this fundamental kind of hunger is to sit down and be, even for a few minutes, wholly present.

If we eat and stay connected with our own experience and with the people who grew and cooked the food, who served the food, and who eat alongside us, we will feel most satisfied, even with a meager meal. This is the gift of mindful eating: to restore our sense of satisfaction no matter what we are or are not eating.

COMMON MISPERCEPTIONS

People get confused about mindfulness. They think that if they just do one thing at a time, like eating without reading, or if they move *veeerrry* slowly and carefully, they are being mindful. We could stop reading, close the book, and then eat slowly but still not be mindful of what we are eating. It depends on what our mind is doing as we eat. Are we just eating, or are we thinking and eating? Is our mind in our mouth or somewhere else? This is a crucial difference.

As we begin to practice mindfulness, it does help a lot to slow down and do only one thing at a time. As we become more skilled in being present, we can be mindful and speedy. In fact, we discover that when we are moving quickly, we need to be much more mindful. To be mindful means to have the mind full, completely full, of what is happening *now*. When you're chopping vegetables with a large, sharp knife, the faster you slice, the more attentive you have to be if you want to keep your fingers!

It's also important to understand that mindful eating includes mindless eating. Within the wide field of mindfulness, we can become aware of the pull toward mindless eating and notice when and how we slip into it. We can also decide, according to this situation and time, how we're going to approach eating. Part of my work as a doctor involves testifying in court cases as an expert witness. Maybe I'm on the way to court and I haven't had time for lunch. I know it will be hard to stay clear on the witness stand and that court is unpredictable. I may be there for hours. I mindfully decide to undertake mindless eating and order a veggie burger from a fast-food window to eat in the car, trying to at least be mindful about not spilling the special sauce on my one good suit. Mindfulness gives us awareness of what we're doing and, often, why we're doing it.

ESTABLISHING A HEALTHIER RELATIONSHIP WITH FOOD

When our relationship with food falls out of harmony, we lose our innate enjoyment of eating. When the relationship has been disordered for many years, it is easy to forget what "normal" eating is like. (Actually it's what normal eating *was* like, because in infancy, almost everyone experienced a natural happiness with eating and an instinctive awareness of how much was satisfying.)

Here are some elements of a healthy relationship with food:

- You feel happy and fully engaged in life when you are not eating. (Food is not your only reliable source of pleasure and satisfaction.)

- If you are not feeling hungry, you don't eat.

- You stop eating when you feel full and are able to leave food on the plate.

- You have intervals of at least several hours when you are not hungry or thinking about food, punctuated by (meal)times when you do feel hungry and take enjoyment in eating.

- You enjoy eating many different kinds of foods.

- You maintain a healthy weight that is steady or fluctuates within a range of five to seven pounds. You don't need to weigh yourself more than once every few months or years.

- You don't obsess about food or count calories in order to decide if you can "afford" to eat something or not.

If few or none of the items on this list apply to you, you're not alone. Many of us have developed unhealthy habits due to a variety of influences in our lives. Fortunately, mindful eating can help restore your natural sense of balance, satisfaction, and delight with food.

PRACTICE

A Mindful Eating Meditation

Anything that we attend to carefully and patiently will open itself up to us. Once we are able to apply the power of a concentrated, focused mind, anything—potentially all things—will reveal their true hearts to us. It is that heart-to-heart connection with ourselves, with our loved ones, and with the world itself that all of us so dearly long for. All it takes is a little bit of courage and the willingness to begin the most delightful of all adventures, the journey of looking, smelling, tasting, and feeling.

In this mindful eating exercise, we will experiment with bringing our full awareness to eating a very small amount of food. It is best to have someone read this exercise aloud to you, one step at a time.

Preparation: For this exercise, you will need a single raisin. Other foods, such as a dried cranberry, a single strawberry, a cherry tomato, or an unusual type of cracker, will also work.

1. Begin by sitting quietly and assessing your baseline hunger: How hungry are you, on a scale of zero to ten? Where do you "look" in your body to decide how hungry you are?
2. Imagine that you are a scientist on a mission to explore a new planet. Your spaceship has landed and found the planet to be quite hospitable. You can breathe the air and walk around without any problem. The surface of the planet seems to be bare dirt

and rock, and no one has seen any obvious life-forms yet. The food supplies on your spaceship are running low, however, and everyone is getting hungry. You have been asked to scout out this planet to look for anything that might be edible.

As you walk around, you find a small object lying on the ground, and you pick it up. Place the raisin (or other food item) on your palm. You are going to investigate it with the only tools you have—your five senses. You have no idea what this object is. You have never seen it before.

3. **Eye hunger.** First investigate this object with your eyes. Look at its color, shape, and surface texture. What does the mind say it could be? Now rate your eye hunger for this item. On a scale of zero to ten, how much hunger do you have for this object based on what your eyes see?

4. **Nose hunger.** Now investigate it with your nose. Smell it, refresh your nose, and sniff it again. Does this change your idea of whether it might be edible? Now rate your nose hunger. On a scale of zero to ten, how much hunger do you have for this object based on what your nose smells?

5. **Mouth hunger.** Now investigate this object with your mouth. Place it in your mouth but *do not bite it.* You can roll it around and explore it with your tongue. What do you notice?

Now you can bite this mysterious object, but only once. After biting it once, roll it around again in your mouth and explore it with your tongue. What do you notice?

Now rate your mouth hunger. On a scale of zero to ten, how much hunger do you have for this object based on what your mouth tastes and feels? In other words, how much does your mouth want to experience more of it?

6. **Stomach hunger.** Now you decide to take a risk and eat this unknown object. You chew it slowly, noticing the changes within your mouth in its texture and taste. You swallow it. You notice whether there are still any bits in your mouth. What does your tongue do when you have finished eating it? How long can you detect the flavor?

Now rate stomach hunger. Is your stomach full or not, satisfied or not? On a scale of zero to ten, rate stomach hunger. In other words, how much does your stomach want more of this food?

7. **Cellular hunger.** Become aware of this food passing into your body. Absorption begins as soon as you begin chewing. Are there any sensations that tell you that this food is being absorbed? How is it being received by the cells in your body? Now rate cellular hunger. On a scale of zero to ten, how much would your cells like to have more of this food?

8. **Mind hunger.** Can you hear what your mind is saying about this food? (Hint: The mind often talks in "shoulds" or "should nots.") Now rate your mind hunger. On a scale of zero to ten, how much would your mind like you to have more of this food?

9. **Heart hunger.** Is your heart saying anything about this food? On a scale of zero to ten, how soothing or comforting is it? Would your heart like you to have more of this food?

You might like to repeat this exercise with a liquid. Pick a drink you have never had before, such as an exotic fruit juice. Take your time and assess each kind of thirst separately.

You might find this exercise difficult at first. As with all aspects of practice, the more you do it, the more your awareness opens up. If you try this exercise with many kinds of food and drink, you will gradually be able to sense and rate the different kinds of hunger more easily. As you continue to practice mindful eating, you will develop skill and confidence in a new and more balanced relationship with food. You will be able to nourish your body, heart, and mind and to regain a sense of ease and enjoyment with eating.

Caring for the Wounded Places

SAKI F. SANTORELLI

The mind in mindfulness also includes the heart, according to Saki Santorelli, executive director of the Center for Mindfulness in Medicine, Health Care, and Society. Discovering that "mind" includes our emotional body and that we can regulate it through careful attention is one of the keys to healing our inner wounded places.

IN THE INTERDEPENDENT DOMAINS of personal health and the health care professions, mindfulness—our capacity to pay attention, moment to moment, on purpose—is an immediately accessible ally. For those in pain as well as those serving to alleviate it, such careful attentiveness is one of the most vital elements of the healing process. On a daily basis, health practitioners find themselves face-to-face with the "bandaged place," the place where a wound lies behind a protective covering. This tends to arrive in the guise of another person's pain. Yet so often it seems as if all of those whom we call patients have concealed and brought with them, into our unknowing presence, an empty mirror. Then when we glimpse their torn and wounded places, we behold, quite unexpectedly, reflections of ourselves.

Likewise, when as patients we are confronted with illness, with the unexpected, and on the receiving end of powerful suggestions from health practitioners about our future, it is easy to turn away from ourselves, losing all sense of direction, no longer trusting our innate wisdom and navigational sensitivities. But if, in these moments, we learn to *stop* and be present, we have a chance to learn a lot.

In these moments, no matter what our role, so much seems to be at stake, so much of our identity ripe for loss, uncertainty, or displacement. And so we often turn quietly away. This is our common habit. It is understandable, because none of us wishes to be hurt. Yet because this tendency is so pervasive, our *intention,* our continually renewing vow to practice being present to the full range of our unfolding lives, is an enormous resource. My own experience suggests that the willingness to stop and be present leads to seeing and relating to circumstances and events with more clarity and directness. Out of this directness seems to emerge deeper understanding or insight into the life unfolding within and before us. Such insight allows us the possibility of choosing the responses most called for by the situation rather than those reactively driven by fear, habit, or long-standing training.

By virtue of being human, each one of us is on intimate terms with *not* being present. Because of this, our intimacy with this felt absence is a powerful ally. This is the terrain of mindfulness practice. Each time we awaken to no longer being present to ourselves or to another person, it *is,* paradoxically, a moment of presence. If we are willing to see the whole of our lives as practice, our awareness of the moments when we are not present, coupled with our intention to awaken, brings us into the present. Given our penchant for absence, opportunities for practicing presence are abundant.

PRACTICES

Turning to the Breath

Over the course of the week, experiment with tuning in to the swing of your breath. Notice that it is possible to make contact with this ever-present rhythm in the common events of your everyday life: taking a shower, folding the laundry, washing dishes, playing with your children, writing a report, going to the doctor or seeing patients, talking with friends and colleagues, and sitting down in front of your computer are all occasions for cultivating wakefulness. Likewise, taking out the garbage, stepping into or leaving your car, and eating lunch are all opportunities to stop, to see, to stay close to your life.

Meditation on the Awareness of Breathing

Meditation practice requires a disciplined, sustained effort. Yet at heart, mindfulness meditation is about care, about a willingness to come up close to our discomfort and pain without judgment, striving, manipulation, or pretense. This gentle, open, nonjudgmental approach is itself both relentless and merciful, asking of us more than we might ever have expected. To practice in such a way, awareness of the breath is an effective, ever-available means for cultivating presence.

Find a comfortable place to sit down. Sitting on the floor or in a straight-backed chair is fine. If you are in a chair, see whether you can ease off the back of the chair and support yourself (unless you have back trouble), sitting upright yet at ease, placing your feet firmly on the floor, allowing your knees and feet to be about hip-width apart. Find a comfortable place for your hands, resting them in your lap. Try folding them together or turning the palms up or down. If you are on the floor, placing a cushion or two under your buttocks can be helpful. This will encourage your pelvis to tilt forward and your knees to touch the floor, thereby providing a strong, stable base of support. Again, find a comfortable place for your hands.

Now you've taken your seat.

Allow yourself to simply be with the feeling of sitting upright, solid, dignified, without pretense, settling into your seat, becoming aware of the flow of your breathing, sensing the rhythm of inhalation and exhalation, the feel of the breath coming into and leaving the body. Become aware of the rise and fall of the belly or the feeling of the breath at the tip of the nostrils or the sense of the whole breath coming in and going out. Rather than thinking about the breath, allow yourself to *feel* the breath—the actual physical sensations of breathing—as the breath comes in and goes out. There's no place to get to, nothing to change. Simply be aware of the breath in the body, coming and going, in and out. Each time you notice that the mind has wandered away from the awareness of breathing, gently and firmly return to the feeling of breathing, to the tide of inhalation or exhalation.

This wandering away might happen fifty times in the next five minutes. This is normal. Still, each time you notice that the mind has wandered, gently and firmly return to the feel of the breath. No need to scold yourself, no need to hold on to whatever enters the mind. Breathing. Riding the waves of inhalation and exhalation. Just this breath . . . and this breath . . . and this breath. Simply dwelling in the flow of the breath. Coming home, returning through the awareness of the breath to your wholeness, your completeness. Right here, right now.

Try working with this practice for five to thirty minutes several times during the next week. If you'd like, try gradually increasing the length of time you devote to "formal" mindfulness practice.

Balancing the Heart-Mind

Sometimes people confuse *mind* in the word *mindfulness* as having to do with thinking about or confining attention to cognition, imagining that we are being asked to engage in some form of introspection, discursive self-analysis, or mental gymnastics. Simply put, mindfulness is bringing a fullness of attention to whatever is occurring, and attention is not the same as thinking.

The Sufi teacher Hazrat Inayat Khan said, "The mind is the surface of the heart, the heart the depth of the mind." Indeed, the language of many contemplative traditions suggests that the words for *mind* and *heart* are not different. Likewise, the artist and calligrapher Kazuaki Tanahashi describes the Japanese character for *mindfulness* as being composed of two interactive figures. One represents mind and the other, heart. Heart and mind are not imagined as separate. From this perspective, Tanahashi translates *mindfulness* as "bringing the heart-mind to this moment."

Whether giving or receiving care, maintaining this heart-mind balance is not easy. All too often we ride the extremes—either we become lost in sympathy and the suffering of another, or we find ourselves coolly observing from a distance, aloof and uninvolved. The qualities of the quiet mind are spaciousness and clarity, the source of our capacity for discerning wisdom. The open heart is tender, warm, and flowing. Together, these attributes allow us to feel deeply and to act wisely. Even when acting means doing nothing. Perhaps compassion, in the fullest sense, is the delicate balancing of a quiet mind and an open heart. There is abundant opportunity in the healing relationship for the cultivation of such a quality of presence. But what does "a quiet mind and an open heart" mean? What does this actually feel like? Even though I cannot know how this feels to you, my sense is that we have all tasted this way of being. It is elusive, yet it is not something we have to get; rather, it is something to be revealed. Something we can cultivate through paying attention. Something to be alert to, both in its presence and in its absence.

PRACTICE

Befriending Self

Mindfulness is an act of hospitality. A way of learning to treat ourselves with kindness and care that slowly begins to percolate into the deepest recesses of our being, while gradually offering us the possibility of relating to others in the same manner. Working with whatever is present is enough. There is no need to condemn ourselves for not feeling loving or kind. Rather, the process simply asks us to entertain the possibility of offering hospitality to ourselves no matter what we are feeling or thinking. This has nothing to do with denial or self-justification for unkind or undesirable actions, but it has everything to do with self-compassion when facing the rough, shadowy, difficult, or uncooked aspects of our lives.

This week try taking some time to explore the possibility of sitting with yourself as if you were your own best friend. Dwelling in the awareness of the breath, allowing thoughts and feelings to come and go, experiment with the possibility of embracing yourself as you would embrace another person who is dear to you and needs to be held. If you like, try silently repeating a phrase on your own behalf. You might offer yourself one or more of the following:

> May I be safe.
> May I be free from suffering.
> May I be peaceful.

Find the words that are right for you in this moment of your life. This may feel awkward, foreign, or lacking in authenticity. None of these feelings need be denied. Nevertheless, if this act of intrapsychic hospitality appeals to you, give yourself the room to work with this practice as a way of caring for yourself. Such a way of working with ourselves is not meant to foster egocentricity or selfishness. It is just asking us to step back into the circle of caring and include ourselves.

PART FOUR

Interpersonal Mindfulness

The Great Mirror of Relationship

DZOGCHEN PONLOP

Our relationships—with our spouse, our children, our colleagues, our friends—are one of the central ways we define who we are. Dzogchen Ponlop, one of the foremost Tibetan meditation masters, shows us how mindfulness and awareness can make our relationships into a mirror that allows us to see who we truly are. From there, we can learn to love more intimately.

OUR SO-CALLED LIFE is nothing more than experience, and experience is relationship. Put simply, we don't have independent existence. We cannot exist without depending on others. When I go to the grocery store and buy an apple, I might feel very independent. I walk in, grab an apple, pay with my own money, and go home and eat it by myself. But in fact, I can only enjoy this apple because it is connected to so many people and conditions: the store owner, the shelf stockers, the truckers, the farmers, all the way back to the seed and the earth. There's so much connection all the time.

Of all the relationships we have in this interdependent experience of ours, the most direct, most emotional, and most apt to bring great joy and suffering is a close, intimate relationship with another human being. We give it great, special prominence in our mind, but it helps to remember that it is the same as the apple. It's about interconnection, interdependence.

Relationship is a great mirror. It is the mirror in which we see ourselves, in which we discover ourselves. That mirror can be distorted. I remember the first time I saw myself in a fun house mirror: "Oh, what happened to me? I'm all stretched out." The mirror can also be very clear. We can see ourselves and what we are up to so directly. That makes relationship a beautiful experience.

When we sit by ourselves, it's easy to enjoy our mental games, fantasies, ego trips, and so forth. We can go on and on and on without any problem. But try that with your partner! Then here comes the mirror. The mirror will reflect and show you your ugly ego trips. A mirror is very neutral—it just reflects. It doesn't take any sides. It is just a mirror for both people.

In this mirror, we discover ourselves—our tendencies, our weaknesses, and our strengths. We discover our good qualities as well as our negative qualities. So this mirror becomes a very precious teacher for us, a very precious path. The mirror of relationship becomes a very precious teaching for us to discover who we really are and where we are on the path and in the world altogether.

This is a lot to take in, so our tendency is to see what we want to see in this relationship mirror. The problem with this approach in a close relationship is that two people are seeing two different things. If I want to see something and she wants to see something else, we're both seeing different things. As a result, we're being thrown off from the balance, the benefit, the preciousness of the relationship, the mirror. We would rather idealize our relationship; we would rather escape. We would rather live in the future than in this very immediate present moment. But if we can practice being in this present moment, relationship can become a path, and the mirror can be a great teacher.

In our relationship with another, we often misunderstand how we are connected. We may think we are two made into one, or we may think we are completely independent. My father taught me that a marriage or partnership, an intimate relationship with another human being, is like two rings coming together. You can illustrate it with your fingers. Make a ring with each hand, then join the rings together. There's a common space in the center. There is mutual responsibility, joy, and sharing, yet at the same time, we must understand there are also the two sides. There is not only the middle; individual space is also necessary.

If we try to overlap these two rings totally, we lose balance. There is a common bond, but there are also two individual mind streams. We must respect that and allow the other independence. The common space respects the individual space. We cannot overpower the other or make them just like us. The other has not only needs, but also individual, karmic habits that we cannot change. They need to initiate change themselves; we cannot forcibly change them. Buddhism teaches us that we cannot change someone's karma; not even Buddha can do that. He said, "I can only show you the path; to do it is totally up to you."

That's the basic principle in a relationship—we share. We share our wisdom, our knowledge; we allow ourselves to be a mirror, but it's up to the individual to make the choice. We must respect that. We must know that the other acts out of a habit pattern, just as we do. Just as we cannot be forcibly changed from the outside, so too with them.

Problems begin when we lose the balance that comes from understanding the interplay of connection and separateness. We lose the sense of mindfulness when we lose the basic balance of the selfless, egoless teaching and become selfish, egocentric, or even egomaniacal.

That's where suffering begins and joy ends, where the joy of relationship ends and the suffering of relationship begins. When a relationship is troubled, that will stimulate our path. We can't expect it to always be perfect. In the mirror of relationship, we discover all these things. We discover the real nature of relationship, and we discover how we go off balance, how we lose the egoless, selfless view, how we lose the sense of love and caring.

Practicing mindfulness and awareness can help us see in the mirror more clearly. Mindfulness can tame the mental wildness that causes us to go so off balance. Mindfulness puts that wild mind in a corral. Once the wild horse of our mind is a little settled, we can train it by tying it to the post of awareness. Then we can train the horse to do all sorts of things, including exert itself on the path of relationship and take joy and delight in loving.

The Natural Warmth of the Heart

Pema Chödrön

Our relationships with others sometimes bring us great difficulty and pain. But if we face these difficulties with mindfulness, Pema Chödrön—author of many best-selling books on fostering courage and compassion—says we have a chance to discover our natural love and warmth.

Before we can know what natural warmth really is, we often must experience loss. We go along for years moving through our days, propelled by habit, taking life pretty much for granted. Then we or someone dear to us has an accident or gets seriously ill, and it's as if blinders have been removed from our eyes. We see the meaninglessness of so much of what we do and the emptiness of so much we cling to.

When my mother died and I was asked to go through her personal belongings, this awareness hit me hard. She had kept boxes of papers and trinkets that she treasured, things that she held on to through her many moves to smaller and smaller accommodations. They had represented security and comfort for her, and she had been unable to let them go. Now they were just boxes of stuff, things that held no meaning and represented no comfort or security to anyone. For me, these were just empty objects, yet she had clung to them. Seeing this made me sad and also thoughtful. After that, I could never look at my own treasured objects in the same way. I had seen that things themselves are just what they are, neither precious nor worthless, and that all the labels, all our views and opinions about them, are arbitrary.

This was an experience of uncovering basic warmth. The loss of my mother and the pain of seeing so clearly how we impose judgments and values, prejudices, likes and dislikes, onto the world made me feel great compassion for our shared human predicament. I remember explaining to myself that the whole world consisted of people just like me who were making much ado about nothing and suffering from it tremendously.

When my second marriage fell apart, I tasted the rawness of grief, the utter groundlessness of sorrow, and all the protective shields I had always managed to keep in place fell to pieces. To my surprise, along with the pain, I also felt an uncontrived tenderness for other people. I remember the complete openness and gentleness I felt for those I met briefly in the post office or at the grocery store. I found myself approaching the people I encountered as just like me—fully alive, fully capable of meanness and kindness, of stumbling and falling down and standing up again. I'd never before experienced that much intimacy with unknown people. I could look into the eyes of store clerks and car mechanics, beggars and children, and feel our sameness. Somehow when my heart broke, the qualities of natural warmth, qualities like kindness and empathy and appreciation, just spontaneously emerged.

People say it was like that in New York City for a few weeks after September 11. When the world as they'd known it fell apart, a whole city full of people reached out to one another, took care of one another, and had no trouble looking into one another's eyes.

It is fairly common for crisis and pain to connect people with their capacity to love and care about each other. It is also common that this openness and compassion fades rather quickly and that people then become afraid and far more guarded and closed than they ever were before. The question then is not only how to uncover our fundamental tenderness and warmth, but also how to abide there with the fragile, often bittersweet vulnerability. How can we relax and open to the uncertainty of it?

The first time I met Dzigar Kongtrül, who is now my teacher, he spoke to me about the importance of pain. He had been living and teaching in North America for more than ten years and had come to realize that his students took the teachings and practices he gave them at a superficial level until they experienced pain in a way they couldn't shake. The Buddhist teachings were just a pastime, something to dabble in or use for relaxation, but when their lives fell apart, the teachings and practices became as essential as food or medicine.

The natural warmth that emerges when we experience pain includes all the heart qualities: love, compassion, gratitude, tenderness in any form. It also includes loneliness, sorrow, and the shakiness of fear. Before these vulnerable feelings harden, before the story lines kick in, these generally unwanted feelings are pregnant with kindness, with openness and caring. These feelings that we've become so accomplished at avoiding can soften us, transform us. The openheartedness of natural warmth is sometimes pleasant (as "I want, I like") and sometimes unpleasant (as "I don't want, I don't like"). The practice is to train in not automatically fleeing from uncomfortable tenderness when it arises. With time, we can embrace it just as we would the comfortable tenderness of loving-kindness and genuine appreciation.

A person does something that brings up unwanted feelings, and what happens? Do we open or close? Usually we involuntarily shut down, yet without a story line to escalate our discomfort, we still have easy access to our genuine heart. Right at this point, we can recognize that we are closing, allow a gap, and leave room for change to happen. In Jill Bolte Taylor's book *My Stroke of Insight,* she points to scientific evidence showing that the life span of any particular emotion is only one and a half minutes. After that, we have to revive the emotion and get it going again.

Our usual process is to automatically revive it by feeding it with an internal conversation about how another person is the source of our discomfort. Maybe we strike out at that person or at someone else—all because we don't want to go near the unpleasantness of what we're feeling. This is a very ancient habit. It allows our natural warmth to be so obscured that we, who have the capacity for empathy and understanding, get so clouded that we can harm each other. When we hate those who activate our fears or insecurities, those who bring up unwanted feelings, and see them as the sole cause of our discomfort, then we can dehumanize them, belittle them, and abuse them.

Understanding this, I've been highly motivated to make a practice of doing the opposite. I don't always succeed, but year by year, I become more familiar and at home with dropping the story line and trusting that I have the capacity to stay present and receptive to other beings. Suppose you and I spent the rest of our lives doing this? Suppose we spent some time every day bringing the unknown people we see into focus and actually taking an interest in them? We could look at their faces, notice their clothes, look at their hands. There are so many chances to do this, particularly if we live in a large town or a city. There are panhandlers we rush by because their predicament makes us uncomfortable; there are multitudes of people we pass on streets and sit next to on buses and in waiting rooms. The relationship becomes more intimate when someone packs up our groceries or takes our blood pressure or comes to our house to fix a leaking pipe. Then there are the people who sit next to us on airplanes. Suppose you had been on one of the planes that went down on September 11. Your fellow passengers would have been very important people in your life.

It can become a daily practice to humanize the people we pass on the street. When I do this, unknown people become very real for me. They come into focus as living beings who have joys and sorrows just like mine, as people who have parents and neighbors and friends and enemies, just as I do. I also begin to have a heightened awareness of my own fears and judgments and prejudices that pop up out of nowhere about these ordinary people whom I've never even met. I've gained insight into my sameness with all these people, as well as insight into what obscures this understanding and causes me to feel separate. By increasing our awareness of our strength as well as our confusion, this practice uncovers natural warmth and brings us closer to the world around us.

When we go in the other direction, when we remain self-absorbed, when we are unconscious about what we are feeling and blindly bite the hook, we wind up with rigid judgments and fixed opinions that are throbbing with *shenpa*, a Tibetan word usually translated as "attachment" but more generally describing the energy that hooks us into our habitual patterns. This is a setup for closing down to anyone who threatens us. To take a common example, how do you feel about people who smoke? I haven't found too many people, either smokers or nonsmokers, who are *shenpa*-free on this topic. I was once in a restaurant in Boulder, Colorado, when a woman from Europe who didn't realize you couldn't smoke indoors, lit up. The restaurant was noisy, bustling with conversation and laughter, and then she lit her cigarette. The sound of the match striking caused the whole place to stop. You could hear yourself breathe, and the righteous indignation in the room was palpable.

I don't think it would have gone over very well with the crowd if I had tried to point out that in many places in the world smoking is not viewed negatively and that their *shenpa*-filled value judgments, not this smoker, were the real cause of their discomfort.

When we see difficult circumstances as a chance to grow in bravery and wisdom, in patience and kindness, when we become more conscious of being hooked and don't escalate it, then our personal distress can connect us with the discomfort and unhappiness of others. What we usually consider a problem becomes a source of empathy. Recently a man told me that he devotes his life to trying to help sex offenders because he knows what it's like to be one of them. As a teenager, he sexually abused a little girl. Another example is a woman I met who said that as a child she hated her brother so violently that she thought of ways to kill him every day. This now allows her to work compassionately with juveniles who are in prison for murder. She can work with them as her equals because she knows what it's like to stand in their shoes.

The Buddha taught that among the most predictable human sufferings are sickness and old age. Now that I'm in my seventies, I understand this at a gut level. Recently I watched a movie about a mean-spirited, seventy-five-year-old woman whose health was failing and whose family didn't like her. The only kindness in her life came from her devoted border collie. For the first time in my life, I identified with the old lady rather than her children. This was a major shift: a whole new world of understanding, a new area of sympathy and kindness, had suddenly been revealed to me.

This can be the value of our personal suffering. We can understand firsthand that we are all in the same boat and that the only thing that makes any sense is to care for one another.

When we feel dread, when we feel discomfort of any kind, it can connect us at the heart with all the other people feeling dread and discomfort. We can pause and tune in to the dread. We can touch the bitterness of rejection and the rawness of being slighted. Whether we are at home or in a public spot or caught in a traffic jam or walking into a movie, we can stop and look at the other people there and realize that, in pain and in joy, they are just like us. Just like us, they don't want to feel physical pain or insecurity or rejection. Just like us, they want to feel respected and physically comfortable.

When you touch your sorrow or fear, your anger or jealousy, you are touching everybody's jealousy, you are knowing everybody's fear or sorrow. You wake up in the middle of the night with an anxiety attack, and when you can fully experience the taste and smell of it, you are sharing the anxiety and fear of all humanity and all animals as well. Instead of your distress becoming all about you, it can become your link with everyone all over the world who is in the same predicament. The stories are different, the causes are different, but the experience is the same. Sorrow has exactly the same taste for each of us; rage and jealousy, envy and addictive craving have exactly the same taste for each of us. And so it is with gratitude and kindness. There can be two zillion bowls of sugar, but they all have the same taste.

Whatever pleasure or discomfort, happiness or misery, you are experiencing, you can look at other people and say to yourself, *Just like me, they don't want to feel this kind of pain,* or *Just like me, they appreciate feeling this kind of contentment.*

When things fall apart and we can't get the pieces back together, when we lose something dear to us, when the whole thing is just not working and we don't know what to do, this is the time when the natural warmth of tenderness, the warmth of empathy and kindness, are just waiting to be uncovered, just waiting to be embraced. This is our chance to come out of our self-protecting bubble and realize that we are never alone. This is our chance to finally understand that wherever we go, everyone we meet is essentially just like us. Our own suffering, if we turn toward it, can open us to a loving relationship with the world.

From Me to Us

RONALD D. SIEGEL

According to psychologist Ronald Siegel, one of the benefits of mindfulness practice is that it can create positive shifts in how we see ourselves, particularly in our relationships to others. As we become more mindful, our sense of connection and empathy grows while our usual, "me-first" attitude gradually diminishes, helping us to resolve conflicts and build healthier, stronger relationships.

HAVE YOU EVER WONDERED why it can be so hard to get along with other people? Why do they insist on being so difficult? The trouble seems to stem from misunderstandings about who we are. Mindfulness practice gradually changes our self-understanding in valuable ways.

While mindfulness practices were originally refined by monks, nuns, and hermits, people are discovering that they have enormous potential for helping ordinary folks get along with each other. They do this in several ways. First, they change our view of who we think we are. Mindfulness practices help each of us feel less like a separate "me" and more like a part of the wider world. This creates a shift in emphasis from "me" to "us" that can go a long way toward reducing conflict. Second, mindfulness practices can help us appreciate how arbitrary our identity, beliefs, and values actually are. This can make us much more flexible. Third, they can help us actually *be with* others—through both their joys and their sorrows. Really listening to other people, without immediately trying to fix or otherwise change things, can do a lot to enhance mutual understanding. Finally, mindfulness practices help us recognize our feelings and choose whether or not to act on them. This helps us respond to others skillfully rather than reflexively, which is particularly useful during tense moments.

WHO AM I?

We're so accustomed to thinking about "me" that we rarely inquire deeply into who we really are. Take five minutes right now to see how central thoughts about yourself are to your stream of consciousness. Begin by following your breath, as you've done before, for a minute or two. Then begin to take note of the content of the thoughts that occur. Just watch how often thoughts of "I want," "I think," "I feel," "I hope," "I like," or "I don't like" arise. Keep making mental notes of this for another few minutes.

Most of us take our identity for granted and don't notice how it's constructed. Anthropologists point out that our sense of self is determined by the culture in which we grow up. In the West, we view individuals as separate entities more than as members of a group such as a family, a community, or the natural world. Healthy psychological maturation in the West is assumed to require that we develop a clear identity and sense of self, good boundaries, and knowledge of our personal needs. Psychologists have traditionally called this accomplishment being "well individuated."

Other cultures, including many African, Asian, and indigenous societies, construct their identities differently. Desmond Tutu, the South African spiritual leader, says that in traditional African societies identity always involves the group. If you ask someone, "How are you?" he or she will answer, "We are fine," or "We're not doing very well." It just doesn't make sense in these cultures for an individual to feel good if the rest of his or her group is suffering.

Of course, even within a society, people vary in how much they're focused on themselves versus other people. Western mental health professionals diagnose individuals as having a narcissistic personality disorder when they are so preoccupied with their rank in the group that they can't get along with others (despite being the "smart monkeys," we act a lot like other primates). These are people whose self-esteem always seems to be on the line. They worry about how they compare and how much respect others show them. Often they treat other people disrespectfully in their attempts to buttress their own self-esteem.

We all know men and women who are like this to varying degrees. We usually start to feel inadequate or competitive around them. Sometimes it's very subtle. These folks just happen to mention things that make us envious. They drop names, mention promotions, talk about their new dress or car, describe their fantastic vacation, or tell us about their child's accomplishments.

But even among healthier people, a preoccupation with building up identity and maintaining self-esteem causes repeated envy, hurt, and conflict. Mindfulness practice helps us see how our view of ourselves as fundamentally separate from one another is at the heart of the problem.

When Albert Einstein developed his theory of relativity, he did much of his work through "thought experiments." He didn't have access to modern particle accelerators and had to figure things out using his imagination. We can perform a thought experiment to see how our usual sense of self is actually based on a misunderstanding. Try answering the questions in the following practice one at a time.

PRACTICE

A Thought Experiment

Imagine you're holding an apple. You take a bite and begin to chew, but then you notice half of a worm is left in the remainder of the apple. You'll probably spit out the partially chewed fruit. At this point, is that partially chewed material "you" or "the apple"? (Choose one.)

Let's now imagine that there was no worm, you continued chewing the apple, and it's now in your stomach, mixed up with digestive juices. Of course, if you're having a bad day, the stuff in your stomach could still come back up. Is that material now "you" or "the apple"? (Again, choose one.)

Imagine next that your digestive system is working well and the apple has passed from your stomach to your intestines, where the sugars in the apple have been absorbed. The sugars travel through your bloodstream and are taken up by cells in your body. The cells use the energy in the sugars to build proteins out of amino acids and create cellular structures. Are those new cellular structures "you" or "the apple"? (Choose again.)

Finally, the fiber in the apple continues its journey through your digestive system. It enters your colon, loses its moisture, and solidifies—ready to be deposited in a familiar white porcelain receptacle. Is this material now "you" or "something else"? (Most of us don't like to identify with our feces, so we know the answer to this one.)

Do you see the challenge of this thought experiment? Where is the line of demarcation between "you" and "the apple"? There is no clear line. Rather, there is an apple/human system in which molecules of the apple are transformed into parts of a human being. We can perform the same thought experiment with everything we eat and every atom of oxygen we breathe. At this very moment, billions of oxygen atoms are changing identity from being "the air" to being "you."

Biologists have given these matters considerable thought. They conclude that our concepts of separate organisms are arbitrary. We see this clearly when looking at an ant colony. Where is the organism: is it the individual ant or the colony? The so-called individuals each have their own roles, but all are needed for the survival of the community. In many ways, the whole colony is the organism. Just as we don't consider the individual cells in our body to be separate individuals, since they all require one another for survival, we might see all the ants as interrelated parts of one colony. Unless we're subsistence farmers, we're all like the ant or body cell—totally dependent on the larger organism for survival.

WHY DON'T WE SEE IT?

Despite understanding this interdependence intellectually, we have trouble living as if it were true. When I'm late for an appointment and the man ahead of me in the convenience store is purchasing twenty-six meticulously chosen lottery numbers, I don't see him as part of "me." In fact, I don't think of us as even vaguely related. I see him as in *my* way. Why?

You probably know René Descartes's famous saying, "I think; therefore I am." There is more truth to this than we often realize. We construct our sense of separate identity largely through thoughts—thoughts of who I am and who you are. While this is, of course, necessary for everyday life (and is why all languages have words for "me" and "you"), it creates a fundamentally distorted view of the world. In fact, all of our concepts are in some ways misleading, for they draw arbitrary distinctions between things that are actually interrelated and interdependent. And as we've seen before, because thinking has been so useful for our survival, we humans think all the time.

By allowing us to gain perspective on our thoughts—to see them coming and going like clouds in the sky—mindfulness practice helps us see the arbitrary nature of the distinctions we draw. Many of the world's religious and philosophical traditions also describe this—it's our penchant for thinking in words that keeps us from seeing our connection to one another and the wider world.

Some people interpret the biblical story of Genesis this way. Adam and Eve were expelled from the Garden of Eden for eating of the Tree of Knowledge of Good and Evil. In this view, the tree represents our human proclivity for thought, for drawing distinctions between things, which is fundamental to how we accumulate knowledge and form judgments. When Adam and Eve ate the fruit, they left paradise and entered into the painful human world, becoming "aware of their nakedness." This might be seen as the onset of our thinking disease, the propensity to live in thoughts and fantasies that sets us up for so much psychological suffering.

Eastern traditions also remind us that words distort reality by creating arbitrary separations and distinctions. The central text of Taoism, the *Tao Te Ching*, begins with a line often translated as "The Way that can be described is not the absolute (true, eternal) Way." It goes on to describe how we create our understanding of reality out of opposing concepts:

> When the people of the world all know beauty as beauty,
> there arises the recognition of ugliness.
> When they all know the good as good,
> there arises the recognition of bad;
> Therefore being and nonbeing produce each other;
> difficult and easy complete each other;
> long and short contrast each other;
>   high and low distinguish each other; . . .

Therefore the wise manage affairs without interfering and teach
beyond the words.[1]

INTERBEING

Mindfulness practice can help us become wise in this way. By no longer
identifying so much with our thoughts and concepts, we're better able to
see the interrelated nature of all things—what biologists call "ecological
systems" and physicists call "fields of matter and energy." In meditation
practice, we can actually observe how our thoughts create a sense of separateness. Once we develop a bit of concentration, the whole world begins to
feel more alive, more interconnected. Plants, animals, and even other people are experienced as part of a vibrant, interactive whole. If we have a theistic perspective, mindfulness helps us connect directly with God or the
Divine. Everything becomes numinous, infused with the spirit of life. From
a scientific perspective, we feel ourselves to be part of nature—which is no
less magical.

It is said that the first teaching that the Buddha offered was a lesson on
mindfulness presented to a group of children. The Zen teacher Thich Nhat
Hanh presents this story as an eating meditation that shows how mindfulness can help us appreciate this sense of interconnectedness. Here is an
excerpt:

> You are all intelligent children and I am sure you will be able to
> understand and practice the things I will share with you. . . . When
> you children peel a tangerine, you can eat it with awareness or
> without awareness. What does it mean to eat a tangerine in awareness? When you are eating the tangerine, you are aware that you
> are eating the tangerine. You fully experience its lovely fragrance
> and sweet taste. When you peel the tangerine, you know that you
> are peeling the tangerine; when you remove a slice and put it in
> your mouth, you know that you are removing a slice and putting it
> in your mouth; when you experience the lovely fragrance and sweet
> taste of the tangerine, you are aware that you are experiencing the
> lovely fragrance and sweet taste of the tangerine. . . .
> A person who practices mindfulness can see things in the tan-

gerine that others are unable to see. An aware person can see the tangerine tree, the tangerine blossom in the spring, the sunlight and rain that nourished the tangerine. Looking deeply, one can see ten thousand things that have made the tangerine possible. Looking at a tangerine, a person who practices awareness can see all the wonders of the universe and how all things interact with one another.[2]

Thich Nhat Hanh calls the reality of the interconnected nature of all things *interbeing*. As we'll soon see, awakening to this reality can do a lot to help us get along with one another.

CONSTRUCTING AN IDENTITY AND A SELF

Developmental psychologists have long studied how we develop a sense of self and what can go wrong in the process. Mostly, we create our sense of who we are out of the responses we get from others. It's no surprise that people who are routinely ignored or criticized by their parents or peers typically develop negative self-images, while those who are loved and appreciated develop positive ones. Our history of success and failure when we tackle challenges—whether academic, artistic, athletic, or social—also shapes how we see ourselves. If I've always gotten As, never got beyond drawing stick figures, regularly dropped the basketball, but still had a lot of friends, I'd view myself as a smart, artistically challenged, uncoordinated, but likable guy. It's as though we are sponges with memories. We absorb all the feedback we receive from others and create a sense of self out of it.

To see this process in action, try the following exercise, which is designed to illuminate your particular sense of self. It works best after a period of concentration practice, so you'll want to devote twenty to thirty minutes to the whole experience.

PRACTICE

Who Am I?

Begin with ten to twenty minutes of focusing your attention on your breath, either at the tip of your nose or in your belly. Try to develop a sense of interest or curiosity in the breath. Whenever your mind wanders and you get caught in a chain of narrative thoughts, gently return your attention to the breath. Try to remain with the breath for full cycles—from the beginning of an inhalation, through the point of fullness, back down to where the lungs are relatively empty and the cycle begins again.

Once your mind is reasonably settled, begin to ask yourself, "Who am I?" Notice whatever words arise in the mind in response and then repeat the question "Who am I?" Continue this process for at least several minutes, until your mind seems to run out of answers. Jot down a few of the responses that came to mind.

At this point, try varying the question slightly and ask, "What am I?" Again, welcome whatever thoughts arise in the mind in response. Continue asking this question until the mind seems to run out of replies. Jot down a few responses.

What did you notice? People often find that the mind goes through familial roles (such as son, daughter, brother, sister, father, mother, wife, husband), social roles (friend, lover, companion), and occupational roles. Sometimes it moves on to more individual categories (man, woman) or qualities (smart, generous, anxious, funny). Sometimes images of the body come to mind. There is no right response. The idea is simply to see some of the elements you use to create this sense of self.

Careful observation reveals that the self is more of a process than a stable entity. As my friend the Buddhist scholar Andrew Olendzki points out, we don't so much *exist* as we *occur*. In each moment that we experience sense contact, perceptions, feelings, and habitual responses, our sense of self is born again. When we add words and describe ourselves in terms of our social roles, strengths, weaknesses, and preferences, we turn this fluid process into a sense of something solid and stable. This is how "selfing" occurs. The mind creates an illusion of continuity out of moment-to-moment experiences, much as a film strings together the separate frames of a motion picture to create the illusion of continuous movement. Mindfulness meditation can help us see this in action and become more relationally flexible as a result.

When we begin to see that our identity is actually a set of patterns formed by experiences over time and our sense of self is re-created in each moment, we can take ourselves more lightly. Combined with the realization of our interdependence or lack of separateness, this shift in attitude can create far more flexibility in relating to others.

NOTES

1. Sanderson Beck, *Wisdom Bible,* retrieved May 27, 2009, from *Literary Works of Sanderson Beck* at www.san.beck.org/Laotzu.html.
2. Thich Nhat Hanh, *Old Path, White Clouds: Walking in the Footsteps of the Buddha* (Berkeley, Calif.: Parallax Press, 1991), 128–29.

Are You Listening?

DAVID ROME AND HOPE MARTIN

If there's anything we need right now, it's less shouting and more listening—open, empathetic, deep listening. To really listen to others, we must first learn to listen to ourselves. David Rome and Hope Martin teach us three techniques for mindfully tuning in to our body, speech, and mind.

WITH CRIES OF "Armageddon!" and "Baby killer!" the great U.S. health care debate in 2010 reached its tortured climax. The debate was adversarial, angry, hateful, even violent—a long-running case study in dysfunctional communication. Politicians on both sides were trapped in scripts that required them to assert fixed political positions and ignore or attack what the other side was saying, rarely sharing their true thoughts and feelings. Cable television pundits leapt into the fray like gladiators, interrupting and out-shouting each other with fierce abandon.

The health care imbroglio may be an extreme example, but it reflects a larger pathology in our culture, one that is driven by combativeness on the one hand and disingenuousness on the other. If we are to survive in the twenty-first century, we must become better communicators, speaking and listening honestly and compassionately across diversity and difference.

Unsatisfying communication is rampant in our society: between spouses; between parents and children; among neighbors and coworkers; in civic and political life; and between nations, religions, and ethnicities. Can we change such deeply ingrained cultural patterns? Is it possible to bring about a shift in the modes of communication that dominate our society? Contemplative practices, with their committed cultivation of self-awareness and compassion, may offer the best hope for transforming these dysfunctional and damaging social habits.

A fruitful place to begin work on shifting our patterns of communication is with the quality of our *listening*. Just as we now understand the importance of regular exercise for good physical health, we need to exercise and strengthen our ability to listen to promote healthy relationships and communication.

Poor, underdeveloped listeners are frequently unable to separate their own needs and interests from those of others. Everything they hear comes with an automatic bias: How does this affect me? What can I say to get things to go my way? Poor listeners are more likely to interrupt; either they have already jumped to conclusions about what you are saying, or it is just of no interest to them. They attend to the surface of the words rather than listening for what is "between the lines." When they speak, they are typically in one of two modes. Either they are "downloading," regurgitating information and preformed opinions, or they are in debate mode, waiting for the first sign that you don't think like them so they can jump in to set you straight. All these behaviors were abundantly on display in the health care debate.

Good listening, by contrast, means giving open-minded, genuinely interested attention to others and allowing yourself the time and space to fully absorb what they say. It seeks not just the surface meaning but where the speaker is coming from—what purpose, interest, or need is motivating his or her speech. Good listening encourages others to feel heard and to speak more openly and honestly.

Carl Rogers, the great American psychologist, taught "active listening," a practice of repeating back or paraphrasing what you think you are hearing and gently seeking clarification when the meaning is not clear. Deep listening, as we present it in our workshops, incorporates some of the techniques of active listening, but it is more contemplative in quality.

This approach involves listening from a deep, receptive, and caring place in oneself to deeper and often subtler levels of meaning and intention in the other person. It is listening that is generous, empathic, supportive, accurate, and trusting. Trust here does not imply agreement, but the trust that whatever others say, regardless of how well or poorly it is said, comes from something true in their experience. Listening deeply is an ongoing practice of suspending self-oriented, reactive thinking and opening one's awareness to the unknown and unexpected. It calls on a special quality of attention that the poet John Keats called "negative capability." Keats defined this as "when a man is capable of being in uncertainties, mysteries, doubts without any irritable reaching after fact and reason."

Our approach focuses first and foremost on *self-awareness* as the ground for listening and communicating well with others. This may seem paradoxical—paying more attention to ourselves in order to communicate better with others—but without some clarity in our relationship to ourselves, we will have a hard time improving our relationships with others. A clouded mirror cannot reflect accurately. We cannot perceive, receive, or interact authentically with others unless our self-relationship is authentic. Likewise, until we are true friends with ourselves, it will be hard to be genuine friends with others.

Deep listening is a way of being in the world that is sensitive to all facets of our experience—external, internal, and contextual. It involves listening to parts to which we are frequently deaf, attending to subtleties of body, speech, and mind.

In order to balance and integrate body, speech, and mind, we teach three different but complementary contemplative disciplines: mindfulness-awareness meditation to clarify and deepen mental functioning; the Alexander Technique to cultivate awareness of the body and its subtle messages; and Focusing, a technique developed by psychologist and philosopher Eugene Gendlin that utilizes "felt-sensing" to explore feelings and nurture intuitive knowing.

MINDFULNESS-AWARENESS MEDITATION

In sitting meditation practice, sometimes called "peaceful abiding," we learn to settle, returning over and over again to the present moment and allowing our thoughts to come and go without acting on them. In the process, we see how our self-absorption keeps us from experiencing the world directly. Letting go of the "web of me" is the first step toward seeing and hearing others more fully.

In our workshops, we give basic instruction in sitting meditation, with particular emphasis on being bodily present. Hope draws on her many years of Alexander practice to help everyone find a sitting posture that is right for them, gently placing her hands on their shoulders, necks, and backs. "Follow my hands," she will sometimes whisper, encouraging students to let the body respond without deliberate effort by letting go of habitual patterns and freeing itself into ease and balance.

During sitting periods, we often read from meditation master Chögyam Trungpa's teachings on the four foundations of mindfulness. These teachings, with their vivid language and images, are extraordinarily evocative of what one actually experiences as one practices mindfulness-awareness:

On mindfulness of body: "The basic starting point for this is solidness, groundedness. When you sit, you actually sit. Even your floating thoughts begin to sit on their own bottoms."

On mindfulness of life: "Whenever you have a sense of the survival instinct functioning, that can be transmuted into a sense of being, a sense of having already survived."

On mindfulness of effort: "The way of coming back is through what we might call the abstract watcher. . . . The abstract watcher is just the basic sense of separateness—the plain cognition of being there before any of the rest develops."

Mindfulness-awareness practice is a way of fundamentally making friends with ourselves based on an attitude of gentle, nonreactive noticing. This attitude is the key to success, not only in sitting meditation, but equally in Alexander work and Focusing.

THE ALEXANDER TECHNIQUE

Meditation helps us to develop equanimity and not be pushed and pulled by our life circumstances. The Alexander Technique takes this attitude off the cushion and into our lives.

Living more fully in our bodies is the anchor to the present moment in all our activities. It allows us to care for and listen to ourselves even while we respond to the many demands of our lives. This is an ideal place from which to listen to others with care and attention.

Our way of perceiving and responding to our world has a physical shape and quality. Generally, that shape consists of either slumping or holding ourselves too rigidly in "good posture." Either way, we are interfering with our freedom and the life-giving movement of our experience. When we interfere with the free functioning of our systems, our sense of well-being and joy gets blocked, and our experience of the body is one of limited mobility, pain, stiffness, and tension.

We are all intrinsically upright, expansive, resilient, and open. Watch any healthy young child, and you will see this is true—children are naturally poised and balanced, they move easily, their spines are long, they move on their joints, and they embody a curiosity and interest in the world. They are alive! This is a far cry from the way most adults experience their bodies. But we were children once too, and we can move like that again.

The Alexander Technique teaches us to notice the ways we interfere with that kind of joy and freedom. Rather than doing more, we learn to let go of what we're doing that gets in our way. Because our habits are so entrenched, they are hard to discern. In fact, they feel right to us. For example, people with lower back pain have no knowledge that they lean way back while standing and moving, thus putting pressure on their lumbar vertebrae. That stance feels perfectly upright to them, and when they are guided to a more balanced upright place in an Alexander lesson, that place initially feels wrong, as if they are falling forward. They can see in the mirror that they are upright, but they don't feel that way.

By becoming intimate with our habits and, in contrast, experiencing the quality of ease and lightness the new place offers, the kinesthetic sense becomes more sensitive and reliable over time. Since kinesthesia provides us with information on our weight, position, and movement in space, it is closely tied with our perception of ourselves and our world. As it becomes more trustworthy, we develop confidence that the feedback we are receiving is sound. We are less prone to interpretation and more in tune with direct experience. This is an essential aspect of skillful listening.

A recent retreat participant described the transformative experience of the Alexander process in this way: "I connected deeply with the relationship between the holding patterns of my body and my state of mind. I was able to observe the subtleties of these holding patterns, how they interconnect throughout my whole being and how they are part of ego's mechanism to shield me from the raw, rugged, and tender aspects of my being. When you acknowledge these experiences and hold them with a sense of appreciation, they soften and allow more space, both in body and mind. The gradual unwinding of patterns of tension and constriction was palpable throughout the group as well."

FOCUSING

Focusing is a contemplative practice that draws from Western philosophy and psychology and cultivates three vital inner skills: self-knowing, caring presence, and intuitive insight. Cultivating these inner skills allows us to bring the wisdom of our whole life experience to bear on solving problems and reaching decisions.

The practice of Focusing involves noticing and welcoming *felt senses.* Felt senses are indistinct sensations that ordinarily lie below the radar of attention but can be noticed and felt if we are receptive to them. Felt senses don't have the clearly defined quality of purely physical sensations like touching a hot stove or stubbing your toe. They are initially quite vague or fuzzy. They are nonconceptual, yet they relate to parts of our lives—work, relationships, fears, creative challenges. They have a quality of "aboutness," even when we can't tell specifically what they are about.

Occasionally a felt sense shows up that can't be missed—like having a "knot" in your stomach, a "lump" in your throat, or a "broken" heart. All of these are distinctly felt in the body yet are clearly "about" events and situations in our lives. But most felt senses are so subtle that we don't notice them. They lie below the level of ordinary feelings, but they can be triggers of strong emotion. An episode of anger may be preceded by an inner tightening, a jittery sensation, a sinking feeling. If we can notice these slight inner sensations before we erupt in anger, we gain psychological space in which to choose our words and actions rather than being overtaken by them. It is the difference between reacting and responding.

Felt senses function as a kind of borderland between the unconscious and the conscious. Being with felt senses in a patient, friendly way primes the pump of intuition. Although intuition, by its nature, is spontaneous and can't be forced, if we know how to enter the borderland of the felt sense, we prepare the ground for intuition to strike. When it does, we gain unexpected insights that can manifest as fresh articulation and action.

In Focusing, we break into partnerships, with each partner taking turns Focusing and listening. The listener's job is simply to be present and, by this presence, to hold a space for the other person to explore his or her felt senses and chosen issues. It is not the listener's job to be helpful, problem solve, commiserate, or evaluate; it is simply to be mindfully present, including being mindful of his or her own felt senses as they arise. The listener also learns how to give simple verbal reflections that help the Focuser check if the words the Focuser has come up with truly and accurately represent the meaning embodied in the felt sense. When assisted in this way, most people discover that they are able to go to and stay at a deeper level in themselves than if they were ruminating alone.

The partners train in both listening to others and listening to themselves. In daily life interactions, the two sides of this equation are equally important. You want to be open and spacious to really hear others; at the same time, you are tracking your inner responses and noting when something doesn't feel right. When you can notice this before you say or do something you may later regret, it is much less likely that you will trigger a negative upsurge in the other person. And because human beings automatically alter their behavior to synchronize with the people they are interacting with, the quality of your listening supports the other person to be more present, at ease, and authentic.

The combination of these three contemplative practices can have potent effects. Practitioners of deep listening learn to contact unresolved, stuck, or wounded places in themselves and to hold them with self-empathy. As they contact how the body holds these situations and listen to the body on its terms, they find meaning and wisdom for how each situation wants to resolve itself. The willingness to touch the discomfort makes for a more resilient, more pliable human being, and as we become better able to tolerate and work with the ups and downs in our own lives, we become more skilled in keeping others company as they navigate their own calm or turbulent seas.

The practice of listening deeply cultivates self-listening as the foundation for listening and communicating well with others. Heightened awareness of the subtleties of one's own body, speech, and mind is the foundation for genuinely receptive, accurate, and compassionate listening and speaking.

If enough people in our culture can learn and practice these inner skills, a shift from highly dysfunctional to highly functional modes of communication can happen, offering hope that we can enjoy healthier, more fulfilling relationships with the people in our personal lives and all those with whom we share community, country, and planet.

Stop, Go, Wait

SUSAN CHAPMAN

Difficulty in effectively communicating our thoughts and feelings lies at the source of many of our relationship problems. Susan Chapman, a psychotherapist and longtime meditator who offers workshops on mindful communication, uses a simple system to understand when we are holding back, when we are opening, and when we need to appreciate our uncertainty and feel our way forward gently. These techniques can improve relations around the office or even save a marriage.

RECENTLY MY FRIEND NANCY, whom I haven't seen in years, sent me an e-mail with some photos attached. "You'll love these," she wrote.

When I opened the photos, I chuckled with delight and clicked back to her, "Yes, I love these pictures so much I've already written a book about them!" The photos circulating through the Internet were of a polar bear and a dog playing together. I first saw them in a *National Geographic* magazine many years ago and was captivated by the story. A dog named Churchill was tied up to a stake in the ice. His owner spotted a starving bear, just out of hibernation, through the window of his cabin. He watched in horror as the bear approached his dog. Feeling powerless to protect his pet from certain death, he grabbed his camera and snapped pictures of the scene unfolding before his eyes. But to his amazement, what he ended up witnessing was how Churchill saved his own life.

As the bear lumbered toward him, Churchill crouched down and wagged his tail. In spite of his ravenous hunger, the bear responded to the signal and switched from predator to playmate. One of the photos shows Churchill and the bear embracing in an affectionate hug as they tumble and roll around the ice. Then the huge polar bear turned and ambled away. Over the next few days, the bear returned to the site several times to play with his new friend.

The *National Geographic* photo essay came into my life at the right moment. I had been preparing to teach a series of workshops on mindful communication, where students would learn practical skills in bringing awareness, insight, compassion, and choice to their communications. In preparation, I was paying close attention to my own interactions, especially with the difficult people in my life.

FROM PREDATOR TO PLAYMATE

When I first saw the *National Geographic* photos, I was observing the defensive strategies I used with the hungry bears in my life. Would Robert, the bullying coworker coming down the hallway, turn into a teddy bear if I adjusted the signals I was sending? Not likely. But I decided to give tail-wagging a try anyway.

In some ways, Robert fit the image of a starving polar bear as he stalked the office, commanding attention and emotionally devouring the rest of us with his crude jokes and predictable opinions. Normally, when he walked into the room, I cringed and put on my mask, which only locked the two of us into another episode in our predator-prey relationship. But when it occurred to me that I could arouse a feeling of friendliness rather than cower, I felt a wave of confidence. Over the following days and weeks, I discovered that I could interrupt my defensive reactions to Robert by bringing up the mental image of Churchill and the polar bear. This interruption in my defensiveness allowed me to relax for a moment. In one such moment, I flashed back to my little brother at age four dressed up as a cowboy wearing a sheriff's badge. A wave of sisterly affection came over me, and with it, a new image of Robert. I saw him as a lonely, confused man who was always hungry because he had no idea how to nourish himself through friendship. Imagining his isolation made me feel sad. Letting my guard down even for a moment or two allowed me to notice the vulnerable messages Robert was *really* communicating behind his bravado. I still did not agree with his bullying tactics, but he became a real human being to me—wounded and frightened, just like the rest of us.

As Robert came into focus for me, positive details about him started to emerge. I appreciated the fact that he was always on time for work, even though his eyes looked tired and swollen, as if he'd been up too late the night before. I noticed that he had good taste in clothes and that his shirts were always clean and ironed. Gradually, I formed a more respectful image of Robert, and my fear of him lessened significantly. I felt my resistance to him dissolve and some compassion grow. Not only did I feel better about Robert, I felt better about myself. Over time, I noticed that Robert seemed to pause by the door of my office more often than he had before, even though he had nothing in particular to say. I had the impression that he was, without knowing why, drawn toward the small amount of warmth I was generating—like a cat to a sunny window ledge.

By merely paying attention to my interactions with Robert, I had learned two lessons. First, I realized how I distort my view of other people when I react defensively. I also saw that when I can open up and see another person in a fresh way, my own self-image transforms. On the surface, these two insights might not seem to be that big a deal. Not as exciting as a dog and a hungry bear rolling around in play. But learning how to switch out of defensiveness into a more humorous, receptive state of mind *is* a big deal; it is the key to happy, harmonious relationships and communities.

MINDFUL COMMUNICATION

Bringing awareness, or mindfulness, to the way we communicate with others has both practical and profound applications. During an important business meeting or in the middle of a painful argument with our partner, we can train ourselves to recognize when the channel of communication has shut down. We can train ourselves to remain silent instead of blurting out something we'll later regret. We can notice when we're overreacting and take a time-out. We begin practicing mindful communication by simply paying attention to how we open up when we feel emotionally safe and how we shut down when we feel afraid. Just noticing these patterns without judging them starts to cultivate mindfulness in our communications. Noticing how we open and close puts us in greater control of our conversations.

Practicing mindful communication brings us face-to-face with our anxieties about relationships. These anxieties are rooted in much deeper, core fears about ourselves, about our value as human beings. If we are willing to relate to these core fears, each of our relationships can be transformed into a path of self-discovery. Simply being mindful of our open and closed patterns of conversation will increase our awareness and insight. We begin to notice the effect our communication style has on other people. We start to see that our attitude toward a person can blind us to who he or she really is.

In my mindful communication workshops, the metaphor we use to notice whether communication is closed, open, or somewhere in between, is the changing traffic light. We imagine that when the channel of communication closes down, the light has turned red. When communication feels open again, we say the light has turned green. When communication feels in-between, or on the verge of closing down, we say the light has turned yellow. Participants learning mindful communication find that the changing traffic light imagery helps them to identify their various states of communication and to recognize the consequences of each.

The Red Light: Defensive Reactions

When I let Robert intimidate me, my red light came on. I became defensive and closed down. When we react to fear by shutting down the channel of communication, we've put up a defensive barrier that divides us from the world. In our mind, we justify our defensiveness by holding on to unexamined opinions that we are right. We tell ourselves that relationships are not that important. We undervalue other people and put our self-interest first. In short, our values shift to "me-first." Closed communication patterns are controlling and mistrustful. We see others as frozen objects that have importance only if they meet our needs.

To make matters worse, when we are closed and defensive, we feel alone and emotionally hungry. Then we look to other people to rescue us from our aloneness. We might try to manipulate and control others to get what we need. Because these strategies never truly work, we inevitably become disappointed with people. We suffer, and we cause others to suffer.

The problem with closed communication is that it increases our distress rather than protects us. Regardless of how self-assured we may feel or appear on the surface, the sense of isolation that our defensive barrier triggers is subconsciously terrifying. If we are indeed isolated individuals, how do we get our supplies? How do we ward off enemies? Suppressing these inner fears makes us even more rigid and out of touch with the flow of energy in our body, mind, and heart. We tighten our muscles and thoughts; we harden our heart.

We're all born with sensitive receptors in our body, heart, and mind that keep us tuned in to the flow of energy and life going on around us and within us. Each of us already has this natural communication system that feeds us information all the time. So when we close down and become defensive—for a few minutes, a few days, months, or even a lifetime—we're cutting ourselves off, not only from others, but also from our natural ability to communicate. Mindful communication trains us to become aware of when we've stopped using our innate communication wisdom, a state symbolized by the red light.

The Green Light: Openness

When I was able to open up and reconnect with my resources and to Robert as a potential playmate, my green light came on. Paying attention to our communication patterns helps us realize the value of openness. Generally, we experience open people as trustworthy, in touch with themselves and others. But openness also has the magic ingredient that enables us to fall in love, to feel empathy and courage. When we're open, we let go of our opinions and enter a larger mind. This larger mind is sometimes described as a fluid awareness, a state of knowing. We discover that the world around us has the same flowing quality. Being connected to this fluid awareness gives us the power to trust our instincts, like Churchill trusted his instincts to wag his tail.

When we're open, we don't regard our individual needs to be in opposition to the needs of others. We experience a "we-first" state of mind because we appreciate that our personal survival depends on the well-being of our relationships. We express this sense of connectedness to others in open communication patterns. Open communication tunes us in to whatever is going on in the present moment, whether it is comfortable or not. Openness is heartfelt, willing to share the joy and pain of others. Because we're not blocked by our own opinions, our conversations with others explore new worlds of experience. We learn, change, and expand.

The Yellow Light: In-Between

When my defensive reactions to Robert became so painful that I began to be curious about them, my yellow light came on. In practicing mindful communication, eventually we ask ourselves, *What exactly causes me to switch from open to closed and then open again?* We begin to discover the state of mind that exists in between open and closed—symbolized by the yellow light. In-between is a place we normally don't want to enter. We find ourselves there when the ground falls out from beneath our feet, when we feel surprised, embarrassed, disappointed, on the verge of shutting down. At this moment, we might feel a sudden loss of trust, an unexpected flash of self-consciousness. Learning to hold steady and be curious at this point is critical to the practice of mindful conversation; meditation master Chögyam Trungpa called this "holding your seat."

THE CRISIS OF UNCERTAINTY

"I don't understand the yellow light," said my friend Kerry's four-year-old daughter one day from the backseat of the car. "I know red means stop and green means go. But when the light is yellow, some people speed up and others slow down."

In mindful communication training, the symbolic yellow light is a reminder to slow down and take a closer look at what happens when something unexpected occurs, when we feel uncertain. What we're more accustomed to doing is to race right through a yellow in-between state and then smack right into a red closed state.

A yellow-light transition can appear anytime. It's possible to switch from a closed state into an open one via the yellow light if we're willing to enter into curiosity, or "not knowing." For instance, one day, during an argument with my husband, I stormed out the door and was halfway around the block when, out of nowhere, I asked myself, *Why am I doing this?* I didn't know the answer and despite my pain, I was curious. Suddenly, I was outside the defensive security of my red light, open to any and all possibilities.

Joining mindfulness with communication makes this kind of turning point more workable. Training our mind boosts our emotional immune system, as it were, so that we are less affected by the ups and downs in our relationships. After we've spent some time observing our patterns of opening up and closing down, we can zero in on this most important area, the stage of in-between. Mindfulness teaches us how to hold steady when we feel hurt or disappointed. It gives us the power to refrain from making matters worse during those times when negative reactions rise up because things aren't going as we planned.

The in-between state of mind is a critical time for bringing peace into our home and workplace. For instance, Jason and Debra wanted to practice mindful communication because they were stuck in negative reactions to each other. After three years of marriage, they felt constantly irritated by one another. After consulting with a meditation instructor, they were surprised by the homework assignment: perform three random acts of kindness for each other every day for the next week. There would be time later for more mindfulness methods, but Jason and Debra first needed to create an atmosphere of appreciation and gratitude in their relationship.

Small acts of kindness that are either shared or withheld when the yellow light is flashing can make or break a relationship. Once we're in the red zone, it's too late to engage in acts of kindness—we're too mistrustful. I've seen this over and over working with couples: they would reach a critical point when they could save their relationship by switching from me-first to we-first thinking. They think about their children, pets, or anything that brings a larger picture to mind. Acts of kindness at this point shift them into a temporary mood of gratitude. Feeling gratitude makes them more interested in moving forward.

The in-between state of mind is where we gain both compassion and insight. It is not only where we witness ourselves closing down, but also where we notice the miracle of opening up again. Why and how does this happen? What exactly is it that makes us stop caring about being right and begin taking an interest in another person's point of view? What causes our defensiveness to dissolve for no reason at all, the way a dream does upon awakening? Mindfulness makes us more curious about this turning point, both in our communication with others and within ourselves.

The key point in mindful communication is to create an environment of insight and compassion when fears and misperceptions arise during the yellow-light state of mind. The reaction of shutting down is triggered by mistrust. If we can hold steady and be a little more aware of our defensiveness, we can learn from all our episodes of reactivity. Defensive reactions backfire on us and make us feel like failures. Being honest and gentle with our own fears is what brings greater softness and appreciation for others. For instance, I became more sympathetic to Robert after examining my own awkward, self-defeating attempts to guard myself from imaginary threats.

The yellow light points to those miracle moments when we can open up and wag our tails to play. We break the spell of our own personal agendas and awaken to a genuine relationship. Such abrupt shifts seem to come out of nowhere in the middle of our most ego-crunching experiences, such as admitting that we've made a mistake.

The yellow light is a moment of choice. When I'm in that zone, I can hear my mind debating which direction to go: *Do I go back and apologize, or do I continue to hold a grudge?* Depending on how much mindfulness I bring, I could tip in either direction. The happiness of my marriage hangs in this balance.

When I think back to the early years and the arguments I had with my husband, I realize that the time line of our twenty-one-year marriage has been a series of turning points. At these turning points, the path of our relationship could have led toward heaven or hell. Our happiness is the result of thousands of small flashes of the yellow light, where we were able to transform disappointments and arguments into opportunities for unmasking, intimacy, and joy.

Parenting with Mindful Awareness

Myla and Jon Kabat-Zinn

If we allow it to, parenting can become a path of inner growth and discovery. The Kabat-Zinns liken parenting to an eighteen-year meditation retreat that challenges us to look deeply at both ourselves and human experience. Their mindful parenting exercises show us how to build richer and more rewarding relationships with our children.

PARENTING IS ONE OF THE MOST challenging, demanding, and stressful jobs on the planet. It is also one of the most important, for how it is done greatly influences the heart and soul and consciousness of the next generation, their experience of meaning and connection, their repertoire of life skills, and their deepest feelings about themselves and their possible place in a rapidly changing world. Yet those of us who become parents do so virtually without preparation or training; with little or no guidance or support; and in a world that values producing far more than nurturing, doing far more than being.

The best manuals on parenting can sometimes serve as useful references, giving us new ways of seeing situations and reassuring us, especially in the early years of parenting or when we are dealing with special problems, that there are various ways to handle things and we are not alone.

But what these books often do not address is the inner experience of parenting. What do we do with our own mind, for instance? How do we avoid getting swallowed up and overwhelmed by our doubts and insecurities, by the real problems we face in our lives, by the times when we feel conflict within ourselves and the times when we are in conflict with others, including our children? Nor do these books indicate how we might develop greater sensitivity and appreciation for our children's inner experience.

To parent consciously requires that we engage in an inner work on ourselves as well as in the outer work of nurturing and caring for our children. The how-to advice that we can draw upon from books to help us with the outer work has to be complemented by an inner authority that we can only cultivate within ourselves through our own experience. Such inner authority only develops when we realize that, in spite of all the things that happen to us that are outside our control, we are still, in large measure, "authoring" our own lives through our choices of response to such events and through what we initiate ourselves. In the process, we find our own ways to be in this world, drawing on what is deepest and best and most creative in us. Realizing this, we may come to see the importance for our children and for ourselves of taking responsibility for the ways in which we live our lives and for the consequences of the choices we make.

Inner authority and authenticity can be developed to an extraordinary degree if we do that inner work. Our authenticity and wisdom grow when we purposely bring awareness to our own experience as it unfolds. Over time, we can learn to see more deeply into who our children are and what they need and take the initiative in finding appropriate ways to nourish them and further their growth and development. We can also learn to interpret their many different, sometimes puzzling signals and to trust our ability to find a way to respond appropriately. Continual attention, examination, and thoughtfulness are essential even to know what we are facing as parents, much less how we might act effectively to help our children to grow in healthy ways.

Parenting is, above all, uniquely personal. Ultimately, it has to come from deep inside ourselves. Someone else's way of doing things will never do. We each have to find a way that is our own, learning from all useful sources along the way. We have to learn to trust our own instincts and to nourish and refine them.

But in parenting, even what we thought and did yesterday that "worked out well" is not necessarily going to help today. We have to stay very much in the present moment to sense what might be required. And when our own inner resources are depleted, we have to have effective and healthy ways to replenish them, to restore ourselves, without it being at the expense of our children.

Becoming a parent may happen on purpose or by accident, but however it comes about, parenting itself is a calling. It calls us to recreate our world every day, to meet it freshly in every moment. Such a calling is, in actuality, nothing less than a rigorous spiritual discipline—a quest to realize our truest, deepest nature as human beings. The very fact that we are parents continually asks us to find and express what is most nourishing, most loving, most wise and caring in ourselves, to be—as much as we can—our best selves.

As with any spiritual discipline, the call to parent mindfully is filled with enormous promise and potential. At the same time, it challenges us to do the inner work on ourselves so we can be fully adequate to the task, so we can be fully engaged in this hero's journey, this quest of a lifetime that is a human life lived.

People who choose to become parents take on this hardest of jobs for no salary, often unexpectedly, at a relatively young and inexperienced age, and often under conditions of economic strain and insecurity. Typically, the journey of parenting is embarked upon without a clear strategy or overarching view of the terrain, in much the same intuitive and optimistic way we approach many other aspects of life. We learn on the job, as we go. There is, in fact, no other way.

But to begin with, we may have no sense of how much parenting augurs a totally new set of demands and changes in our lives, requiring us to give up so much that is familiar and to take on so much that is unfamiliar. Perhaps this is just as well, since ultimately each child is unique and each situation different. We have to rely on our hearts, our deepest human instincts, and the things we carry from our own childhood, both positive and negative, to encounter the unknown territory of having and raising children.

And just as in life itself, when faced with a range of family, social, and cultural pressures to conform to frequently unstated and unconscious norms, and with all the inherent stresses of caring for children, we often find ourselves—in spite of all our best intentions and our deep love for our children—running more or less on automatic pilot. To the extent that we are chronically preoccupied and invariably pressed for time, we may be out of touch with the richness, what Thoreau called the "bloom," of the present moment. This moment may seem far too ordinary, routine, and fleeting to single out for attention. Living like this, it is easy to fall into a dreamy kind of automaticity as far as our parenting is concerned, believing that whatever we do will be okay as long as the basic love for our children and desire for their well-being is there. We can rationalize such a view by telling ourselves that children are resilient creatures and that the little things that happen to them are just that, little things that may have no effect on them at all. Children can take a lot, we tell ourselves.

But as I (Jon) am reminded time and again when people recount their stories in the Stress Reduction Clinic and in mindfulness workshops and retreats around the country, for many people, childhood was a time of either frank or subtle betrayals, of one or both parents out of control to some degree—often raining down various combinations of unpredictable terror, violence, scorn, and meanness on their children because of their own addictions, deep unhappiness, or ignorance. Sometimes, in the deepest of ironies, accompanying such terrible betrayals come protestations of parental love, making the situation even crazier and harder for the children to fathom. For others, there is the present pain of having been invisible, unknown, neglected, and unappreciated as children.

We believe that parents can best meet their needs by cultivating mindfulness, which can lead to deeper insight into and understanding of our children and ourselves. Mindfulness has the potential to penetrate past surface appearances and behaviors and allow us to see our children more clearly as they truly are, to look both inward and outward, and to act with some degree of wisdom and compassion on the basis of what we see. Parenting mindfully can be healing and transformative—for both children and parents.

From the perspective of mindfulness, parenting can be viewed as a kind of extended and, at times, arduous meditation retreat spanning a large part of our lives. And our children, from infancy to adulthood, can be seen as perpetually challenging live-in teachers, who provide us with ceaseless opportunities to do the inner work of understanding who we are and who they are, so that we can best stay in touch with what is truly important and give them what they need most in order to grow and flourish. In the process, we may find that this ongoing, moment-to-moment awareness can liberate us from some of our most confining habits of perception and relating, the straitjackets and prisons of the mind that have been passed down to us or that we have somehow constructed for ourselves. Through their very being, often without any words or discussion, our children can inspire us to do this inner work.

Being a parent is particularly intense and demanding, in part, because our children can ask things of us no one else could or would in ways that no one else could or would. They see us up close as no one else does and constantly hold mirrors up for us to look into. In doing so, they give us the chance to see ourselves in new ways over and over and to work at consciously asking what we can learn from any and every situation that comes up with them. We can then make choices out of this awareness that will nurture both our children's inner growth and our own at the same time. Our interconnectedness and our interdependence enable us to learn and grow together.

To bring mindfulness into our parenting, it is helpful to know something about what mindfulness is. Mindfulness means moment-to-moment, nonjudgmental awareness. It is cultivated by refining our capacity to pay attention, intentionally and in the present moment, and then sustaining that attention over time as best we can. In the process, we become more in touch with life as it unfolds.

Ordinarily, we live much of our lives on automatic pilot, paying attention only selectively and haphazardly, taking many important things completely for granted or not noticing them at all, and judging everything we do experience by forming rapid and often unexamined opinions based on what we like or dislike, what we want or don't want. Mindfulness brings to parenting a powerful method and framework for paying attention to whatever we are doing in each moment and seeing past the veil of our automatic thoughts and feelings to a deeper actuality.

Mindfulness is a meditative discipline, and there are many such disciplines. We might think of them all as various doors into the same room. Each doorway gives a unique and different view into the room; once inside, however, it is the same room, whichever door we came through. Meditation, whatever the method or tradition, means tapping into the order and stillness embedded in and behind all activity, however chaotic it may appear, using our faculty of attention. It is not, as is so commonly thought, an inward manipulation—like throwing a switch or merely relaxing—into some "special state" in which everything feels different or better, or in which your mind goes "blank" or you suppress your thoughts. It is a systematic and sustained observation of the whole field of our experience or of some specific element of it.

While it received its most elaborate articulation in the Buddhist tradition, mindfulness is an important part of all cultures and is truly universal, since it is simply about cultivating the capacity we all have as human beings for awareness, clarity, and compassion. There are many different ways to do this work of cultivation. There is no one right way, just as there is no one right way to parent.

Mindful parenting involves keeping in mind what is truly important as we go about the activities of daily living with our children. Much of the time, we may find we need to remind ourselves of what that is or even admit that we may have no idea at the moment, for the thread of meaning and direction in our lives is easily lost. But even in our most trying, sometimes horrible moments as parents, we can deliberately step back and begin afresh, asking ourselves as if for the first time and with fresh eyes, "What is truly important here?"

In fact, mindful parenting means seeing if we can *remember* to bring this kind of attention and openness and wisdom to all our moments with our children. It is a true practice, its own inner discipline, its own form of meditation. And it carries with it profound benefits for both children and parents to be discovered in the practice itself.

For us to learn from our children requires that we pay attention and learn to be still within ourselves. In stillness, we are better able to see past the endemic turmoil, cloudiness, and reactivity of our own minds, in which we are so frequently caught up, and so cultivate greater clarity, calmness, and insight that we can bring directly to our parenting.

Parents have their own needs and desires and lives, just as children do. Yet, too often, in both big and little ways, the needs of the parent in any given moment may be very different from those of the child. These needs, all valid and important, are simply different and are often in conflict. The clash of needs in any given moment may result in a struggle of wills over who is going to get their way, especially if we, the parents, are feeling stressed, overburdened, and exhausted.

Rather than pitting our needs against those of our children, parenting mindfully involves cultivating an awareness in such moments of how our needs are *interdependent*. Our lives are undeniably deeply connected. Our children's well-being affects ours, and ours affects theirs. If they are not doing well, we suffer, and if we are not doing well, they suffer.

This means that we have to continually work to be aware of our children's needs as well as our own, emotional as well as physical, and, depending on their ages, to work at negotiations and compromises with them and within ourselves so that everybody gets something of what they need most. Just bringing this kind of sensitivity to our parenting will enhance our sense of connectedness with our children. Our commitment to them is felt through the quality of our presence, even in difficult times. We may find that our choices in moments of conflicting and competing needs will come more often from this heartfelt connection and, as a result, will have greater kindness and wisdom.

TWELVE EXERCISES FOR MINDFUL PARENTING

1. Try to imagine the world from your child's point of view, purposefully letting go of your own. Do this every day for at least a few moments to remind yourself of who this child is and what he or she faces in the world.

2. Imagine how you appear and sound from your child's point of view, that is, what it's like having you as a parent today, in this moment. How might this modify how you carry yourself in your body and in space, how you speak, what you say? How do you want to relate to your child in *this* moment?

3. Practice seeing your children as perfect just the way they are. See if you can stay mindful of their sovereignty from moment to moment and work at accepting them as they are when it is hardest for you to do so.

4. Be mindful of your expectations for your children, and consider whether those expectations are truly in the children's best interest. Also, be aware of how you communicate those expectations and how they affect your children.

5. Practice altruism, putting the needs of your children above your own whenever possible. Then see if there isn't some common ground

where your true needs can also be met. You may be surprised at how much overlap is possible, especially if you are patient and strive for balance.

6. When you feel lost or at a loss, remember to stand still, as recommended in David Wagoner's poem: "The forest knows / Where you are. You must let it find you." Meditate on the whole by bringing your full attention to the situation—to your child, to yourself, to the family. In doing so, you may go beyond thinking, even good thinking, and perceive intuitively with the whole of your being (your feelings, intuition, body, mind, and soul) what really needs to be done. If that is not clear in any moment, maybe the best thing is not to do anything until it becomes clearer. Sometimes it is good to remain silent.

7. Try embodying silent presence. This will grow out of both formal and informal mindfulness practice over time if you attend to how you carry yourself and what you project in body, mind, and speech. Listen carefully.

8. Learn to live with tension without losing your own balance. In *Zen and the Art of Archery*, Eugen Herrigel describes how he was taught to stand at the point of highest tension effortlessly without shooting the arrow. At the right moment, the arrow mysteriously shoots itself. Do this by practicing moving into any moment, however difficult, without trying to change anything and without having to have a particular outcome occur. Simply bring your full awareness and presence to this moment. Practice seeing that whatever comes up is "workable" if you are willing to stand in this way in the present, trusting your intuition and best instincts. Your child, especially when young, needs you to be a center of balance and trustworthiness, a reliable landmark by which he or she can take a bearing within his or her own landscape. An arrow and a target need each other. Forcing doesn't help. They will find each other better through wise attention and patience.

9. Apologize to your child when you have betrayed a trust in even a little way. Apologies are healing. An apology demonstrates that you have thought about a situation and have come to see it more

clearly—or perhaps more from your child's point of view. But be mindful of being "sorry" too often. It loses its meaning if you are always saying it or make regret into a habit. Then it can become a way for you not to take responsibility for your actions. Be aware of this. Cooking in remorse is, on occasion, a good meditation. Don't shut off the stove until the meal is ready.

10. Every child is special, and every child has special needs. Each sees in an entirely unique way. Hold an image of each of your children in your heart. Drink in their being, wishing them well.

11. There are very important times when we need to practice being clear and strong and unequivocal with our children. Let this come as much as possible out of awareness and generosity and discernment rather than out of fear, self-righteousness, or the desire to control. Mindful parenting does not mean being overindulgent, neglectful, or weak; nor does it mean being rigid, domineering, and controlling.

12. The greatest gift you can give your child is your self. This means that part of your work as a parent is to keep growing in self-knowledge and awareness. We have to be grounded in the present moment to share what is deepest and best in ourselves. This is ongoing work, but it can be furthered by making a time for quiet contemplation in whatever ways feel comfortable to us. We only have right now. Let us use it to its best advantage for our children's sake and for our own.

Mindfulness for Children

SUSAN KAISER GREENLAND

A child is a natural when it comes to "beginner's mind"—the open, receptive state of being that can come from practicing mindfulness. Just like adults, though, children can easily let this mind slip away, and sometimes we adults can pressure them into losing their freewheeling, natural state. Here are a few hands-on techniques for helping children rediscover the simple peace of their minds.

AT 7 A.M. ON A COOL WINTER DAY in Los Angeles, I was in an elementary school classroom sitting on a chair designed for a seven-year-old. There was a translator on one side of me and a security guard on the other, and I was teaching a group of mostly Latina moms simple breath awareness techniques to help them feel better, both physically and mentally, in the midst of the enormous pressures they shouldered each day. These moms were single, victims of domestic violence and spousal abuse. My job was to teach them self-directed mindfulness techniques that they would in turn teach their children—if not through direct instruction, then through example, which is by far the most powerful teaching method we possess as parents.

These women did not get out of bed for this early-morning meeting because they had a passionate interest in mindfulness. Few if any of them had heard about mindfulness before reading the flyer from the shelter, and after reading about it, many did not have a favorable impression. Most were devout Catholics, and some thought mindfulness was a mystical religion. Others thought it was some New Age, California thing. They were skeptical but nonetheless got to the classroom very early in order to lie on a cold floor and give mindfulness a try, because they would do pretty much anything within their power to help their kids have a chance at a better life. At the end of the class, one after another, they spoke about what a relief it was to take the time for themselves to calm and quiet their minds and bodies.

At the time, I was a relative newcomer to teaching mindfulness to kids and families, and I would sometimes look around the room and wonder, *How can I be so certain that these simple breathing techniques, the same ones that helped me get through a particularly traumatic time in my own life, will be of help to anyone else?* It was one thing to work with privileged kids whose parents were able to provide an abundance of enrichment activities for them. After all, teaching kids mindfulness isn't going to hurt anyone, and at least it helps them see something in a new way, however briefly.

I didn't feel the same way teaching in the domestic violence center. In underserved areas, the resources of time and energy are as scarce as money, and for my own peace of mind, I had to be 100 percent certain that what I was teaching would help these families—and not just a little. It had to be such a big help that it not only justified asking these kids and moms to get out of bed early in the morning, but, more important, it justified getting their hopes up.

Almost a decade later, I've seen the benefits of mindfulness manifest in many different cultures, every age group, and across continents. I don't have those doubts anymore.

Finding What's Already There

The natural clarity of everyone's mind can be hidden by the restless mental chatter of daily experience. Imagine you're looking at the surface of a pond. When the water is still, you can see through it to the sand and stones on the bottom. But on a windy day, when there are waves and ripples on the surface of the water, you can't see what's underneath. Mental restlessness can be like wind on the surface of a pond, making ripples and waves that hide the still, clear mind below. Introspection calms the waves so that we can once again see through the still water to the bottom of the pond. The process of introspection settles restless thoughts and emotions, allowing us to discover the stillness and mental clarity that is already there. It's not easy to explain this concept to children with words alone, but you can get the point across with the aid of a bottle of water and some baking soda.

PRACTICE

Clear Mind Game

Take a clear glass bottle full of water, put it on a table, and ask your children to look through and see what's on the other side. They'll probably see you or whatever's sitting on the tabletop. Pour a cupful of baking soda into the water and shake the bottle. What does it look like now? Can they still see through to the other side? Probably not; the baking soda clouds the water and obscures their vision. Just like baking soda in water, thoughts and emotions can create havoc in our heads and cloud our otherwise clear minds. After a minute or two, take another look at the water. What happens when you leave it alone? Sure enough, the more the water rests, the more the baking soda settles, and the clearer the water becomes. Soon, all the baking soda will settle to the bottom of the bottle, and your children will be able to see through the glass again. The same holds true with our minds. The longer we rest in the steady rhythm of our breathing, the more our thoughts and emotions settle down and the clearer our minds become.

In his book *Zen Mind, Beginner's Mind,* Suzuki Roshi describes a clear mind as "beginner's mind," a mind like a child's. Beginner's mind reflects a mental state that is open and receptive, one of nonreactive, nonconceptual awareness. It's not empty, but it's a lens through which we experience life directly and clearheadedly. I explain this way of seeing and experiencing life by comparing two different perspectives on a rainbow. Someone who knows that a rainbow exists but has never seen one personally has a conceptual perspective that is quite different from that of someone who has actually seen and experienced the magic of a rainbow in the afternoon sky.

A beginner's mind is open and receptive to new ideas, not closed down by adhering rigidly to what we believe to be true. Putting preconceived concepts and ideas aside to look at something with fresh eyes is one of the most difficult qualities to cultivate in mindfulness practice, and it isn't easy to describe. But I stumbled upon a way to do so when I least expected it. Making breakfast one morning when my kids were younger, I opened up a cylindrical box of Quaker Oats cereal and was taken by surprise. Instead of finding oatmeal, I found a treasure trove of brightly colored and shiny glass jewels that my daughter had hidden away. Somehow her Quaker Oats treasure chest had made its way back into the kitchen cupboard. When I saw what was inside, my expectations were jettisoned, and I experienced a moment of nonconceptual knowing—a flash of awareness—in that shattering of the bustle of my morning routine. "Aha," I said to myself. This is a way to begin a discussion with kids about beginner's mind. So I put the oatmeal box in my backpack and headed out to teach. Since then I've used a Quaker Oats box many, many times as a visual aid in a mindfulness game I call What's Inside the Box.

PRACTICE

What's Inside the Box

Place a box of Quaker Oats or other cereal in the middle of a circle of children, or on a table with your own children, and ask them to guess what, besides cereal, could possibly be inside the box. I've heard guesses that ranged from oatmeal to lizards. After everyone has had a turn guessing, ask the kids questions about what it feels like not to know what's in the box. Do they want to know? Have there been times in their lives when something was going on and they didn't know what it was? What was that like? How does it feel to be really curious and eager to discover?

Sit with the kids and pay attention to what it feels like not to know something. Ask them how their bodies feel when they don't know what is going to happen next. Is it comfortable? Is it uncomfortable? Does anyone feel excited? Ask them if it feels like they have butterflies in their stomachs. See if you and the kids can feel the energy and thrill of not-knowing fill the room. If you can, just sit there and breathe, taking it all in.

Beginner's mind is the most natural thing in the world, but many of us have had it conditioned out of us long before adulthood. It is a child's default mind-set, but sometimes we inadvertently condition it out of them too. When working with kids, teenagers especially, I'm reminded of a refrain from the song "Anyone Can Whistle" by Stephen Sondheim: "What's hard is simple. What's natural comes hard." Even with the best intentions, we don't always make life simple for kids.

Many of the children I teach are extremely accomplished. They get good grades, make the varsity team, solo at the concert, perform amazing feats of community service, score well on their standardized tests; you name it, they nail it. Worldly success comes relatively easily to these kids. No wonder. Many of them have watched their moms and dads model achievement since they were little. Here's the good news: by modeling hard work, we've helped make difficult things, like working hard, come naturally to our kids. The flip side is that in doing so, we sometimes make natural things—like finding the way back to a childlike, open, and curious beginner's mind—very, very hard.

Every day, as parents, we struggle with questions for which there are no easy answers and with mysteries that we do not understand. Helping our children make healthy choices is one of our most difficult jobs and one of our most profound responsibilities. Whether we realize it or not, what we do with our kids, how we talk to them, and how we schedule their time influences their characters and points them in a certain direction. It may be creative, academic, artistic, athletic, spiritual, or any one of a number of things, but what that path is, and where it points, will affect our children for years to come—often for their whole lives. How can we help our children choose their paths with integrity?

When I started practicing mindfulness with my children, my goal was to follow the precedent established by Mindfulness-Based Stress Reduction and teach self-directed, calming techniques to help them become more attentive, balanced, and aware. I hoped mindfulness would help kids see their lives clearly, set thoughtful goals, provide them with tools to achieve their goals, and become more reflective and caring adults.

Mindful awareness does not depend on reaching a peaceful mental state. Plenty of times I have sat on a cushion for an extended period of time and achieved nothing even approaching a calm, concentrated mental state. This isn't failure, but an integral part of the process of developing mindfulness. It happens to everybody. The point of mindful introspection is *to bring awareness to what happens in your mind and body (your thoughts, emo-*

tions, and physical sensations, for example), not to control your mind. It is a process-oriented practice. This is the polar opposite of the school day during which children are often compelled to direct every bit of their energy to a static, rigid goal, one often measured by standardized test scores. Mindfulness is a different way of looking at learning than the approach taught in most schools, and I've seen it foster the love of learning in children.

A Mindful Consumer Can Help Change the World

Daniel Goleman

Psychologist Daniel Goleman has radically changed how we think about intelligence, asking us to broaden our definition beyond analytic ability to include emotional intelligence, social intelligence, and now ecological intelligence. He suggests that the key to stopping environmental destruction and climate change is to be mindful at the moment we're deciding whether or not to buy something.

MINDFUL SHOPPING is a potentially important practice, a socially engaged act that could collectively help us save the world from its greatest threat: us.

It seems likely that if we practice mindfulness, we will become more in tune with our world ecologically. We will get more in touch with our actual needs and will be driven less by our desires. As a result, we will consume less and decrease our overall impact on the environment. But I think there is a level of mindfulness, or ecological intelligence, that goes beyond just decreasing our acquisitiveness. It relates to what happens when we do buy something. So the question is, When we consume, how can we consume more mindfully?

The key step in socially engaged shopping is to be mindful in the moment we're about to make a decision about whether to buy something rather than going through the store in our usual trance. At the very point of buying, we need to pay attention rather than act on impulse. Our mindfulness can then allow us to take in the bigger picture.

To become mindful shoppers, we need to start by reviewing some of our common, unexamined perceptions and paradigms, beginning with our way of thinking about "stuff"—the material things we buy, use, and throw away every day. Turning our minds to stuff and how we use it opens a vast opportunity for practice that, to my knowledge, few of us have taken advantage of.

One of my favorite Buddhist teachings is the metaphor of the chariot. It asks, Where is the chariot? Is it in its wheels and axle? Is it in the spokes? Is it in the poles that connect it to the horse and the frame? In the carriage? The answer is that the chariot is found in none of these. It is nowhere. The chariot is an illusion. It's not a thing; it's a process. The chariot is just a frozen moment in time when those parts come together. It's one moment in a long history of each of those parts, and each of them will continue in some way after the chariot is no longer used.

This ancient metaphor shows us the very kind of shift we need to make in thinking about the things we buy and use. We're not buying products. We're participating in a process that often started long before the moment of purchase. The modern version of the metaphor of the chariot can be found in a very technical, but nonetheless extremely relevant field called industrial ecology. It is a discipline carried out by chemists, engineers, physicists, and other scientific researchers who look in a very fine-grained way at the life history of a consumable and break it down into the discrete steps that result in the product that you and I buy at our neighborhood store, mall, car dealership, or restaurant.

Take the example of a drinking glass. If you did what industrial ecologists call a life-cycle assessment, you would find that there are 1,959 discrete steps in the life of an average drinking glass. It begins with all the processes involved in the extraction of raw materials and continues through various manufacturing, transportation, and retail processes, culminating in our use and disposal. Each step of the way can be examined to determine the myriad impacts of the glass on the environment in the form of emissions to the air, water, and soil; the contribution to greenhouse gases; the energy tied up in it; its embodied toxicity; its embodied water, and so on. Industrial ecologists look at every angle and determine the ecological impact of each step in the life of the glass. The sum total gives you a kind of karmic score for the glass, the debt to nature that you take on when you buy it.

When we begin to understand things in this more global way, it challenges what we tend to think of and call "green." It's often a mirage. An organic cotton T-shirt may be called green because the growers didn't use pesticides or chemical fertilizers when growing the cotton. That's on the good side of the ledger, to be sure, but if we look into the life cycle of the T-shirt, we discover that organic cotton fibers are shorter than other fibers, so you need to grow a lot more cotton per T-shirt. Cotton is typically raised in arid parts of the world, and it's a very thirsty crop, so a lot of water is implicated in the production of the T-shirt.

Also, if it's a colored T-shirt, we have to take into account that textile dyes tend to be carcinogenic. When we consider all these angles, we may come to see that if you change one thing about a product and leave 999 unchanged, it's not green. It's perhaps just a little bit greener.

Understanding the life cycle of products in this way is a means of directing our contemplative mind to the true impact involved in our buying decisions. It lets us know the karmic weight of any given object. Therefore, it's a way of helping us buy in a more socially engaged way, in a way that takes more responsibility for our impacts.

Another ancient metaphor from the Buddhist tradition can also help shed light on what's involved in becoming a mindful shopper. It's known as Indra's net. At each connection point in this infinite web is a jewel, and each jewel reflects every other jewel in the web. Everything is interconnected, and everything is reflected in every other thing. Nothing is totally independent.

That view of interconnectedness can help us understand the supply chain: a company gets its stuff from such and such a place, which gets components from other places, which employs immigrants from yet other places. The history of any given item likely extends throughout the world. It can also make us rethink what "local" really means. Some researchers, for example, did a life-cycle analysis on locally grown tomatoes in Montreal. It showed that the seeds were developed in France, grown in China, then flown to Ontario, where the seeds were sprouted. The sprouts were trucked to Montreal, sold in a nursery, planted, and sold as local. Apart from asking, "How green is green?" then, we also need to ask, "How local is local?"

Considering the scope of the life cycle for any given item and the vast interconnectedness of the supply chain may make the shopping decision seem overwhelming and daunting, but we are not alone in our efforts to become mindful, socially engaged consumers. We can get help. There is now a way to know the relative ecological merits and demerits of many competing products through a website and an iPhone app called GoodGuide, started by an independent group at the University of California–Berkeley. It aggregates 200 databases and compares 60,000-plus consumer items—toys, foods, personal care products, and so on. They're adding new categories continuously. This kind of tool helps us to pay attention to the karmic virtues of one competitive choice versus another.

Even Walmart has announced that it wants to develop a sustainability index for all its products. It may take four or five years for this concept to reach the shelves of Walmart and other retailers, but if it becomes an industry standard, it will make it easier to be a mindful shopper.

Another wonderful resource that's available now is Skin Deep, a Web database that reports on toxic chemicals in personal care products. Skin Deep looks at the fifty different ingredients in a given shampoo through the lens of a medical database and sees if there are any negative findings. It then ranks the products in terms of safety. One of the lowest shampoos on the list is one of the most expensive. Even though it has a greenish-looking label and a botanical name, its ingredients are really bad.

That moment when we are about to be drawn in by the label and the name—the buying moment—is critical. As a psychologist, I would call mindfulness at that moment "looking into the backstory." It means looking into the ecological truths about the things we're considering buying. One hair dye may have lead in it, while another doesn't—that means something. One sunblock might have a chemical that becomes a carcinogen if it is exposed to the sun. An "organic" dairy product might come from an industrial-sized dairy farm that employs some of the worst feedlot practices. The moment you realize the bigger picture surrounding your purchase, the moment you find your preference for a brand turning to disgust, you are led to a more mindful buying decision.

For example, I've taken to using a stainless-steel water bottle rather than buying plastic bottles of water and then throwing them away. The new math of industrial ecology helps me to understand the impact of such a decision. If you bought a stainless-steel bottle and used it only sparingly, from an ecological standpoint, it would be better to buy the plastic, because the stainless steel is very ecologically intensive at first. The steel is made from a combination of pig iron, nickel, and chromium, all of which have to be mined or obtained from recycling. Also, raw chrome ore, it turns out, is a carcinogen and tends to be mined in parts of the world such as Kazakhstan, South Africa, and India where the workers may not be well protected. You have to calculate that into the karmic load of the stainless-steel bottle.

However, if you use the bottle repeatedly, each time saving a disposable plastic bottle, the math will switch over in favor of the stainless at a certain point. At various points along the way, the ecotoxicity for the stainless becomes less, the greenhouse gases less, and so on. By five hundred or so uses, there is no measure left that favors the plastic bottle, including overall metal depletion, which is surprising for something made of metal. Where is any metal depleted in making a plastic bottle? The industrial ecologists include the metal used up in the machinery that manufactures the plastic, which gives us an idea of just how fine the industrial ecologists make these measures.

By drawing on the ongoing work of industrial ecologists and using the guides and indexes that are increasingly available for products, we can become mindful shoppers, not only decreasing our acquisitiveness through mindfulness, but also taking into account the bigger picture when we do buy. I see three key steps to mindful shopping. Step one: pay attention to your impacts. Step two: buy the ecologically better product. Step three: share what you know as widely as you can. Any organized group could collectively improve its buying habits and create a broader impact.

To the extent that more people shop mindfully, it will have a telling impact on the market. Market share will shift toward the more ecologically virtuous products. Brand managers will pay attention, creating a virtuous cycle whereby our choices based on sound, transparent information influence the market. It will pay for companies to innovate, to change their practices, to go after our dollar by upgrading the ecological impacts of what they're trying to sell us.

Finally, our mindful shopping habits could shift the debate within the corporate world about sustainability, which is stalled right now. Most voices for corporate social responsibility say that companies should pay attention to ecological impacts because it's the morally and ethically correct thing to do. The counterargument is that the first duty of corporations is to their investors. But if doing good also becomes what is most economically advantageous, that debate will be over. They will make the better choice because we've made the better choice.

Taking Responsibility for the World's Well-Being

The Fourteenth Dalai Lama

The Dalai Lama says that all beings are equal in seeking happiness and peace. Yet as individuals and as nations, we too often put ourselves first and value our own well-being over everyone else's. This self-cherishing mind is the root of all suffering, both personal and collective. His Holiness proposes a new approach to global politics based on fostering a kind heart and a calm, clear mind that leads to taking responsibility for the happiness of all people.

BROADLY SPEAKING, there are two types of happiness and suffering: mental and physical. Of the two, I believe that *mental* suffering and happiness are the more acute. Hence, I stress the training of the mind to endure suffering and attain a more lasting state of happiness. However, I also have a more general and concrete idea of happiness: a combination of inner peace, economic development, and, above all, world peace. To achieve such goals, I feel it is necessary to develop a sense of "universal responsibility," a deep concern for all, irrespective of creed, color, sex, or nationality.

The premise behind this idea of universal responsibility is the simple fact that, in general terms, all others' desires are the same as mine. Every being wants happiness and does not want suffering. If we, as intelligent human beings, do not accept this fact, there will be more and more suffering on this planet. If we adopt a self-centered approach to life and constantly try to use others for our own self-interest, we may gain temporary benefits, but in the long run, we will not succeed in achieving even personal happiness, and world peace will be completely out of the question.

In their quest for happiness, humans have used different methods, which all too often have been cruel and repellent. Behaving in ways utterly unbecoming to their status as humans, they inflict suffering upon fellow humans and other living beings for their own selfish gains. In the end, such shortsighted actions bring suffering to oneself as well as to others. To be born a human being is a rare event in itself, and it is wise to use this opportunity as effectively and skillfully as possible. We must have the proper perspective, that of the universal life process, so that the happiness or glory of one person or group is not sought at the expense of others.

All this calls for a new approach to global problems. The world is becoming smaller and smaller—and more and more interdependent—as a result of rapid technological advances and international trade, as well as increasing transnational relations. We now depend very much on each other. In ancient times, problems were mostly family-size, and they were naturally tackled at the family level, but the situation has changed. Today we are so interdependent, so closely interconnected with each other, that without a sense of universal responsibility, a feeling of universal brotherhood and sisterhood, and an understanding and belief that we really are part of one big human family, we cannot hope to overcome the dangers to our very existence—let alone bring about peace and happiness.

It is no longer possible for any nation to solve its problems satisfactorily alone; too much depends on the interest, attitude, and cooperation of other nations. A universal humanitarian approach to world problems seems the only sound basis for world peace. What does this mean? We begin from the recognition mentioned previously that all beings cherish happiness and do not want suffering. It then becomes both morally wrong and pragmatically unwise to pursue only our own happiness, oblivious to the feelings and aspirations of all others who surround us as members of the same human family. The wiser course is to think of others also when pursuing our own happiness. This will lead to what I call "wise self-interest," which hopefully will transform itself into "compromised self-interest" or, better still, "mutual interest."

The development of a kind heart (a feeling of closeness for all human beings) does not involve the religiosity we normally associate with conventional religious practice. It is not only for people who believe in religion but is for everyone regardless of race, religion, or political affiliation. It is for anyone who considers himself or herself, above all, a member of the human family and who sees things from this larger and longer perspective. This is a powerful feeling that we should develop and apply; instead, we often neglect it, particularly in our prime when we experience a false sense of security.

When we take into account a longer perspective (the fact that all people wish to gain happiness and avoid suffering) and keep in mind our relative unimportance in relation to countless others, we can conclude that it is worthwhile to share our possessions with others. When you train in this sort of outlook, a true sense of compassion—a true sense of love and respect for others—becomes possible. Individual happiness ceases to be a conscious self-seeking effort; it becomes an automatic and far superior by-product of the whole process of loving and serving others.

Another result of spiritual development, most useful in day-to-day life, is that it gives a calmness and presence of mind. Our lives are in constant flux, bringing many difficulties. When faced with a calm and clear mind, problems can be resolved successfully. When, instead, we lose control over our minds through hatred, selfishness, jealousy, and anger, we lose our sense of judgment. Our minds are blinded, and at those wild moments, anything can happen, including war. Thus, the practice of compassion and wisdom is useful to all, especially to those responsible for running national affairs, in whose hands lie the power and opportunity to create the structure of world peace.

Such human qualities as morality, compassion, decency, wisdom, and so forth have been the foundation of all civilizations. These qualities must be cultivated and sustained through systematic moral education in a conducive social environment so that a more humane world may emerge. The qualities required to create such a world must be inculcated right from the beginning, from childhood. We cannot wait for the next generation to make this change; the present generation must attempt a renewal of basic human values. If there is any hope, it is in the future generations, but not unless we institute major change on a worldwide scale in our present educational system. We need a revolution in our commitment to and practice of universal humanitarian values.

In this regard, there are two important things to keep in mind: self-examination and self-correction. We should constantly check our attitude toward others, examining ourselves carefully, and we should correct ourselves immediately when we find we are in the wrong.

Finally, a few words about material progress. I have heard a great deal of complaint against material progress from Westerners, and yet, paradoxically, it has been the very pride of the Western world. I see nothing wrong with material progress per se, provided that people are always given precedence. It is my firm belief that in order to solve human problems in all their dimensions, we must combine and harmonize economic development with spiritual growth.

However, we must know its limitations. Although materialistic knowledge in the form of science and technology has contributed enormously to human welfare, it is not capable of creating lasting happiness. In America, for example, where technological development is perhaps more advanced than in any other country, there is still a great deal of mental suffering. This is because materialistic knowledge can only provide a type of happiness that is dependent upon physical conditions. It cannot provide the happiness that springs from inner development.

Creating a Mindful Society

BARRY BOYCE

At the Shambhala Sun *magazine, we've been hearing more and more stories of people who are transforming their professions and communities by applying mindfulness. So we began a regular department called "Mindful Society." As the editor of this section, it has been my job to meet and interview these individuals and to write about the emergence of mindfulness in different facets of American life. In nearly thirty years of journalism, no assignment has given me more pleasure. In this final chapter, I'll tell you about some of the people and organizations I've encountered and how they're changing our society bit by bit. These are the people in your neighborhood—and they want to make it a better place.*

MINDFULNESS PRACTITIONERS do not exist in splendid isolation. They are part of the larger society they live in and contribute to. As people from many walks of life—health care practitioners, therapists, social activists, musicians, artists, lawyers, judges, police officers, firefighters, soldiers, high-tech professionals, entrepreneurs, homemakers, politicians, you name it—learn mindfulness, they're inspired to bring the insight they've gained into their workplace and into the area of endeavor they're engaged in. As Jon Kabat-Zinn said earlier in this book:

Three or four hundred years ago, . . . people practicing meditation did so under fairly isolated conditions, mostly in monasteries. Now meditation is practiced and studied in laboratories, hospitals, and clinics, and it is even finding its way into primary and secondary schools. . . . Mindfulness work is spilling into areas way beyond medicine and health care and also beyond psychology and neuroscience.

As people practicing mindfulness begin to feel it has helped them see the workings of their minds and their motivations more clearly—and to make better choices in their lives—they want to offer that possibility to others. As one mindfulness practitioner wrote to me:

When I began to realize I was not my thoughts, it was so liberating. When overly critical thoughts coursed through my brain, I couldn't necessarily push them away, but the mindfulness technique allowed me to be aware of them and also aware of a greater peace and clarity within. It showed me a place I could operate from with more confidence. Then I asked myself, "Why didn't they teach me this in school?" In fact, why are we not teaching it in schools now? It should be available to people in the workplace. A little bit of mindfulness in a few places could bring big changes to our society.

I have been on a mission to find a little bit of mindfulness in a few places that could bring big change to our society. I've been talking to and learning from a lot of enthusiastic people. At a gathering of mindfulness teachers and practitioners recently, a colleague of mine quickly sketched a diagram for me as we sat in the hallway between sessions. She drew a circle showing elements in the human life cycle—birth, infancy, childhood, schooling, higher education, career, family life, community life, leadership, retirement, old age, death. We have many institutions, she said, to support the many stages and facets of life. Wouldn't it be great, she asked, if the level of mindfulness of the people in each of these institutions were raised? If there were more mindfulness surrounding childbirth and early childhood, we might see less child abuse and possibly less divorce. Mindfulness in the schools might decrease bullying, help children learn better, and help teachers burn out less. Mindfulness in hospitals might help doctors and nurses become better listeners. And so on.

That colleague is Nancy Bardacke, and I've been very taken with her vision of mindfulness enhancing as many elements of society as possible. Here are a few short profiles of people trying to do just that in a variety of areas. Appropriately, the first is about Nancy and her focus on the activities that surround the birth of a child.

Nancy Bardacke was a nurse-midwife with a background in yoga and meditation when she took a Mindfulness-Based Stress Reduction (MBSR) course for health professionals and decided it was time to develop a comparable program for childbirth. She kept the essential elements and morphed it into something that would work for expectant couples. According to Bardacke, "Whereas MBSR addresses an individual's health, in our program two—really three—people are involved." She began Mindfulness-Based Childbirth and Parenting (MBCP) in Oakland, California, in 1998 and has taught it continuously since then. It includes an introductory session, nine weekly classes before birth, an all-day practice session, and a reunion class following birth. She also offers one-day and weekend courses for parents and health professionals.

"Pregnancy, birth, and early parenting is *the most* transformative period in the adult life cycle," Bardacke said, when I talked to her about the significance of her work. "The experiences that emerge can be some of the most stressful of people's lives. Nothing really prepares you for it. Mindfulness skills help everyone involved navigate this transition and are a foundation, not only for the uncertainties of the birth itself, but also for the new life of parenthood that follows."

Bardacke feels confident that longitudinal studies of mindfulness applied to the childbirth process will show a range of benefits to the mother, the child, and the couple. She feels it is time for this methodology to become more widespread and has started a professional development and training program for MBCP. "Most people having children take childbirth education," she explains. "What a wonderful opportunity to teach skills that can last a lifetime. This is bigger than just focusing on mindful birth. Through practice, we can interrupt intergenerational patterns of dysfunction. This is violence prevention, shaken-baby prevention, family breakup prevention. It's another means of helping create a more peaceful society."

One of the most exciting applications of mindfulness today is in grade-school classrooms, where the rise of bullying and other forms of antisocial behavior has alarmed parents, teachers, and government leaders. While efforts are under way to teach simple forms of meditation to schoolchildren, the most promising initiatives focus on using contemplative techniques to help teachers reduce stress and improve their emotional awareness, concentration, and responsiveness.

A pioneer in progressive children's education and a Fulbright Scholar, Linda Lantieri has been an educator in New York City for forty years. After 9/11, she established a program in twelve schools in and around Ground Zero to help strengthen the inner resilience of students, teachers, and families dealing with the trauma. She is spearheading an effort to build on the successes of the social and emotional learning (SEL) movement and add a dimension of deep inner resiliency, or "spirit," as she likes to call it. Currently she serves as the founding director of the Inner Resilience Program (IRP), whose mission is to cultivate the inner lives of students, teachers, and schools by integrating social and emotional learning with contemplative practice. Linda prefers to think and talk in terms of "nurturing young people's inner lives, which includes activities that we might call 'contemplative' and 'mindful,' but it can include a lot more." One of the challenges of this developing field, she says, "is building common ground and finding a common lexicon for discussing students' and teachers' ultimate questions about meaning and purpose, the spiritual dimension of learning, and the connectedness we have that goes beyond our own mind and emotions. This work includes techniques for quieting the mind, but also uses the arts, storytelling, and spending time in nature, and I've certainly noticed that it is not at all difficult to get children excited about this kind of work."

Another leader in K–12 education is Patricia Jennings, director of the Initiative on Contemplation and Education at the Garrison Institute in upstate New York and a research associate in the Prevention Research Center at Pennsylvania State University. Garrison's professional development program for teachers, Cultivating Awareness and Resiliency in Education (CARE), received a nearly million-dollar grant in 2009 from the U.S. Department of Education's Institute for Education Sciences (IES). "We will provide a great service," Jennings told me, "if we can help teachers apply mindfulness to their emotions in the intense classroom environment. If teachers can notice emotion within their bodies, they can stop and make choices. Instead of seeing children with challenging behavior as problems, they can experience them as human beings who need compassion. Over time, that will change how they lead their classrooms."

A small but growing cadre of university professors who integrate contemplative disciplines into academic training are staking out a unique position in the long-standing debate about what is "higher" in higher education. Through a variety of innovative programs, they've been bringing contemplative disciplines onto university campuses as a way to increase students' attention and decrease stress, give deeper meaning to university education as a means to self-knowledge, and foster community and cooperation as a salve to the competitive atmosphere of academia. Harold Roth, founder of the Contemplative Studies Initiative at Brown University, told me, "I'm very encouraged by how this movement is gaining momentum. We're at the beginning of the development of a major new academic field, one that will potentially be quite significant in changing the face of higher education in North America. It asks us to consider deeply what a *higher* education really means."

The Contemplative Studies Initiative brings together traditional academic third-person inquiry and the first-person inquiry of the great contemplative traditions. While Roth's dream of a full-fledged major in contemplative studies lies further down the road, at present, students can do an independent study with a concentration in contemplative studies. The introduction to contemplative studies course that Roth teaches attracts more than eighty students each year, but to keep the course manageable, he caps it at thirty-five. He also leads "meditation labs," which emphasize the scientific and exploratory nature of contemplative practice. In 2009, seven students in the medical school chose a contemplative study concentration. One studied the effect of yoga practice on postpartum depression, and another focused on developing a program to bring mindfulness into clinical settings on a much wider basis.

The Mind-Body Awareness Project (MBA) in Oakland, California, founded by Noah Levine, brings mindfulness practice to troubled inner-city youth. I went into the Alameda County Juvenile Justice Center to attend a mindfulness class for offenders taught by MBA instructors Amani Carey-Simms and Jon Oda. MBA program director Chris McKenna also came to observe the class. The attendees were mainly members of inner-city gangs. Their average age was fourteen or fifteen years old. Carey-Simms and Oda didn't teach mindfulness according to the conventional game plan used in most other settings. Instead, they talked about martial arts movies and songs that would be familiar to young people, then slowly and deftly brought the attendees around to mindfully exploring their own feelings.

McKenna, whose prior work was with child soldiers and victims of torture, told me, "These young gang members are trauma victims. They've known no other world but street justice from a very young age. When they're incarcerated, we have a brief opportunity to interrupt what's been going on in their lives and introduce some mindfulness." Having made a connection with a young person, MBA counselors try to follow up with them when they're on the outside and get them to attend a retreat outside the city. "I've experienced many different approaches to working with people in these kinds of extreme circumstances," McKenna said, "and mindfulness is by far the most powerful intervention I've ever worked with."

Adam Bernstein—a bass guitar player, music educator, and meditator in Brooklyn, New York—has discovered that mindfulness practice is an excellent means to help music students quiet the chatter in their minds a bit and learn how to listen for real. More than that, Bernstein realized, jazz-playing itself has a quality of mindfulness and awareness—and having a regular meditation practice could help players extend that quality to their daily lives. Bernstein started the Jazz Mindfulness Program for instrumentalists and singers from ages twelve to eighteen. Bernstein leads two fourteen-week programs each year. The students meet one night a week for two hours, with a short meditation followed by instruction and improvisational practice. Each program ends with a concert.

"One of the hardest things for musicians, and probably jazz musicians in particular," Bernstein says, "is coming down off the high of playing. That's led to a lot of self-abuse. I've had to work with that myself, on how to just be with myself. Music has always been a release for young people, but I'd love my students to learn mindfulness at a young age, so they can have the joy of the music and also get beneath the chatter and the judgment that can suppress the creative, open mind. My youngest student, Olivia, was telling us the other day how she was tearing herself apart with judgments about her schoolwork and stressing out. Then she said she noticed her breath and was able to calm herself. That's what we're trying to do for these young people."

More than fifteen years ago, Elana Rosenbaum, a longtime Mindfulness-Based Stress Reduction teacher, was diagnosed with non-Hodgkin's lymphoma. Her cancer led her to many arduous courses of treatment, including a stem-cell transplant, and took her to the brink of death. It also took her deeply into the practice of mindfulness and made her one of the most sought-after teachers of mindfulness for cancer patients. "When I was diagnosed with cancer," she told me, "it was a great shock, because the thought was that if you meditated and ate right, you wouldn't get sick, and in my crowd, I was the first one to get a serious illness. We often used to say, 'This too shall pass' around the stress-reduction clinic, but we weren't usually talking about human life itself. I made up my mind then to live what I had been teaching."

Rosenbaum teaches cancer patients a range of mindfulness meditations, including a body scan. She feels it's important for patients to transform their experience of pain by understanding the simplicity of sensation. While she was initially concerned about how very ill people would relate to a body scan, she now finds it essential: "I thought they might experience their body as betraying them, but I discovered that the body scan is a very effective way to develop a friendly relationship with what is happening." Rosenbaum feels mindfulness should be part of the curriculum in medical and nursing schools. She believes it would also be helpful for health care professionals to have short periods of time in their offices when they regularly practice mindfulness and ask others to join in if they wish. She would like to train volunteers who would be willing to sit with patients in different medical settings and practice mindfulness. She has been traveling the country training nurses, occupational therapists, psychologists, social workers, and other members of the caring professions, including some from the military.

Frank Ostaseski has been involved in improving end-of-life care for a long time. The founder of the Zen Hospice Project, he also created the Metta Institute, in Sausalito, California. Its primary program is the End-of-Life-

Care Practitioner Program, whose goal is to establish a national network of educators, advocates, and guides for those facing life-threatening illnesses and the individuals and systems that serve them.

"Our work," he says, "is about reclaiming the spiritual dimensions of the dying process. I've always thought there is a natural match between people who are cultivating the listening heart in meditation and people who really need to be heard—the dying. We reach out to people working in medical institutions, in environments far less supportive than Zen Hospice. How can they take spiritual practices into their workplace and benefit themselves and the people they serve? Many people enter health care with a deep intention to serve and to reduce suffering. They want an internal process like mindfulness that supports them as they go forward. In the dying process, there's little that can be done medically, so it becomes a natural place for caregivers to find inner resources that may be applied in the rest of health care. The lessons learned at the time of dying can have an impact for the rest of us in our everyday lives. I dream of a day when hospices are like YMCAs and corner churches—so broadly accepted they won't be considered special at all."

Mirabai Bush is the cofounder of the Center for Contemplative Mind in Society, in Northampton, Massachusetts, and serves as its executive director. Under her leadership, the center has developed programs bringing contemplative and mindfulness-based practices into five key areas of society: academia, social justice, law, business, and research. The center is also a major sponsor of retreats and meetings in these and other arenas.

Bush is an accomplished teacher and an energetic "connector," putting people and projects in touch with each other. When Google was looking for a new way to bring contemplative practice to its engineers after stress reduction had failed as a motivator, Chade-Meng Tan called Bush. Before too long, Bush says, "we decided to develop a course on mindfulness-based emotional intelligence. The real goal was to bring mindfulness to Google, but we knew it had to appeal to the engineers. Dan Goleman gave a talk on the connection between mindfulness and emotional intelligence. We then advertised a course. In the first four hours, 150 people signed up for Google's Search Inside Yourself: A Mindfulness-Based Emotional Intelligence Program. SIY includes an introductory class, a full day of mindfulness practice, and six two-hour sessions, each a week apart. Class sizes range from twenty to fifty, depending on the time of year and whether an entire team or department has signed on for the course. The course begins with the "Neuroscience of Emotional Intelligence," which shows participants that there is a growing body of scientific literature on the effects of training attention and emotion. In addition to basic mindfulness, the course includes instruction in journaling as a means of nonjudgmentally noticing mental content, mindful listening, walking meditation, mindful e-mailing, and a variety of other contemplative techniques. The latter stages of the course emphasize empathy (using loving-kindness meditation) and social skills, including how to carry on difficult conversations.

Because of the success of the course at its headquarters, Google has been taking the course to locations around the world. Eventually, Bush says, "it can most likely be adapted for other corporate environments, because we've been learning a lot about how mindfulness can work at the office. But it's not one size fits all. What motivates people will be different in different workplaces. SIY is a good curriculum and if it's exported—and we've been talking about how to do that—it won't simply be a Google thing."

Traditional legal education focuses on overcoming external challenges. Now an increasing number of lawyers are training themselves to work on their inner challenges in an effort to improve their law practice, benefit clients and colleagues, provide better training for other lawyers, and, ultimately, yield better justice. The leading initiative in this area is the Law Program of the Center for Contemplative Mind in Society. The program sponsors annual retreats for lawyers, judges, professors, and students that combine sitting and walking meditation, yoga, qigong, talks, and discussion.

The Law Program's leading light is Charles Halpern, a renowned public interest lawyer who is chair of the board of the Center for Contemplative Mind in Society. In 1982, when he became the founding dean of the City University of New York's law school, he started practicing meditation to work with the resulting stress. Since 2002, he's been leading a weekly meditation group at the law school at the University of California–Berkeley, together with Doug Chermak, the Law Program's director. Chermak, an environmental lawyer in Oakland, told me that the crux of the program is "effective and sustainable lawyering" and "the meditative perspective." He says the central question is, "How does meditation affect the quality of your listening, your ethics, and any kind of interaction you would have as a legal professional?"

Elizabeth Stanley represents the ninth generation of her family to serve in the U.S. Army. In 1996, Stanley left the service with the rank of captain following postings in Korea and Germany and two deployments as a peacekeeper in the Balkans. After her military service, she earned an MBA from the MIT Sloan School of Management and a PhD in government from Harvard; she is now assistant professor of security studies at Georgetown's Walsh School of Foreign Service. In 2002, Stanley began practicing yoga, and after a few months, her yoga instructor suggested she attend an eight-day *metta* (loving-kindness) retreat at the Insight Meditation Society (IMS). For the first few days, Stanley found the experience of sitting meditation almost unbearably difficult, despite having experienced the rigors of deployment. Things began to turn around, though, when she gave herself permission to leave if she felt it was just too difficult to continue. She stayed, and the rest of the retreat became her initiation into mindfulness. She has returned to the IMS for many intensive retreats and also took temporary ordination as a nun and trained in Burma for two months. She completed teacher training in Mindfulness-Based Stress Reduction in 2008 and taught a program together with Jon Kabat-Zinn in 2009.

For Stanley, mindfulness has been central to her approach to dealing with the effects of the stress from her military service and has become a focus of her research into alternatives to current approaches to national security. As she explains, "My research has focused on the United States' overreliance on technology in national security, a cultural tendency born from the desire to feel certain, in control, and safe. This tendency has led to a devaluation of human-centric approaches to security, especially in terms of providing troops with skills to remain balanced, nonreactive, and clear-seeing, despite the extreme stress, uncertainty, and confusion of the counterinsurgency environment."

The intersection of her personal experiences with her professional research has led her to the conclusion that a blending of mindfulness and other related mind-body training could help troops develop a kind of mental fitness to "cope with the physiological and psychological effects of extreme or prolonged stress." She has been conducting research with military units to demonstrate that mindfulness can help people in high-stress environments draw on their natural resiliency and not fall as easily into poor, reactive decision making at critical moments, which often leads to disastrous results and needless long-term damage. Stanley designed a program called Mindfulness-based Mind Fitness Training (MMFT) that adapts mindfulness training for use with troops and others in high-stress environments (such as police officers and firefighters). For MMFT to gain acceptance in this context, Stanley knew, "mindfulness alone was not enough. The training needed to integrate mindfulness with other skills for regulating stress activation in the autonomic nervous system." Body-based training helps trainees to be aware of and work with how energy moves in the body in response to stressors in the environment. In that way, body disciplines help trainees to discover and support the body's inherent resilience. "Mindfulness," she says, "helps them to stabilize their attention and accept things, just as they are, and those two qualities support the body and mind's self-regulation and return to balance."

Tim Ryan, a fourth-term Democratic U.S. congressman from the Youngstown-Akron area of Ohio, attended a week-long mindfulness retreat for leaders led by Jon Kabat-Zinn in 2008, immediately following his reelection. He deposited his two BlackBerrys at the door and immediately spent thirty-six hours in complete silence. Although Ryan had practiced yoga and meditation prior to the retreat, the intense practice period proved to be a watershed for him, and it inspired him to bring mindfulness to the U.S. Congress, including setting up a small meditation room on Capitol Hill. "I realized how helpful this practice could be," he told me. "Now when I'm listening to people, I can more often cut through the distraction and listen to them with my whole body and mind." Ryan also began to feel that if more people could practice mindfulness in schools, workplaces, hospitals, military bases, and other government institutions, "it could have a transformational effect across our entire country at a time when we most desperately need it."

When he took office in 1993, at age twenty-nine, Ryan was the youngest representative in the U.S. Congress. He is a member of the "30 Something" working group, which includes House Democrats who have not yet reached the age of forty. It was organized by House Speaker Nancy Pelosi to engage younger people in politics by focusing on issues important to them. Ryan thinks mindfulness and health are issues of prime importance to young people. He has become a zealous advocate for the support of contemplative practices in government-supported programs in health and social services. Several schools in Ryan's district now receive funding to implement Linda Lantieri's Inner Resilience Program.

As the featured speaker at a gala event celebrating the Center for Mindfulness entering its fourth decade of work, Ryan emphasized the cost savings that could come from mindfulness-based interventions in health care. He also asked for the attendees' support in helping put mindfulness on the health care agenda in Washington. In another message to a group of leaders discussing the state of contemplative practice in America, he said, "Washington is starting to understand the power of mindfulness, compassion, and the contemplative. We need you to knock on our doors and tell us how these practices benefit the world and what we can do to help." When I asked Congressman Ryan if he ever got any political blowback for being a publicly declared meditator, he said, "What can I say? I exhaled, and I paid attention to it. Shoot me."

I've mentioned just a few of the many people I've met and interviewed over the past several years who are applying some form of mindfulness in their work or experimenting with doing so. There are many others: doctors, restaurateurs, entrepreneurs, social workers, corporate leaders, high-tech workers, rabbis, priests, ministers, Sufi masters, journalists, student counselors. And the list is growing. It's still small in the grand scheme of things, but it is a bona fide revolution.

Mindfulness is a personal discipline. We often do it by ourselves, in silence. And yet, as it starts to decrease our stress, relax the hold our fixations can have on us, and brighten our outlook, it usually causes us to look outward more often. We are motivated to deepen our connections with others and to be more helpful, as our focus on our own problems lessens. This phenomenon—which causes some people to say that mindfulness blossoms into "heartfulness"—is what creates the groundwork for a mindful society. But mindfulness is not a trademark or a brand name. It's an innate quality that can appear in many guises. Authentic mindfulness is never stingy and self-confirming; it seeks to rediscover itself in the works of others. A yearning for a more mindful way of being can be seen in many disciplines and movements that exhibit mindfulness but don't necessarily carry the label, including, for example, social and emotional learning, the slow food movement, contemplative arts and education, alternative dispute resolution, and innovative methods for strategic thinking and organizational development.

Developing a mindful society is not about having a meditation center on every corner. It's about finding as many ways as possible to draw out our inherent ability to be present fully for what's going on in any given moment, which helps us discover peacefulness and openness as inherent qualities that all people possess. Eventually, as mindfulness practitioners we desire to see the peace discovered in mindfulness writ large—in our home life, our workplace, our community, our institutions, our society. It starts with our own body, breath, thoughts, and concerns, but the circle of mindfulness quickly grows, and there are no limitations on how far it can go. Mindfulness is not a *me* thing. It's a *we* thing.

Resources

GUIDED AUDIO INSTRUCTION IN MINDFULNESS MEDITATION

Elisha Goldstein, *Mindfulness Solutions for Stress, Anxiety, and Depression* (Mindful Solutions, 2007)

Jon Kabat-Zinn, *Guided Mindfulness Meditation* (Sounds True, 2005)

———, *Mindfulness for Beginners* (Sounds True, 2006)

Jack Kornfield, *Meditation for Beginners* (Sounds True, 2004)

Carolyn McManus, *Mindfulness Meditation and Body Scan* (Wellness Series, 2003)

Susan Piver (ed.), *Quiet Mind: A Beginner's Guide to Meditation* (Shambhala, 2008)

Thich Nhat Hanh, *Calm, Ease, Smile, Breathe* (Parallax, 2009)

FREE ONLINE AUDIO AND VIDEO MINDFULNESS INSTRUCTION

These websites offer audio and video instruction in mindfulness and/or discussions of its benefits.

Canadian Mental Health Association audio links on the benefits of MBSR
www.cmhawpg.mb.ca/mbsr.htm

The Cognitive Neuroscience of Mindfulness Meditation
www.youtube.com/watch?v=sf6Q0G1iHBI

Talk and Guided Meditation by Jon Kabat-Zinn at Google
www.youtube.com/watch?v=3nwwKbM_vJc

Mindful Awareness Research Center's Mindful Meditations
marc.ucla.edu/body.cfm?id=22

The Shambhala Sun Foundation's website dedicated to mindfulness
www.mindful.org

Sounds True's interactive guide to meditation
   www.withinsight.com
STOP: A Short Mindfulness Practice by Elisha Goldstein
   www.youtube.com/watch?v=PhwQvEGmF_I
UCSD's Guided Audio Files for MBSR practice
   health.ucsd.edu/specialties/psych/mindfulness/mbsr/audio.htm
University of Missouri–Columbia Mindfulness Practice Center
   www.umsystem.edu/ums/curators/wellness/mindfulness/guided.htm

Online Courses in Mindfulness

These organizations offer distance classes in mindfulness practice online.

Duke Integrative Medicine
   www.dukeintegrativemedicine.org
   (Search for "foundations home study")
eMindful
   www.emindful.com
Mindful Living Programs
   www.mindfullivingprograms.com/index.php
Mindfulness Awareness Research Center (MARC) at the
UCLA Semel Institute for Neuroscience and Human Behavior
   marc.ucla.edu

Media

The following websites and publications offer articles, reports, audio, video, and social networking on mindfulness practice and mindfulness research.

The Center for Investigating Healthy Minds
Regular updates on neuroscience research on mindfulness and contemplative practices.
   www.investigatinghealthyminds.org/cihmFindings.html
Greater Good: The Science of a Meaningful Life
A quarterly online magazine reporting on the psychology, sociology, and neuroscience of well-being.
   www.greatergood.berkeley.edu

Mindful: Living with Awareness and Compassion
A website and occasional free periodical with mindfulness instruction
  and reports on innovative mindfulness programs and research
  results.
  www.mindful.org
The Mindful Society
A special section in the Shambhala Sun magazine reporting on people and
  organizations doing pioneering work in bringing mindfulness into
  mainstream society.
  www.shambhalasun.com
Mindfulness Research Guide and Mindfulness Research Monthly
A database and monthly publication updates on mindfulness research.
  www.mindfulexperience.org

Organizations and Centers

The following organizations offer classes, workshops, conferences, and professional trainings in mindfulness and related contemplative disciplines.

The Center for Contemplative Mind in Society
15 Conz Street, Suite 1
Northampton, MA 01060
Website: www.contemplativemind.org

Center for Investigating Healthy Minds
Waisman Center
University of Wisconsin–Madison
1500 Highland Ave.
Madison, WI 53705-2280
Website: www.investigatinghealthyminds.org

Center for Mindfulness in Medicine, Healthcare, and Society
The University of Massachusetts Medical School
55 Lake Avenue North
Worcester, MA 01655
Website: www.umassmed.edu/cfm

Duke Integrative Medicine
DUMC Box 102904
Durham, NC 27710
Website: www.dukeintegrativemedicine.org

Garrison Institute
Rt. 9D at Glenclyffe
Garrison, NY 10524
Website: www.garrisoninstitute.org

The Mind & Life Institute
7007 Winchester Circle, Suite 100
Boulder, CO 80301
Website: www.mindandlife.org

Mindful Living Programs
6 Governors Lane, Suite A
Chico, CA 95926
Website: www.mindfullivingprograms.com

Mindfulness Awareness Research Center (MARC)
UCLA Semel Institute for Neuroscience and Human Behavior
760 Westwood Plaza, Rm. 47-444, Box 951759
Los Angeles, CA 90095-1759
Website: marc.ucla.edu

The Penn Program for Mindfulness
3930 Chestnut Street, 6th Floor
Philadelphia, Pennsylvania 19104
Website: www.pennmedicine.org/stress

University of Arkansas at Little Rock
The Mindfulness-Based Campus-Community Health Program
2801 S. University Avenue
Little Rock, Arkansas 72204
Website: www.ualr.edu/mindfulness

UCSD Center for Mindfulness
Moores UCSD Cancer Center
3855 Health Science Dr. #0658
La Jolla, CA 92093-0658
Website: mindfulness.ucsd.edu

University of Minnesota Center for Spirituality and Healing
420 Delaware St. S.E.
Mayo Memorial Building
5th floor, MMC #505
Minneapolis, MN 55455
Website: www.csh.umn.edu

Contributors

JAN CHOZEN BAYS, MD, has studied and practiced Zen Buddhism since 1973. She has been a Zen teacher since 1983 and the teacher for the Zen Community of Oregon since 1985. In 2002 she helped to found Great Vow Zen Monastery and currently is the co-abbot. She is also a pediatrician, mother, and wife. She is the author of *Mindful Eating: A Guide to Rediscovering a Healthy and Joyful Relationship with Food* and *Jizo Bodhisattva*.

TONI BERNHARD received a JD from the School of Law at the University of California–Davis in 1982 and, as a faculty member, served as the law school's dean of students from 1992 to 1998. She contracted a chronic illness in 2001, and her experiences in coping with daily life with chronic illness led her to write *How to Be Sick: A Buddhist Inspired Guide for the Chronically Ill and Their Caregivers*.

BARRY BOYCE is senior editor of the *Shambhala Sun* and editor of www .mindful.org. He is also a freelance writer and writing teacher, as well as a member of the Denma Translation Group, which produced a critically acclaimed and best-selling translation of *The Art of War* by Sun Tzu. He is coauthor of *The Rules of Victory: How to Transform Chaos and Conflict—Strategies from* The Art of War and editor of *In the Face of Fear: Buddhist Wisdom for Challenging Times*.

JEFFREY BRANTLEY, MD, is the founder and codirector of the Mindfulness Based Stress Reduction program at Duke Integrative Medicine. He teaches intensive courses on mindfulness meditation and conducts extensive experiential programs and group lectures. He is the author of *Calming*

Your Anxious Mind: How Mindfulness and Compassion Can Free You From Anxiety, Fear, and Panic and is the coauthor with Wendy Milstine of the Five Good Minutes series and *Daily Meditations for Calming Your Anxious Mind.*

EDWARD ESPE BROWN has been practicing Zen since 1965 and has also done extensive vipassana practice, yoga, and qigong. He was ordained as a priest by Suzuki Roshi in 1971 and is the founder and teacher of the Peaceful Sea Sangha. He is an accomplished chef and author of *The Tassajara Bread Book, Tassajara Cooking, The Tassajara Recipe Book,* and *Tomato Blessings and Radish Teachings.*

MADELINE BRUSER graduated from the Juilliard School in 1970 and has studied mindfulness meditation and its relationship to artistic and educational processes since 1977. She has led the annual Meditation for Musicians Retreat in Vermont since 2004. She is the founder of the Golden Key Music Institute and author of *The Art of Practicing: A Guide to Making Music from the Heart.*

VIDYAMALA BURCH is the founder and codirector of Breathworks, an organization offering mindfulness-based approaches to pain and illness. She has been meditating since 1985 and is preparing for ordination into the Triratna Buddhist Order. She is the author of *Living Well with Pain & Illness: The Mindful Way to Free Yourself from Suffering.*

MICHAEL CARROLL is an authorized teacher in the lineage of the renowned Tibetan meditation master Chögyam Trungpa and a consultant and business coach for many large firms and nonprofit organizations. He is the author of *Awake at Work: 35 Practical Buddhist Principles for Discovering Clarity and Balance in the Midst of Work's Chaos* and *The Mindful Leader: Awakening Your Natural Management Skills through Mindfulness Meditation.*

SUSAN CHAPMAN is a licensed marriage and family therapist who has been practicing mindfulness meditation for more than thirty-five years. She is the founder of Green Light Conversations, which presents training programs applying the principles of mindfulness to conversations, relationships, and communities. She is currently working on a book on mindful communication.

PEMA CHÖDRÖN is one of America's leading Buddhist teachers and the author of many best-selling books, including *The Places That Scare You*, *When Things Fall Apart*, and *Start Where You Are*. Born Deirdre Blomfield-Brown in 1936, she raised a family and taught elementary school before becoming ordained as a nun in 1981. Pema Chödrön's root teacher was Chögyam Trungpa, who appointed her abbess of the monastery he founded in Cape Breton, Nova Scotia, Canada.

DALAI LAMA. See Tenzin Gyatso below.

ZOKETSU NORMAN FISCHER is a Soto Zen priest in the Suzuki Roshi lineage and a well-known writer and poet. A former abbot of the San Francisco Zen Center, he is a founder and teacher of the Everyday Zen Foundation. His most recent books are *Sailing Home: Using Homer's Odyssey to Navigate Life's Perils and Pitfalls* (prose) and *I Was Blown Back* (poetry).

STEVE FLOWERS, MFT, is the director of the Mindfulness-Based Stress Reduction Clinic in Chico, California, and has been teaching the course for more than eleven years. He is in private practice as a psychotherapist specializing in the treatment of stress-related conditions. Along with Bob Stahl, PhD, he is the codirector of Mindful Living Programs, which provides retreats for health professionals. He is the author of *The Mindful Path through Shyness: How Mindfulness and Compassion Can Help Free You from Social Anxiety, Fear, and Avoidance*.

ELISHA GOLDSTEIN, PhD, teaches mindfulness-based programs in his own psychology practice and through InsightLA. He is the coauthor with Bob Stahl of *A Mindfulness-Based Stress Reduction Workbook*.

JOSEPH GOLDSTEIN is a guiding teacher and cofounder of the Insight Meditation Society in Barre, Massachusetts. He lectures and leads retreats around the world, and he is the author of *One Dharma: The Emerging Western Buddhism* and *The Experience of Insight*. His most recent book is *A Heart Full of Peace*.

DANIEL GOLEMAN, PhD, is an internationally known psychologist who lectures frequently to professional groups, to business audiences, and on college campuses. Working as a science journalist, he reported on the brain and behavioral sciences for the *New York Times* for many years. He is the author of *Emotional Intelligence* and *Ecological Intelligence: How Knowing the Hidden Impacts of What We Buy Can Change Everything.*

SUSAN KAISER GREENLAND teaches mindful awareness to children and teens, as well as educators, parents, therapists, and health care professionals. She also consults with organizations on teaching mindful awareness in an age-appropriate and secular manner. She developed the Inner Kids mindful awareness program for children and families, and she and her husband co-founded the Inner Kids Foundation to teach mindful awareness in Los Angeles schools. She is the author of *The Mindful Child: How to Help Your Kid Manage Stress and Become Happier, Kinder, and More Compassionate.*

TENZIN GYATSO, the Fourteenth Dalai Lama, is the spiritual and temporal leader of the Tibetan people and a winner of the Nobel Peace Prize. He is also a profound Buddhist teacher who is the author of many best-selling books, including *Worlds in Harmony: Compassionate Action for a Better World.* His most recent works are *In My Own Words: An Introduction to My Teaching and Philosophy* and *Ethics for a New Millennium.*

THICH NHAT HANH is a renowned Vietnamese Zen monk, poet, peace advocate, and founder of the Engaged Buddhist movement. The author of more than forty books, including *The Miracle of Mindfulness, Peaceful Action, Open Heart: Lessons from the Lotus Sutra,* and *You Are Here.* He resides at practice centers in France and the United States.

ROBERT HOWARD has been a professional gardener for more than thirty years. He is the former director of the Naropa Garden Institute Project and author, with Eric Skjei, of *What Makes the Crops Rejoice: An Introduction to Gardening.* The late Eric Skjei was a professional writer specializing in contemplative topics.

ANDY KARR is a teacher, writer, and photographer who has practiced meditation and the contemplative arts for the better part of four decades.

He is the author of *Contemplating Reality: A Practitioner's Guide to the View in Indo-Tibetan Buddhism* and coauthor with Michael Wood of *The Practice of Contemplative Photography: Seeing the World with Fresh Eyes.*

JON KABAT-ZINN, PHD, is a scientist, writer, and meditation teacher engaged in bringing mindfulness into the mainstream of medicine and society. He was the founding executive director of the Center for Mindfulness in Medicine, Health Care, and Society at the University of Massachusetts Medical School, as well as the founder and former director of its world-renowned Stress Reduction Clinic. He is the author of several best-selling books, including *Full Catastrophe Living* and *Wherever You Go There You Are.* His most recent book is *Coming to Our Senses: Healing Ourselves and the World through Mindfulness.* He is the coauthor with his wife, Myla Kabat-Zinn, of *Everday Blessings: The Inner Work of Mindful Parenting.*

MYLA KABAT-ZINN, RN, has worked as a childbirth educator, birthing assistant, and environmental advocate. She is the coauthor with her husband, Jon Kabat-Zinn, of *Everyday Blessings: The Inner Work of Mindful Parenting.*

JACK KORNFIELD, PHD, trained as a Buddhist monk in Thailand, Burma, and India. He is a cofounder of the Insight Meditation Society in Barre, Massachusetts, and of the Spirit Rock Meditation Center in northern California. He is the author of *A Path with Heart* and *After the Ecstasy, the Laundry.* His most recent work is *The Wise Heart: A Guide to the Universal Teachings of Buddhist Psychology.*

ELLEN LANGER, PHD, is a professor of psychology at Harvard University. She has studied the illusion of control, decision making, aging, and mindfulness theory. She is the author of eleven books including *Mindfulness, The Power of Mindful Learning,* and *Counterclockwise: Mindful Health and the Power of Possibility.*

HOPE MARTIN is a teacher in the Shambhala Buddhist tradition. She has also taught deep listening and the Alexander Technique for more than a decade. She currently teaches in her studio in New York City.

Karen Maezen Miller is a mother, wife, writer, and Zen teacher in the lineage of Zen master Taizan Maezumi Roshi. A trained journalist, she had a twenty-year career as the owner of a marketing and public relations agency. She is the author of *Momma Zen: Walking the Crooked Path of Motherhood* and *Hand Wash Cold: Care Instructions for an Ordinary Life.*

Susan Moon has been a Zen student since 1976, practicing in the lineage of Suzuki Roshi and currently with Zoketsu Norman Fischer's Everyday Zen sangha. She is the former editor of *Turning Wheel,* the journal of socially engaged Buddhism. She is also the author of *This Is Getting Old: Zen Thoughts on Aging with Humor and Dignity.*

Kristi Nelson is a trainer and consultant with the Center for Mindfulness in Medicine, Health Care, and Society and The Soul of Money Institute. She is also currently writing a workbook on values-aligned fundraising.

Lawrence Peltz, MD, is an addiction psychiatrist and the medical director of the Bournewood-Caulfield Center, a drug and alcohol treatment facility in Woburn, Massachusetts. He is also a trained teacher of Mindfulness-Based Stress Reduction and speaks regularly to mental health professionals about mindfulness and recovery. He's currently at work on a book on this subject.

Dzogchen Ponlop is a meditation master and scholar in the Kagyu and Nyingma schools of Tibetan Buddhism. He is the president of Nalandabodhi, a network of meditation centers, and founder of the Nitartha Institute, a course of Buddhist study for Western students. He is also the author of *Rebel Buddha, Wild Awakening,* and *Mind Beyond Death.*

Matthieu Ricard was a translator and senior student of Dilgo Khyentse Rinpoche, the twentieth century's foremost teacher of the Great Perfection (Dzogchen) tradition of Tibetan Buddhism. He is a participant in current scientific research on the effects that meditation has on the brain. He is also the author of *The Monk and the Philosopher, The Quantum and the Lotus,* and more recently *Happiness: A Guide to Developing Life's Most Important Skill.*

DAVID ROME is senior fellow at the Garrison Institute in Garrison, New York. He is a certified Focusing trainer, and in 2000, he started teaching deep listening, combining meditation and Focusing. He served as personal secretary to meditation master Chögyam Trungpa for nine years and is the former president of Schocken Books and former senior vice president for planning at Greyston Foundation.

SAKI F. SANTORELLI, ED.D, MA, is associate professor of medicine, executive director of the Center for Mindfulness in Medicine, Health Care, and Society and director of the Stress Reduction Program at the University of Massachusetts Medical School. He is the author of *Heal Thy Self: Lessons on Mindfulness in Medicine.*

DANIEL SIEGEL, MD, is a graduate of Harvard Medical School, director of the Mindsight Institute, and codirector of the UCLA Mindful Awareness Research Center. He is the author of *The Developing Mind, The Mindful Brain: Reflection and Attunement in the Cultivation of Well-Being,* and *Mindsight: The New Science of Personal Transformation.*

RONALD D. SIEGEL, PSYD, is assistant clinical professor of psychology at Harvard Medical School, where he has taught for more than twenty-five years, and is also on the faculty of the Institute for Meditation and Psychotherapy. He is a coauthor of *Back Sense: A Revolutionary Approach to Halting the Cycle of Chronic Back Pain,* which integrates Western and Eastern approaches for treating chronic back pain. He is also the author of *Mindfulness and Psychotherapy* and *The Mindfulness Solution: Everyday Practices for Everyday Problems.*

STEVE SILBERMAN'S articles have appeared in *Wired,* the *New Yorker,* and *Time.* He has written about autism, bacterial evolution, the Beat Generation, and the Grateful Dead. He is currently working on a book about neuroscience and human diversity.

SUSAN SMALLEY, PHD, is the founder and director of the Mindful Awareness Research Center at UCLA, bringing twenty years of experience as a professor and behavior geneticist to the emerging area of mindfulness research. She is the coauthor with Diana Winston of *Fully Present: The Science, Art, and Practice of Mindfulness.*

BOB STAHL, PHD, directs Mindfulness-Based Stress Reduction programs for physicians and health care professionals, as well as for those seeking relief from chronic stress and illness. He is a longtime practitioner of mindfulness meditation. He is the coauthor with Elisha Goldstein of *A Mindfulness-Based Stress Reduction Workbook.*

CLAUDE ANSHIN THOMAS is a Zen Buddhist monk and Vietnam War veteran. He was first introduced to mindfulness by Thich Nhat Hanh in the early 1990s and was ordained in the Japanese Soto Zen tradition by Bernie Glassman in 1995. He is the founder of the Zaltho Foundation, whose purpose is to promote peace and nonviolence. He is also the author of *At Hell's Gate: A Soldier's Journey from War to Peace.* Thomas actively works with veterans in the United States and abroad, teaching them how mindfulness can help with the effects of combat.

CHÖGYAM TRUNGPA (1940–1987) escaped his native Tibet in 1949, eventually moving to North America, where he founded Vajradhatu, a worldwide network of meditation centers. A prolific writer, poet, calligrapher, and artist, he became one of the most influential Buddhist teachers to come to the West. He was the author of such classics as *Cutting through Spiritual Materialism, The Myth of Freedom, Born in Tibet, Training the Mind and Cultivating Loving-Kindness,* and *Shambhala: The Sacred Path of the Warrior.*

DIANA WINSTON is the director of mindfulness education at UCLA's Mindful Awareness Research Center. She is a member of the Spirit Rock Teachers Council, founder of the Buddhist Alliance for Social Engagement program, and former associate director of the Buddhist Peace Fellowship. She has practiced vipassana since 1989, including a year as a Buddhist nun in Burma. She is the author of *Wide Awake: A Buddhist Guide for Teens* and coauthor with Susan Smalley of *Fully Present: The Science, Art, and Practice of Mindfulness.*

MICHAEL WOOD studied photography at Sheridan College School of Visual Arts, and worked as a commercial photographer in Toronto. Meditation profoundly affected the way he experienced his perceptions, inspiring him to found the Miksang Institute for Contemplative Photography. He is the coauthor with Andy Karr of *The Practice of Contemplative Photography: Seeing the World with Fresh Eyes.*

Credits

JAN CHOZEN BAYS, "What is Mindfulness?" Adapted from *Mindful Eating* by Jan Chozen Bays, © 2009 by Jan Chozen Bays. Reprinted by arrangement with Shambhala Publications Inc. Boston, MA. www.shambhala.com.

JAN CHOZEN BAYS, "Mindful Eating." From *Mindful Eating* by Jan Chozen Bays, © 2009 by Jan Chozen Bays. Reprinted by arrangement with Shambhala Publications Inc., Boston, MA, www.shambhala.com.

TONI BERNHARD, "Sickness Is Like the Weather." © Toni Bernhard, 2010. Reprinted from *How to Be Sick: A Buddhist Inspired Guide for the Chronically Ill and Their Caregivers*, with permission from Wisdom Publications, 199 Elm St., Somerville, MA. 02144. wisdompubs.org.

BARRY BOYCE, "Creating a Mindful Society." Original material. © 2010 Barry Boyce.

JEFF BRANTLEY, "Mindfulness FAQ." Adapted with the consent of the author from "Frequently Asked Questions about Mindfulness and Meditation" at the website of the University of California at San Diego Center for Mindfulness (http://mindfulness.ucsd.edu/abtmindfulness.htm). Adaptation © 2010 by Jeff Brantley.

EDWARD ESPE BROWN, "Let Your Passion Cook." From the March 2010 issue of the *Shambhala Sun*.

Mindful.org

Mindful.org is a website that provides the latest information on bringing mindfulness practice into our everyday lives. Created by the publishers of the *Shambhala Sun* magazine, mindful.org offers mindfulness-based approaches to physical health, emotional well-being, relationships, family life, work life, and much more—drawn from diverse sources and perspectives.

Visit mindful.org to

- discover simple practices from leading meditation teachers to help you bring awareness and compassion to everyday life

- learn about the latest science on the benefits of meditation

- discover how mindfulness is being applied in personal and professional life

- make friends with fellow mindfulness practitioners

- find blogs, commentary, audio, video, social networking, and much more.

About the Shambhala Sun

The *Shambhala Sun* is an award-winning bimonthly magazine dedicated to the wisdom of meditation and how it can be applied to all our important issues and pursuits—from livelihood, parenting, and relationships to politics, social action, and the arts. Inspired by Buddhist teachings, the magazine is devoted to the principle that true wisdom is not the property of any one religion or culture.

The *Shambhala Sun* is the place where ancient wisdom shares the stage with some of today's finest writers and thinkers. It regularly features mindfulness teachings, reports on unique applications of mindfulness in its Mindful Society department, and offers an annual issue devoted to mindful living.

Visit www.shambhalasun.com to learn more about the magazine, start a subscription, enjoy the Sun Space blog, learn about news and special events, sign up for a free e-newsletter, and more.

About Shambhala Sun Books

Shambhala Sun Books presents themed anthologies featuring the best writing available on bringing the wisdom of mindfulness and meditation into everyday life. Other volumes in this series include:

In the Face of Fear: Buddhist Wisdom for Challenging Times, edited by Barry Boyce

Right Here with You: Bringing Mindful Awareness into Our Relationships (forthcoming), edited by Andrea Miller